Beginner's Guide to Unity Shader Graph

Create Immersive Game Worlds Using Unity's Shader Tool

Álvaro Alda

Apress®

Beginner's Guide to Unity Shader Graph: Create Immersive Game Worlds Using Unity's Shader Tool

Álvaro Alda
Guadalajara, Spain

ISBN-13 (pbk): 978-1-4842-9671-4   ISBN-13 (electronic): 978-1-4842-9672-1
https://doi.org/10.1007/978-1-4842-9672-1

Copyright © 2023 by Álvaro Alda

Managing Director, Apress Media LLC: Welmoed Spahr
Acquisitions Editor: Spandana Chatterjee
Development Editor: Laura Berendson
Editorial Project Manager: Mark Powers
Copy Editor: April Rondeau

Cover designed by eStudioCalamar

Cover image by Hassan Here on Unsplash (www.unsplash.com)

Distributed to the book trade worldwide by Apress Media, LLC, 1 New York Plaza, New York, NY 10004, U.S.A. Phone 1-800-SPRINGER, fax (201) 348-4505, email orders-ny@springer-sbm.com, or visit www.springeronline.com. Apress Media, LLC is a California LLC and the sole member (owner) is Springer Science + Business Media Finance Inc (SSBM Finance Inc). SSBM Finance Inc is a **Delaware** corporation.

For information on translations, please e-mail booktranslations@springernature.com; for reprint, paperback, or audio rights, please e-mail bookpermissions@springernature.com.

Apress titles may be purchased in bulk for academic, corporate, or promotional use. eBook versions and licenses are also available for most titles. For more information, reference our Print and eBook Bulk Sales web page at http://www.apress.com/bulk-sales.

Any source code or other supplementary material referenced by the author in this book is available to readers on GitHub (https://github.com/Apress). For more detailed information, please visit https://www.apress.com/gp/services/source-code.

Paper in this product is recyclable

To my father, figurehead, friend, and mentor, and to my mother, who always has supported me in all my adventures.

Table of Contents

About the Author

 **Álvaro Alda** is a game developer with over four years of experience. He is currently working for Popcore, a pioneering German hypercasual game company. He has also worked at LabCave, a Spanish mobile game company. In his spare time, he likes to work on personal projects, which has led to the release of his three games, one of which appeared on national Spanish television. He has also created tools for developers and artists for video games.

About the Technical Reviewer

**Simon Jackson** is a long-time software engineer and architect with many years of Unity game development experience, as well as an author of several Unity game development titles. He loves to both create Unity projects as well as lend a hand to help educate others, whether it's via a blog, vlog, user group, or major speaking event.

His primary focus at the moment is the Reality Toolkit project, which is aimed at building a cross-platform mixed-reality framework to enable both virtual reality and augmented reality developers to build efficient solutions in Unity and then build/distribute them to as many platforms as possible.

Acknowledgments

No words are enough to represent how these people have supported me all my life, especially in the roughest moments, and have been important pillars to lean on when needed.

To my parents. You are always there giving me any support needed and a kind word to cheer me up when I am in my lowest moments. To my father, Luis Angel Alda, who is still my mentor and friend and who introduced me to the amazing world of video games. And to my mother, Paky Sanchez-Seco, who has always had a big smile and who has always been an inspiration, the strongest woman I have ever known.

To my girlfriend, Oriana Romero, my travel companion, the love of my life, who has always been there making me a better person every day, the bravest person I have ever known, thanks with all my heart.

To my friends, the most incredible people in my life. Whenever I had a hard day at work or a bad moment in my life, you were always there to bring out my best smile and make me disconnect from the daily routine with your presence . . . and a couple of beers. To my colleague Ruben Torres, who always supported me and inspired me to make my own projects and to start my own adventures.

Thank you all for being a part of my journey, for believing in me, and for contributing to my growth and success. I am truly blessed to have such incredible individuals in my life.

With heartfelt gratitude,
Álvaro

Introduction

Welcome to the fascinating world of Shader Graph! Whether you are a beginner or an intermediate user, this book aims to be your comprehensive guide to understanding and harnessing the power of shaders in Unity's Shader Graph.

Shaders play a vital role in creating visually stunning and immersive experiences in game development and computer graphics. They enable us to manipulate how light interacts with objects, simulate complex materials and textures, and bring life to virtual worlds. With the introduction of Shader Graph, Unity has provided a powerful and user-friendly tool that allows developers and artists to create custom shaders without the need for complex coding.

In this book, we will embark on a journey together, exploring the fundamental concepts and techniques of shader development using Shader Graph. We will start with the basics, assuming no prior knowledge of shaders, and gradually progress to more advanced topics. Whether you are an aspiring game developer, a 3D artist, or simply someone intrigued by the magic behind captivating visuals, this book will equip you with the knowledge and skills needed to create your own shaders and bring your creative vision to life.

You will learn everything related to Shader Graph in Unity, from creating a single scan line effect to creating outstanding complex materials, such as cartoon water, bubble particles, holograms, and much more.

You will study shader principles, including mathematical foundations and shader theory, such as how they work, where they run, and why they are useful. Then, you will learn how to create them using Shader Graph in the latest version available. Using this amazing visual scripting tool, you will be able to visually enhance your games or portfolio to make a step further in this incredible world of video games.

Throughout the book, we will provide step-by-step instructions, hands-on examples, and practical tips to reinforce your understanding of Shader Graph. Additionally, we will showcase real-world applications and examples to inspire your creativity and help you see the immense potential of shaders in game development, simulations, and visual effects.

By the end of this book, you will have a solid foundation in shader development using Shader Graph, empowering you to create stunning visual effects, realistic materials, and captivating environments in your Unity projects.

So, without further ado, let's dive into the exciting world of Shader Graph and unlock the limitless possibilities that shaders offer in bringing your creative visions to reality!

CHAPTER 1

Introduction to Shaders

Shader programming has become an indispensable tool for modern video game development, enabling developers to create stunning, realistic graphics and immersive game worlds. Shaders are essential for implementing effects such as lighting, shadows, reflections, and texture mapping, and they have become an integral part of the game development pipeline. But what exactly are shaders, and how do they work? In this chapter, we will explore the foundations of using shaders in video games, starting with an overview of the history and evolution of shader technology. We will then delve into the basic principles of shader programming, discussing the different types of shaders and their respective roles in the rendering pipeline. By the end of this chapter, you will have a solid understanding of the fundamentals of shader programming. This lays the groundwork for examining more advanced topics in the field of video game development.

What Is a Shader?

In video game development, a shader is a small program that runs on the graphics processing unit (GPU) and is responsible for calculating the colors and properties of every pixel on the screen. Shaders are used to create a wide variety of visual effects, such as lighting, shadows, reflections, and texture mapping. They are essential for achieving the realistic and immersive graphics that modern games demand. Shaders work by manipulating the geometric and material properties of 3D models, as well as the properties of light sources and the camera, to calculate the final color of each pixel. They were introduced by Pixar in 1988 and were originally created to calculate **shadows** projected by 3D elements.

© Álvaro Alda 2023

Á. Alda, *Beginner's Guide to Unity Shader Graph*, https://doi.org/10.1007/978-1-4842-9672-1_1

Nowadays, shaders have drastically evolved into liquid shaders, texture shaders, dynamic surface shaders, and more, thanks to the current technology we can access. In Figure 1-1, you can find a sample of a dynamic cartoon water shader that we are going to develop together throughout this book.

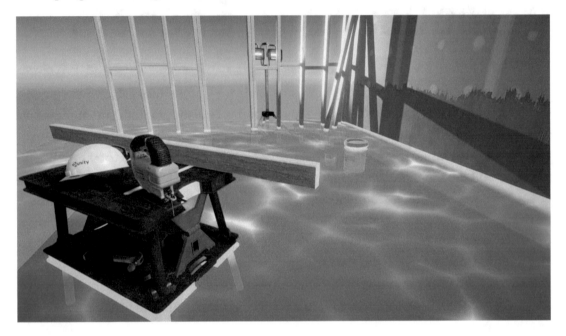

Figure 1-1. *Toon water shader*

But, *how do I create shaders?* you may ask.

Computational Objects and Meshes

In 3D computational graphics, a mesh is a collection of vertices and faces that define the geometric structure of a three-dimensional object or surface. It is a fundamental representation used in computer graphics, simulation, and computational geometry. Every object is represented by a mesh, which is defined by vertices and triangles or quads (two triangles), as you can see in Figure 1-2.

Figure 1-2. *From left to right: vertices, triangles, and complete shaded sphere mesh*

A mesh consists of the following two key components:

- **Vertices**: These are the points in 3D space that define the shape and position of the object. Each vertex is represented by its coordinates (x, y, z) and may also store additional attributes, like color or texture coordinates.

- **Faces**: These are the polygonal surfaces that enclose a region in space. Faces are composed of three or more vertices connected by edges. Common face types include triangles (three vertices), quadrilaterals (four vertices), or more complex polygons.

Vertices

The vertices of an object are a set of points in space that define the area of its surface in either two-dimensional or three-dimensional space. The position of a vertex in Unity is set according to the center of the object. We will use the vertex position information to create several shader effects, like procedural snow, procedural animation, morphing of meshes, and more (Figure 1-3). "Procedural" refers to a method of generating images, textures, or other visual elements using algorithms rather than manually created data or assets.

Figure 1-3. *Flag effect achieved by deforming the vertices of a plane*

Vertices have additional information that will be useful for creating amazing shading effects later in this book, as follows:

- Normals

- UV coordinates

- Vertex color

Normals

Imagine an arrow pointing up from your desktop table. That arrow is the *normal* of your table. A normal is a perpendicular vector/arrow on the surface of a polygon (we will define the concept of a vector later on).

As you can see in Figure 1-4, normals are represented pointing outward from the face of the polygon, which indicates the side of the face that is going to be rendered.

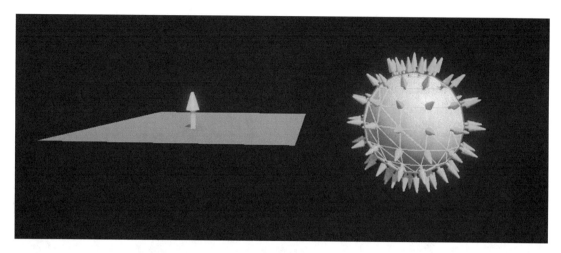

Figure 1-4. *Representation of the normals of a plane and a sphere*

Note   Rendering is the process that happens when the computer device changes the screen pixels' color and illumination in order to represent on screen a 3D or 2D object.

The normal vector plays a crucial role in determining how light interacts with the surface of a 3D object. When light hits a surface, its behavior is influenced by the orientation of the surface, which is defined by the normal vector at each vertex. By calculating the angle between the incoming light and the normal vector, it becomes possible to determine how much light is reflected, absorbed, or refracted by the surface.

UV Coordinates or Texture Coordinates

Do you remember changing the skin of your main character in a video game? This can be achieved thanks to the UV coordinates of the mesh of that character.

UV coordinates means "texture coordinates in a 2D space," where "U" and "V" are the axes of this 2D space. This notation refers to the way that textures are mapped onto 3D models, allowing the GPU to apply the correct colors and patterns to each pixel of the model's surface. The "U" and "V" coordinates are usually represented as floating point values ranging from 0 to 1, and they determine the position of each pixel on the texture map that is being applied to the model.

When you create a mesh in a **CAD**[1] program like Blender or Maya you generate the UV coordinates for each vertex. This process is called *UV mapping*. Think of it as cutting a paper and unfolding it to form the shape of a mesh, like in Figure 1-5. Normally these programs assist you in that task, since, depending on the mesh, this process can become quite tricky.

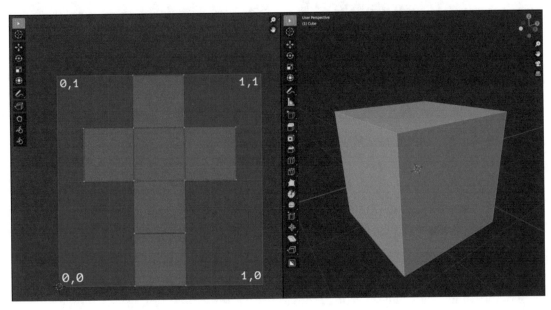

Figure 1-5. *UV-mapped cube, defining the UV coordinates of each pixel (Blender generated)*

Figure 1-5 shows how the cube was "cut" in order to be unfolded in a 2D representation.

Any texture can be painted on top of that unwrapped representation of the cube so as to display that texture in the actual 3D model, like in Figure 1-6, where I used handmade dice texture.

---

[1] CAD (computer-aided design) programs help a developer to design a 2D or 3D product. We can find 2D CAD programs like Photoshop, Krita, Illustrator, and 3D ones like Blender, Maya, and Fusion360.

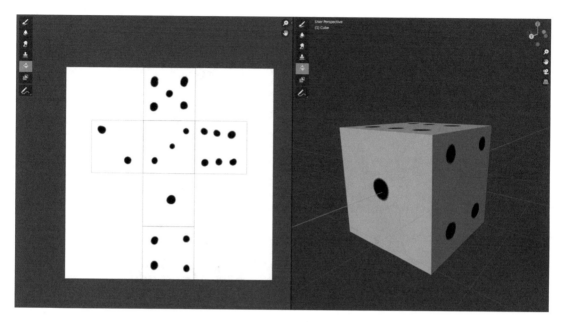

Figure 1-6. *UV-mapped cube textured with a dice texture*

Vertex Color

CAD programs can assign color information to each vertex when exporting the object to either be affected by illumination inside the 3D engine or be changed by the developer using a shader.

These colors can be accessed by the shader to, for example, be applied directly to paint the object. They can be also used to select a certain group of vertices defined by their color to modify another property of that specific area. In Figure 1-7, you can check an object with the vertices colored using Blender.

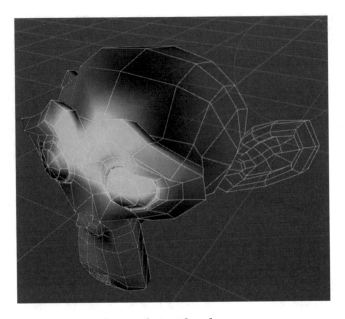

Figure 1-7. *Painted vertices of a mesh in Blender*

Triangles and Polygons

Polygons, and specifically triangles, are the fundamental building blocks of 3D objects in computer graphics. A polygon is a flat, two-dimensional shape with straight sides, and a triangle is a type of polygon with three sides. In 3D graphics, polygons are used to represent the surfaces of 3D objects, and triangles are the most commonly used type of polygon. This is because triangles have a number of properties that make them well suited for 3D modeling and rendering. For example:

- **Triangles are planar**: All three points of a triangle lie on the same plane, which makes them easy to render and manipulate in 3D space.

- **Triangles have a fixed orientation**: They have a well-defined front and back side, which makes it easy to apply different materials and textures to different parts of a model.

- **Triangles are simple**: They have a small number of sides and vertices, which makes them computationally efficient to work with.

In addition to triangles, other types of polygons, such as quads and *n*-gons can be used in 3D modeling, but they are generally less common than triangles. The more polygons or triangles a mesh has, the more details we can find in its surface, but the GPU will require more time and resources to paint it on screen. You can compare in Figure 1-8 a dense mesh (left) with a low polygonal mesh (right).

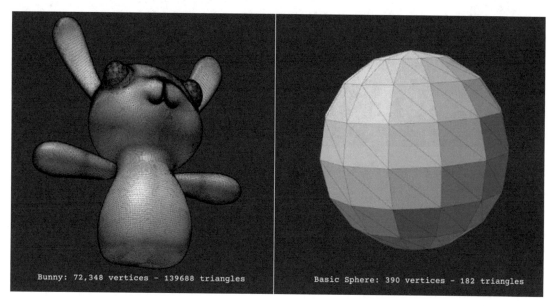

Bunny: 72,348 vertices - 139688 triangles   Basic Sphere: 390 vertices - 182 triangles

Figure 1-8. *High poly mesh (left) vs. low poly mesh (right)*

Programming Shaders

Now that we have learned what a mesh is and its constituent parts, we are ready to know how to program a shader and which elements run those programs inside a rendering device, like a computer or a mobile phone.

In our computer, there are several processing units, but we will talk about two of them: the **CPU**, or **central processing unit**, which processes general logic, physics, and main gameplay mechanics; and the **GPU**, or **graphics processing unit**, which takes care of shading computation and mathematical floating point calculations. Whereas the CPU has only one thread to make calculations (sequential), the GPU can have up to 10,000 threads, which means that the GPU can work on 10,000 tasks at the same time. Check a visual analogy of a single thread turning a red box into a green sphere in Figure 1-9.

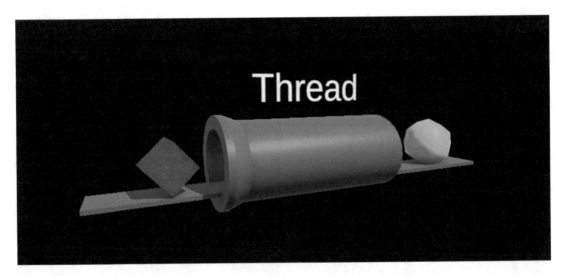

Figure 1-9. *Analogy of a thread performing an operation (turning a red box into a green sphere)*

Running one function in each frame is an easy operation for a CPU, but a screen-coloring effect function needs to be performed once for each pixel in a screen. For instance, in a 2880x1800 monitor running at 60 frames per second, the calculation adds up to 311,040,000 operations per second! That would be a lot of work for a CPU, which would get stuck and take a long time to process those operations, since it would have to perform them one by one sequentially (see comparative in Figure 1-10).

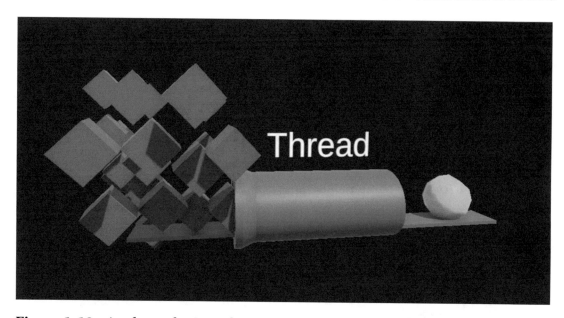

Figure 1-10. *Analogy of a CPU thread getting stuck by a huge load of operations*

To avoid this problem, shaders will run in the **GPU**. A GPU is a device that computers, consoles, and mobile phones use to take care of rendering and making mathematical floating coma operations, letting the CPU calculate physics, player inputs, and the general logic of our game. A GPU works in **parallel**; in other words, it can perform multiple operations at the same time (Figure 1-11).

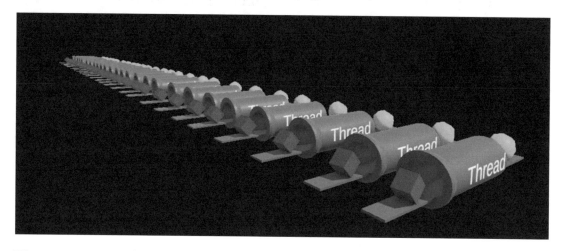

Figure 1-11. *Analogy of a mult-threaded GPU processing the operations*

Vertex-Fragment Shader

In video games, there are several types of shaders that are commonly used to achieve different visual effects. Here are some examples:

- **Vertex shaders**: These shaders operate on individual vertices in a 3D model, transforming their positions, orientations, and colors based on mathematical calculations.

- **Pixel/fragment shaders**: Also known as fragment shaders, these shaders operate on individual pixels in a 3D scene, determining their final colors based on complex calculations involving textures, lighting, and other environmental factors. Pixel shaders are used to create detailed textures, realistic reflections, and other complex visual effects. They will use shared information output by the **vertex shader.**

- **Geometry shaders**: These shaders operate on the geometry of a 3D model, generating additional geometry and modifying existing geometry in real time. Geometry shaders are often used to create particle effects, deformable objects, and other dynamic visual elements like procedural grass or hair.

- **Compute shaders**: These shaders perform general-purpose computing tasks on the GPU, allowing developers to perform complex calculations and simulations that would be difficult or impossible to do on the CPU. Compute shaders are used to implement advanced physics simulations, artificial intelligence algorithms, and other complex systems in video games, like GPU particles and fluid simulation.

In this book we are going to focus especially on **vertex shaders** and **fragment shaders** since we are going to create only visual effects that deform and color the surface of the objects.

Shader Programming Languages

As we just saw, the GPU lets us make mathematical calculations quickly because they are being processed in parallel. This "great power comes with a great responsibility," (Spiderman) meaning that shaders must be written in a special language that only the GPU will understand.

Some examples of programming languages used to write shaders are **OpenGL** (open graphics language), **CG** (C for graphics), and **HLSL** (high-level shaders language), among others. They are quite similar, and their structures are pretty much the same. Unity uses CG for its basic built-in render pipeline and HLSL for the universal render pipeline.

In the following code snippet, we see an example of a shader in HLSL, which takes the color of the vertices of a mesh and applies it to the corresponding pixel coordinate as output:

```
//This is obtaining information from the vertex
struct vertex_to_pixel
{
    float3 color : COLOR;
};

//This is using the vertex info to return a color to the pixel
float4 main(in vertex_to_pixel IN) : COLOR
{
    return float4(IN.color, 1.0);
};
```

Although this is a book about shaders development, we are not going to focus on writing any code in any language. In the software version 2018.1 of Unity a new, visual way of programming shaders was introduced, **Shader Graph.**

Shader Graph

Shader Graph is a new Unity tool to create shaders that takes advantage of what developers call *visual programming*. Visual programming is a technique to program code without writing it, taking advantage of a graphic user interface (GUI) that allows you to connect nodes that perform certain operations and achieve a resulting shader in real time. In Figure 1-12, you can see a sample of a material that changes the color of an object.

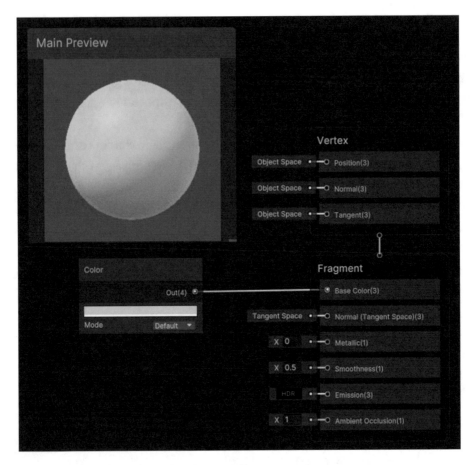

Figure 1-12. *Color changing shader graph*

As you can see, we access the fragment shader directly, changing the output color of the fragments of an object. A Shader Graph will generate in real time a brand-new shader program with both Vertex and Fragment shader steps without your writing a single line of code.

In the next chapter, we will introduce Shader Graph in depth by creating our first shader in a real Unity 3D project.

Shaders' Mathematical Foundations

I know you want to start creating shaders right away, but we first need to learn just the most basic mathematical concepts to know what we are doing in the next chapters. First of all, we will explain *vectors* and the operations we can make with them to obtain spectacular results in our shaders. Finally, we will cover the different coordinate systems we can use.

Vectors

A vector is a mathematical concept that represents a direction and a magnitude. Normally we use vectors to represent physical phenomena like speed, force, and acceleration.

We can represent vectors as an arrow (direction) with a determined length (magnitude), as you can see in Figure 1-13.

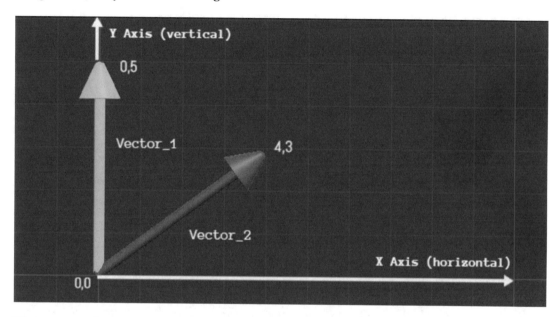

Figure 1-13. *Vector_1 and Vector_2 represented in a coordinate system*

The vectors shown in the figure are represented by the cartesian coordinates *x* (horizontal) and *y* (vertical); thus, we can consider them as two-dimensional vectors.

Vectors are written as a tuple of real numbers named *components*, which are the projection of the vectors in each axis; for example, the Vector_2 of Figure 1-12 is Vector_2 = (4,3), meaning 4 units long in the horizontal axis and 3 units long in the vertical axis.

Vector_1 only has vertical component, therefore we can represent it as Vector_1 = (0,5).

In game programming vectors are used to give the characters speed, apply forces to particles, make the camera look to the player, and more. In Figure 1-5 we saw the normal of a vertex represented by a vector.

Adding Vectors

We can add two vectors together by adding the corresponding components of each one:

Vector_1 + Vector_2 = (0,5) + (4,3) = (4+0, 5+3) = (4,8).

Each operation with vectors will have a meaningful visual representation that will help us to understand them better and to achieve effects when implemented in shaders. The way to add them graphically is by using the *parallelogram method* (Figure 1-14).

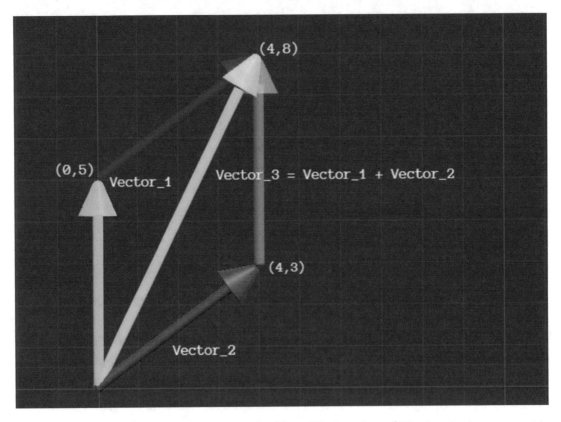

Figure 1-14. *Visual representation of adding Vector_1 and Vector_2*

Scalar Product

The scalar product, or dot product, consists of the multiplication of both vectors, thus obtaining a scalar value (a real number) as a result of that operation. There are two ways of calculating the scalar product:

```
Vector_1 • Vector_2 = (4 · 0 + 5 · 3) = (0 + 15) = 15
Vector_1 • Vector_2 = |Vector_1| * |Vector_2| * cos(Alpha)
```

|vector| is the magnitude of the vector and is calculated with this formula:

$$|\text{Vector\_1}| = \sqrt{4^2 + 3^2} = \sqrt{16 + 9} = \sqrt{25} = 5$$

$$|\text{Vector\_2}| = \sqrt{0^2 + 5^2} = \sqrt{25} = 5$$

We can say both vectors are five units long; therefore they have the same length.

But what is cos(Alpha)? Alpha is the angle between both vectors, and the cosine is an operation that determines the projection of a vector over the other vector. We can achieve it graphically by tracing a line from one vector end to a perpendicular point of the second vector (Figure 1-15).

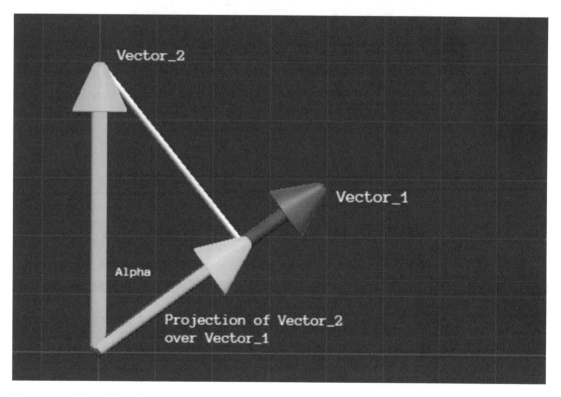

Figure 1-15. *Visual representation of a scalar product*

This is very handy because the scalar product will be at the maximum when Vector_1 and Vector_2 are parallel and will be zero when they are perpendicular. Thus, this operation serves as a mathematical interpretation of how these vectors are respectively oriented with each other.

It is vital to calculate how much light is hitting a vertex so as to color it with a radiant color. Light is hitting a vertex because the normal of that vertex is parallel to the light vector, thus `cos(alpha)` = `1` (Figure 1-16).

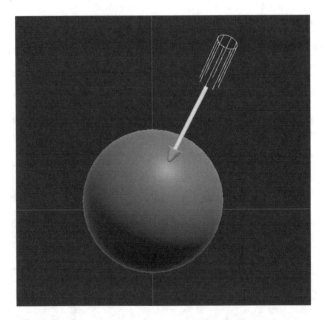

Figure 1-16. *Light hitting parallel to the normal of the vertex*

For simplicity of representation, the operations use examples of two-dimensional vectors, but these operations are achieved the same way using a three-dimensional approach by just adding a third component to them:

```
Vector_4 = (vx, vy, vz);
```

Coordinate Systems

In computer graphics, coordinate spaces are used to describe the position and orientation of objects in a 3D scene. There are several coordinate spaces that are commonly used in 3D graphics, including object space, world space, and view space. Each of these spaces has its own unique properties and use cases; therefore, understanding how they work is essential for creating realistic and immersive 3D environments. We will talk about three of them in this book:

- Object space

- World space

- View space

Object Space

Object space refers to the coordinate system that is local to a particular object in a 3D scene. In object space, the object's vertices are defined relative to the center of the mesh they are forming.

The vertex positions of a mesh take the object mesh origin as the reference origin position (0,0,0) (Figure 1-17).

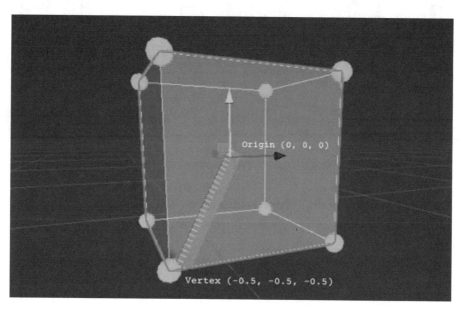

Figure 1-17. *Down-left vertex represented in object space*

Knowing the cube is one unit length on each side, the position of the bottom-down vertex from the center of the cube is as follows:

```
vertex = (-0.5, -0.5, -0.5)
```

World Space

World space, however, is a global coordinate system that is used to describe the position and orientation of objects relative to the overall scene.

The world-space coordinates put the origin at the world position (0,0,0), as we can see in Figure 1-18. The position of the vertex is different since it is relative to the center of the scene, not to the center of the cube mesh.

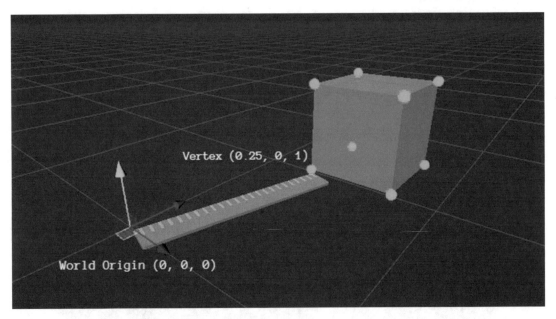

Figure 1-18.   *Vertex represented in world space*

Now, you may think that the vertex position has changed, but actually, what did change is the reference we use to measure its position.

View Space

View space, also known as camera space, is a coordinate system that is used to describe the position and orientation of objects relative to the camera that is viewing the scene, taking the camera position as the origin of coordinates (0,0,0), as shown in Figure 1-19.

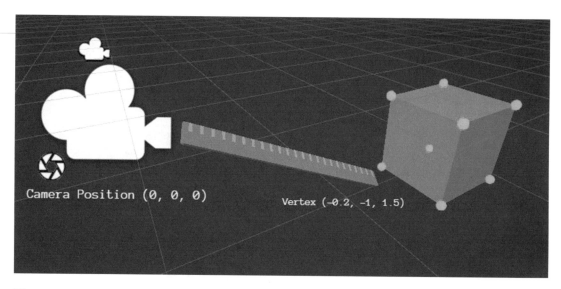

Figure 1-19. *Vertex represented in view space*

This coordinate system is very useful if we want to apply effects that depend on the point of view of the user, like fog or vanishing particles.

Summary

Nicely done! You have just passed through the most boring part of this book with flying colors. You now have a better understanding about what a shader is and how it is written, the main tool that we are using to achieve that without writing a single line of code, and the different coordinate spaces we will use in this book.

I think it is time to "get our hands dirty" and start learning how to create our first project in Unity 3D and make your first shader with Shader Graph.

CHAPTER 2

Shader Graph

Now that you know the foundations of shaders, it is time to start making them. In this more interactive chapter, we will create your first project in Unity 3D and your first shader. Then, we will review the Shader Graph inspector to get to know the main tool we are going to use along with this book.

Create a Unity 3D Project

First, you need to install Unity on your computer. Download it from the Unity official webpage at `https://unity.com/download`.

Double-click on the executable you just downloaded, and an assistant to install **Unity Hub** will pop up in your machine. **Unity Hub** is the interface that allows you to create and organize Unity projects in your computer, as you can see in Figure 2-1.

© Álvaro Alda 2023
Á. Alda, *Beginner's Guide to Unity Shader Graph*, https://doi.org/10.1007/978-1-4842-9672-1_2

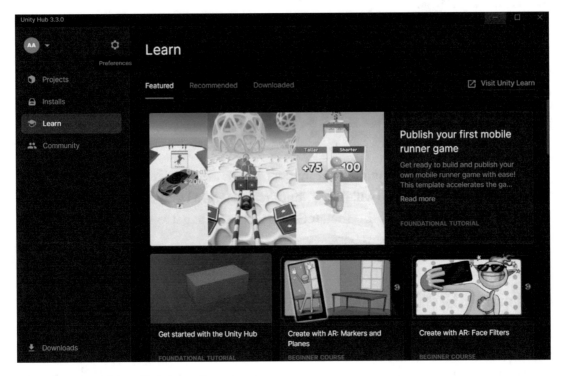

Figure 2-1. *Unity Hub interface*

- Now, we need to install the Unity Editor version we will work with. For that, click on **Installs** in the left-hand menu. It will send you to the **Installs** section, where you can install, uninstall, or modify Unity Editor versions.

- Click on **Install Editor** at the top-right corner and click on the LTS (long term support) version **2021.3.22f1.** LTS versions are stable and have "almost" no bugs. When writing this book, **2021.3.22f1** is the latest version, **try to use this or greater LTS version to follow the project**.

- In the left-hand panel of Unity Hub click on **Projects**, from which you can select the project template you want to use as the starting point of your unit project. Scroll down until you find **3D (URP)**, then click **Download Template** to be able to create 3D URP projects.

  We are going to select this URP template since by default it has all the packages we will need downloaded to develop the shaders in this book (Universal Render Pipeline, Shader Graph...).

- When the template is downloaded, at the bottom right, it will let you select a name for your project and a location where the project is going to be created. After that just click the **Create Project** button, and the project will be created and opened right away.

Congratulations, your brand-new Unity project is ready to be filled with tons of outstanding visual effects. Next time you open Unity Hub, your project will be listed under the Projects section, which you can open by clicking it.

Unity Editor

If you followed the previous steps correctly, you will find yourself looking at something similar to Figure 2-2.

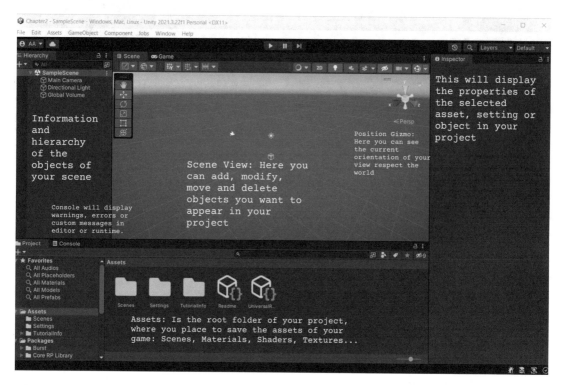

Figure 2-2. *Unity Editor*

Unity Editor is fully customizable. You can drag and drop every tab and set up your layout as you like. You can also change the assets icons sizes using the bottom-right slider. You can do much more, but Editor customization is a topic out of the scope of this book.

When you feel confident with Editor we will create our first shader.

Create Your First Shader

Let's create the first shader in your brand-new project. First of all, we will create the object that will interact with our shader. Right-click in the **Hierarchy** tab and select **3D Object ➤ Capsule** (Figure 2-3).

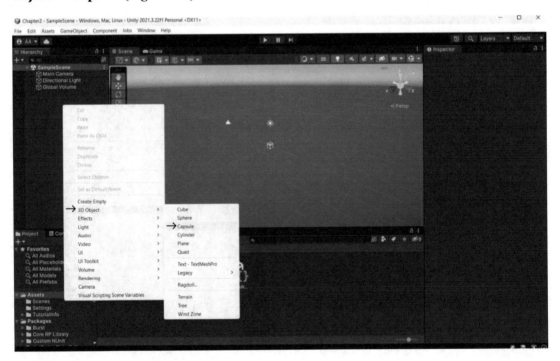

Figure 2-3. *Create a capsule*

Doing this will create a lovely capsule in the Scene view (Figure 2-4). As you can also see in that figure, the Inspector tab will show the components of the capsule when the object is selected, including the following:

- **Transform**: This is a component that every object in the scene has. It allows us to control its position, rotation, and scale inside the scene.

- **Mesh Filter**: This will load the mesh we want to display. In this case a capsule was automatically selected, but we can change it to display any mesh we want; for example, a cube.

- **Mesh Renderer**: This component will take one or more materials as reference and will apply them to the object.

- **Capsule Collider**: The collider will create the bounds to let our object interact with other objects in the scene through Unity physics.

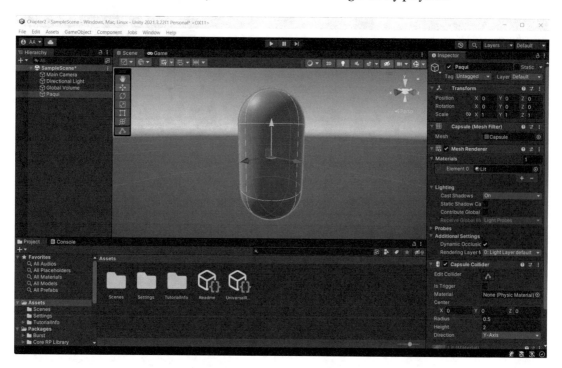

Figure 2-4. *Capsule created, and its components*

To create a shader graph, we can right-click anywhere inside the Assets folder in the Project tab (lower part of the screen) and click on **Create ➤ Shader Graph ➤ URP ➤ Lit Shader Graph** (Figure 2-5).

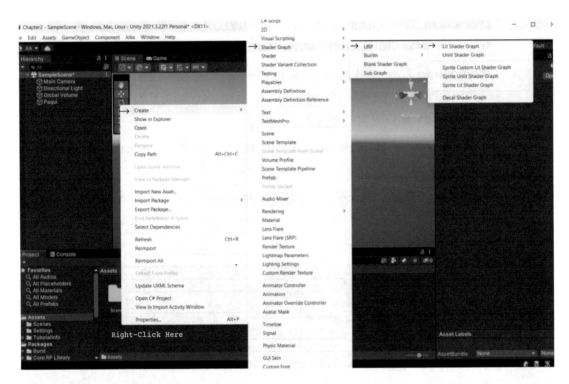

Figure 2-5. *Create a shader graph*

The shader graph asset will appear in the Assets tab, as shown in Figure 2-6.

Figure 2-6. *Shader graph in the Assets root*

If you double-click it, you will open the Shader Graph editor, as shown in Figure 2-7.

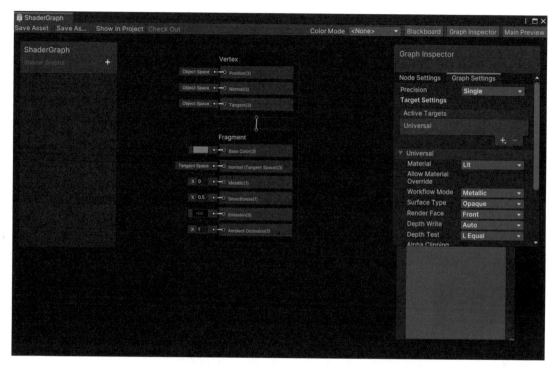

Figure 2-7. *Shader Graph editor*

This window will appear attached to the Unity Editor, but you can drag the top-left tab to take it out and amplify the window for convenience.

The main things you should notice are the two main blocks in the middle, called **Vertex** and **Fragment.** These blocks are going to be studied in detail at the end of this chapter, but we will use them now just to change the color of our object. Click directly on the gray box to the left of the Base Color field in the Fragment block section of the Shader Graph editor, and a color palette will be displayed so you can change the color, as shown in Figure 2-8.

Figure 2-8. *Changing base color in the Fragment shader*

Now we are going to create a color input node. Creating an input node instead of changing the default input of the current node will be more versatile, since we can create a property related to the new node and change it from any part of our code or from the Inspector tab in the Unity Editor.

To make a new color node, right-click in any empty spot inside the Shader Graph editor and select **Create Node**. Then a pop-up will be displayed showing all the nodes we can create. At the top part of that pop-up there is a Search tab where you can look for a specific node. In our case, by typing Color we can find several options.

Go to the one under **Input ➤ Basic** and left-click on it (Figure 2-9). Then, a color node will be created.

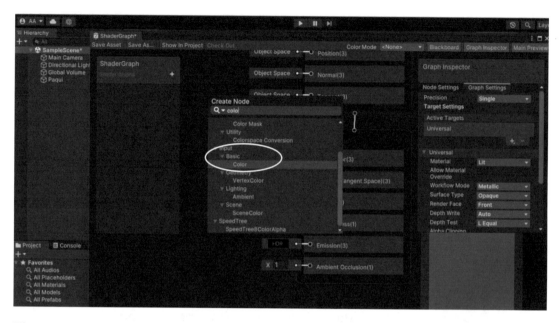

Figure 2-9. *Creating a color node*

If you click in the color square inside the color node, you can change the color output. Then, by dragging from the output of the node to the input of the **Base Color** in the **Fragment node**, as shown in Figure 2-10, you will assign that node output to the **Base Color** value.

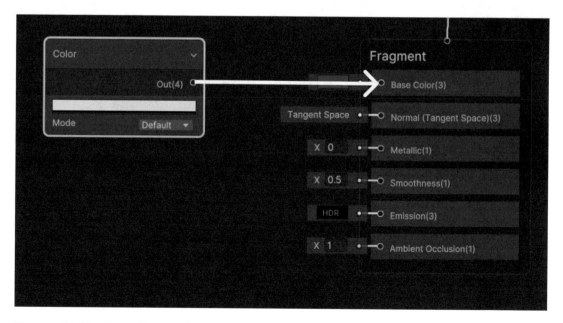

Figure 2-10. *Creating and setting a custom color for base color*

Finally, click on **Save Asset** at the top-left corner. The shader is ready to be used in our capsule, but first we need to create a material that will be fed with the shader.

Create a Material

In video games, materials and shaders are closely related and work together to create the final appearance of 3D objects. A material defines the visual properties of an object, such as its color, texture, and transparency, or any custom variables that the shader can access.

When a material is applied to an object in a game engine, it is linked to a specific shader that controls how the object is rendered. The shader takes the properties defined in the material and uses them to calculate the final appearance of the object.

There are two ways of associating a shader to a material:

1) Create a material by right-clicking on top of the shader in the Assets folder and then click **Create ➤ Material.** The material created will have the shader loaded by default (Figure 2-11).

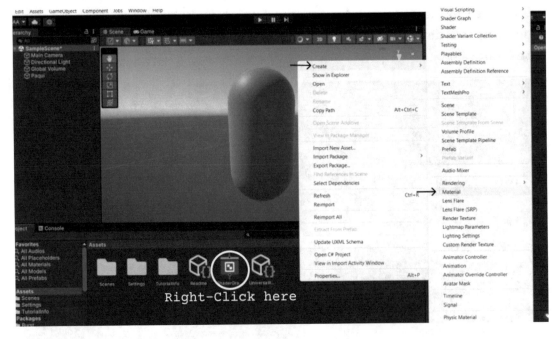

Figure 2-11. *Creating a material from a shader*

2) The other way to achieve the same result material is by right-clicking anywhere inside the Assets folder on the project tab in the lower portion of the screen and by clicking **Create ➤ Material**. You will create a default material with a default selected pipeline **lit shader** on it. To assign the shader, click on the created material and click in the top part of the inspector; then, navigate to **Shader Graphs ➤ "The name of your shader"** and click again over it to assign to the material (Figure 2-12).

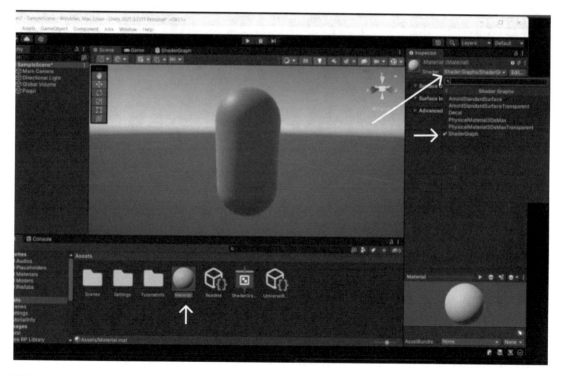

Figure 2-12. *Assign shader to a default material*

Now, you can either drag the material asset to your capsule in the scene, drag the material to the object in the hierarchy, or assign the material to the Mesh Renderer component as in Figure 2-13.

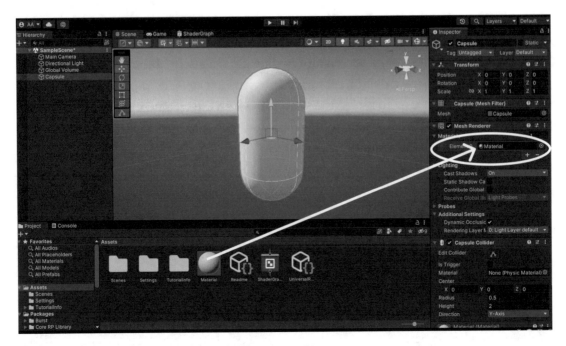

Figure 2-13. *Assign a material to the capsule*

Mesh renderers can have more than one material assigned to them because it allows greater flexibility and customization in the appearance of 3D objects. By assigning multiple materials to a single mesh renderer, developers can create more complex and detailed visual effects.

For example, imagine a 3D model of a car. By assigning different materials to different parts of the car, such as the body, windows, and tires, developers can create a more realistic and detailed representation of the car. The body might have a metallic material with a glossy finish, while the windows might have a transparent material to simulate glass, and the tires might have a rubber material with a matte finish.

Congratulations! You have created your first shader, "fed" your first material with it, and assigned the material to your first object in your first Unity project. Now, let's dig into the different pipelines that Unity offers their users to work with.

Rendering Pipelines

A rendering pipeline in Unity is a system that controls how the game engine renders graphics on screen. It consists of a series of steps, each of which processes data related to the game's visual appearance. The rendering pipeline in Unity is responsible for taking 3D models, textures, and other assets and transforming them into the 2D images that appear on the screen.

Unity offers several different rendering pipelines, each with its own advantages and limitations. The most popular rendering pipelines in Unity are the Built-in Render Pipeline, the **Universal Render Pipeline (URP)**, and the High-Definition Render Pipeline (HDRP).

URP Pipeline

We will mostly use URP in this book since this pipeline uses modern rendering techniques, such as GPU instancing, dynamic resolution scaling, and occlusion culling, to optimize rendering performance. It is perfect for making really performant games for mobile platforms and visually outstanding games for PC or consoles. It will also allow us to take advantage of several tools, like **Shader Graph** for URP and **VFX Graph** (a visual scripting tool for GPU- run particles).

Its lightweight and efficient design, combined with its user-friendly workflow, makes it a popular choice among developers.

Upgrading a Project to URP

Previously, we have shown how to create a URP project via Unity Hub. But maybe you have mistakenly created a Built-in Render Pipeline project or you just want to upgrade an old project you created a while ago to URP.

I will create a Built-in Pipeline project from Unity Hub, as shown in Figure 2-14, and then I will upgrade it to URP.

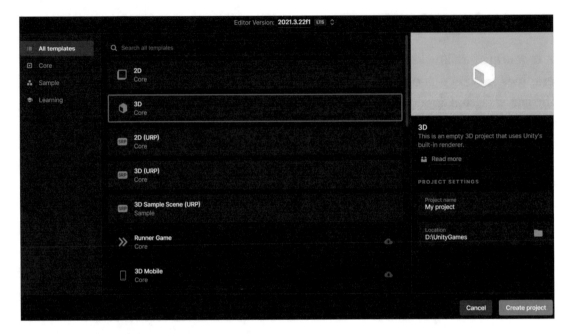

Figure 2-14. *Creating a Built-in project*

I will also create a new material with a green base color assigned to it and name it "Old Material" (Figure 2-15).

Figure 2-15. *Material created in Built-in Pipeline*

Now that we have our project in the Built-in Render Pipeline, let's install the URP package.

Install URP Package

With the project Unity Editor opened, we will access the Package Manager window by clicking **Window ➤ Package Manager** in the top toolbar.

This will open a window where you can check all the packages Unity pre-installed in your project (Figure 2-16).

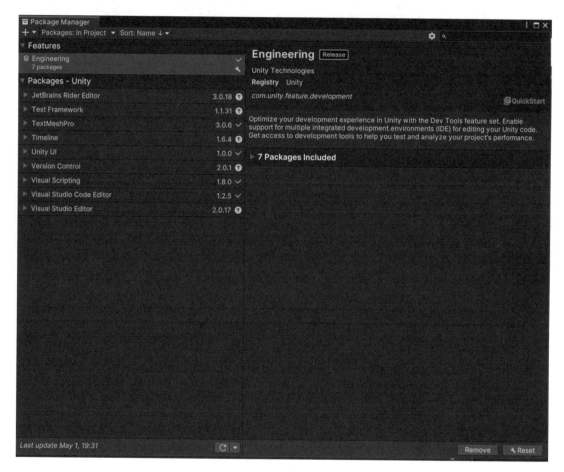

Figure 2-16. *Package Manager window*

To install a new package, go to the top-left dropdown that displays "Packages: In Project" and select **Unity Registry** (Figure 2-17).

Figure 2-17. *Unity Registry packages*

After that, scroll down in the left-hand section until you find the package "Universal RP." Then, select it and click on the **Install** button at the bottom right of the Package Manager window, as shown in Figure 2-18.

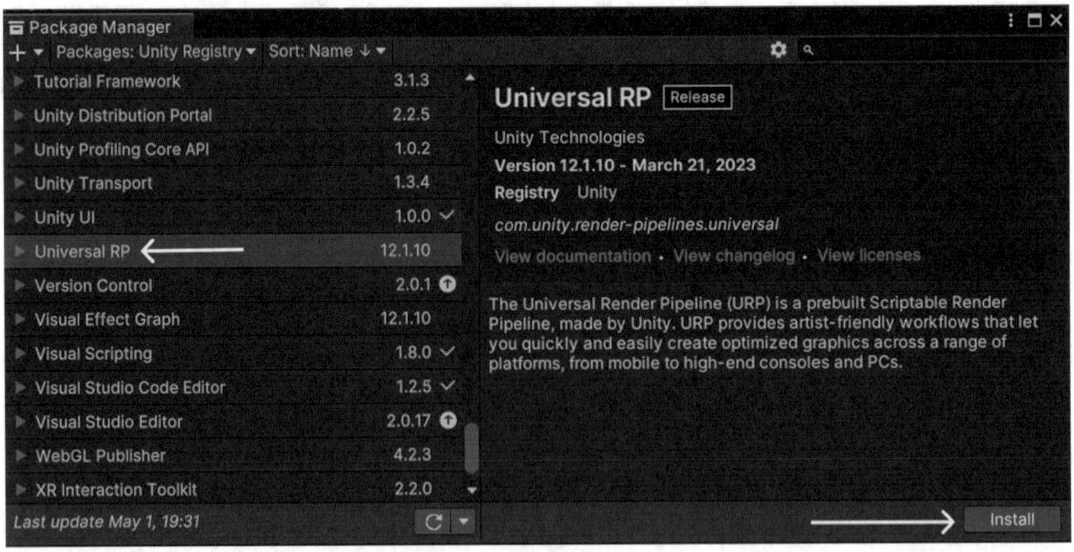

Figure 2-18. *Selecting URP package to install*

After clicking the Install button, a compiling progress bar will appear; when completed, you will have your UR Pipeline correctly installed in your project. The **Shader Graph** package will also be installed because URP has dependencies on it.

Now, we have to tell the graphic pipeline that we want to use URP as our default pipeline and to stop using the Built-in one.

Set Up a URP Asset

Now, we need to assign a URP asset to the graphic settings of our game to establish Universal Render as our new pipeline.

Inside the Project tab, right-click and select **Create ➤ Rendering ➤ URP Asset (with Universal Renderer).** You will now see how two scriptable objects will be created, as shown in Figure 2-19.

Figure 2-19. *Created URP settings assets*

If you click on "New Universal Render Pipeline Asset" you can change and set every setting you want related to how the game looks (shadows, depth texture, opaque texture, lighting settings, and more).

This is the best thing that scriptable render pipelines like URP and HDRP have to offer: an extensive and easy-to-use user interface via which to tweak every rendering setting that will give the final look to the resulting game (Figure 2-20).

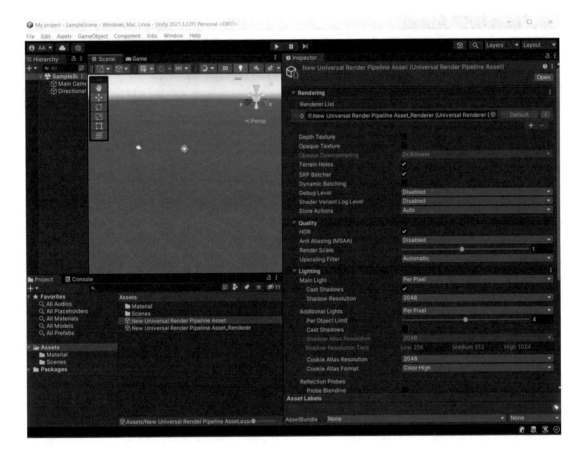

Figure 2-20. *URP asset settings*

Now that we have created the URP asset, we can go to the top toolbar of the Unity Editor and click on **Edit ➤ Project Settings ➤ Graphics**. Then you can drag and drop the recently created asset to the "Scriptable Render Pipeline Settings" section, as shown in Figure 2-21.

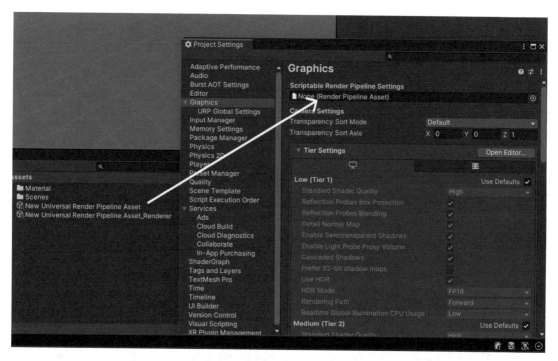

Figure 2-21. *Assigning URP asset to the Graphics settings*

This will make a pop-up appear saying that "changing the render pipeline will take time." Click on Continue, and then your game will be running in the almighty Universal Render Pipeline. But we have a problem . . . our previous materials are not working properly, and are outputting an ugly magenta color that symbolizes that there is an error happening.

Upgrade Previous Materials

Our previous materials were set with calculations of libraries made for the Built-in Render Pipeline, meaning that they are not compiling in our new URP, instead outputting an unlit magenta color (Figure 2-22).

Figure 2-22. *Material not compiling*

Note   The color magenta is used to represent that a shader is not compiling correctly, because magenta is out of the spectrum of visible colors. Your brain creates that color by making an average from red and violet (limits of the color spectrum). Technically, the color magenta doesn't exist.

To fix this annoying issue, select the material or materials that are "broken" and navigate to **Edit ➤ Rendering ➤ Materials ➤ Convert Selected Built-in Materials to URP** (Figure 2-23).

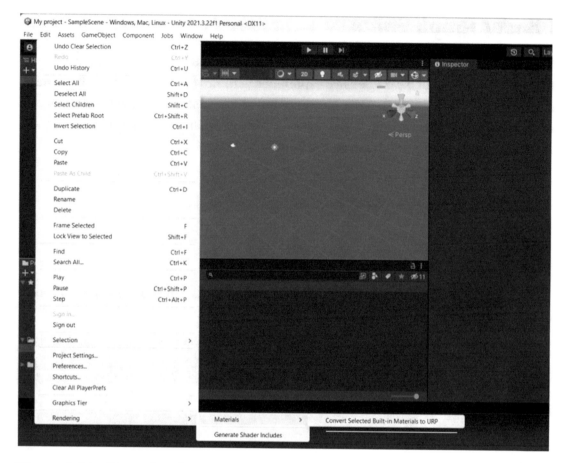

Figure 2-23. *Upgrade selected materials section*

When clicked, a pop-up will appear, warning you that the material and shader will be overwritten, so be sure to have a backup if you might want to switch back to the Built-in Render Pipeline. Then, click on **Proceed**, and the materials will be upgraded to URP and working again as before.

Now that we have everything set up in our desired pipeline, it is time to study our main tool during this book, the **Shader Graph Editor**.

Shader Graph Editor

The Shader Graph Editor is designed to be user-friendly and accessible, even for developers who do not have extensive experience with shader programming. It provides a library of pre-built nodes that can be combined and modified to create a wide range of visual effects. In this section, we will take a look at the main parts of the interface that will help us along in our shader development steps.

- Main Preview

- Blackboard

- Graph Inspector

- Master Stack

The three first interfaces can be toggled on and off by clicking the top-right buttons in the Shader Graph Editor, as in Figure 2-24.

Figure 2-24. *Shader Graph tools top bar*

Main Preview

The Main Preview tab will show the final result of the created shader assigned to a predefined mesh (Figure 2-25). It allows developers to see the effects of their shader design changes in real-time, without the need to compile and run the game each time. You can change the preview mesh by right-clicking inside the **Main Preview** window and selecting the desired mesh.

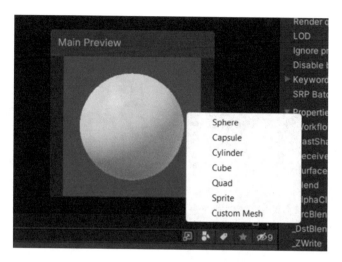

Figure 2-25. *Main Preview*

Blackboard

The Blackboard window serves as a central hub for managing the properties and variables used in the shader graph. Developers can create and edit properties and variables directly in the Blackboard window and then use them in different nodes throughout the graph. It provides a convenient way to manage and modify shader properties and variables. Instead of having to search through different nodes in the graph to modify a particular value, developers can simply locate the corresponding property or variable in the Blackboard window and make changes there.

Let's add the color node to the blackboard by right-clicking on top of the color node and selecting **Convert to ➤ Property**, as you can see in Figure 2-26.

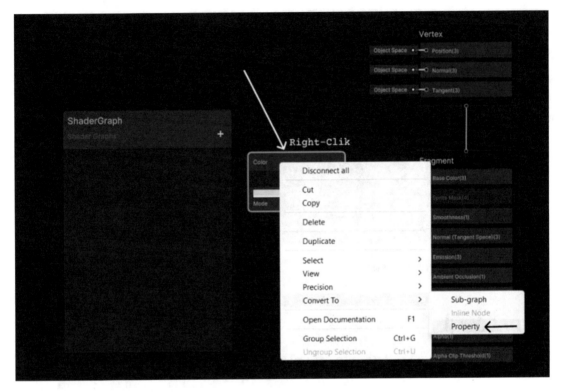

Figure 2-26. *Converting the color input node into a property*

Once you have created the color property, it will be placed in the blackboard (Figure 2-27).

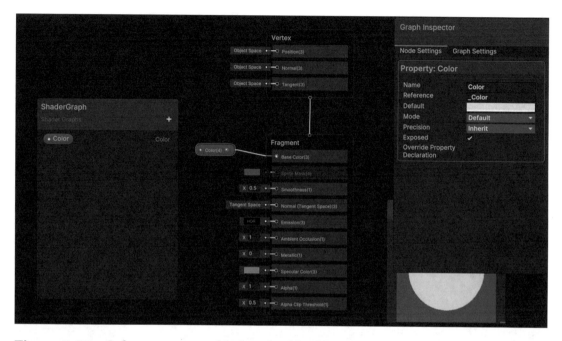

Figure 2-27. *Color property added to the blackboard*

You can also create properties by clicking on the "+" button at the top-right of the blackboard, selecting a type, and giving it a name. Once created, the property can be dragged onto the canvas to automatically create a new node for the property inside the Shader Graph Editor, to be used as an input node.

Also, as you can see in Figure 2-28, when selecting a property in the blackboard or in the Shader Graph Editor, the different attributes of that property will be shown inside the **Nodes Settings** tab of the **Graph Inspector**.

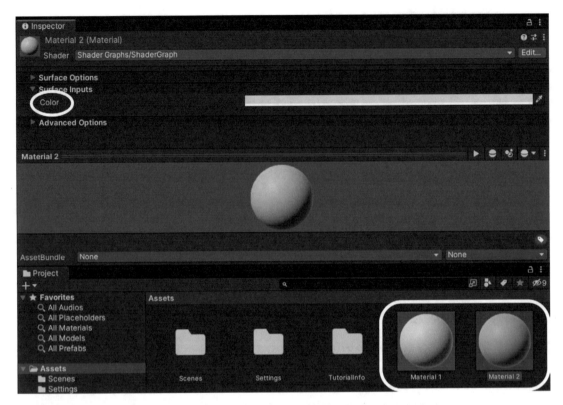

Figure 2-28. *Different materials with the same shader referenced*

Now, the color property is going to be exposed and editable. In Figure 2-28, we can see two different materials with the same shader but with different color property values assigned, inside the Unity Editor Assets folder under the Project tab.

Graph Inspector

Graph Inspector inside Shader Graph is a panel that provides additional controls and settings for the currently selected node or group of nodes in the shader graph, as well as general control over the overall shader properties.

Graph Inspector is a contextual window, meaning that it displays different options and controls depending on the type of node or group of nodes selected. For example, selecting a texture node will display options for setting the texture's resolution, tiling, and filtering properties, while selecting a math node will display options for setting the operation type, input values, and output ranges.

Graph Inspector is divided into the following main parts:

- Graph Settings

- Node Settings

Graph Settings

This part of Graph Inspector lets you change the general rendering settings of your shader (Figure 2-29).

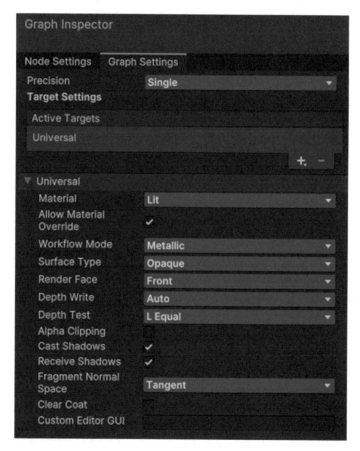

Figure 2-29. *Graph Settings tab*

- **Precision**: This setting allows you to change the precision of the floating coma values that use the shader to apply calculations. Single is more precise than Half but will use more computer resources.

- **Active Targets**: This will change the pipeline that your shader will run; as we are going to use URP, I don't recommend tweaking this setting.

- **Material**: This will let you change the type of material to generate from:

  - Lit: A 3D material that interacts with lighting generating realistic shading in your object

  - Unlit: If you don't want your shader to interact with lighting, or to be affected by it, this is the setting to choose; it will be more performant than the previous one.

  - Sprite Lit and Unlit: Are the same as the previous ones but for sprites, which are 2D elements

  - Decal: Will generate a shader that will behave like a "sticker" to an object that will also interact with light, creating a 3D illusion effect.

- **Allow Override Material**: This toggle will expose all the graph settings in the graph inspector of Unity under the foldout **Surface Options.**

- **Workflow Mode**: This will allow you to change between metallic (reflections in the material) or specular (change the color of the specular light reflection).

- **Surface Type**: Here you can set your object to transparent if you want to create vanishing effects or make your object disappear at any moment.

- **Render Face**: Here you can select the side of the polygons of the mesh to be rendered. You can choose the back face (for example, if you want to see a force field from inside of it) or the front side as default, or both sides.

- **Depth Write and Depth Test**: These two parameters will require a further explanation when needed, but, basically, they let you establish how the vertex will be evaluated depending on the distance to the camera, taking into account how deep in the z-axis that vertex is (fog calculations, transparent and semitransparent color mixing, etc.).

- **Alpha Clipping**: This will set up a threshold to change from totally opaque to totally transparent.

- **Cast Shadows & Receive Shadows**: They are self-explanatory.

- **Fragment Normal Space**: We won't pay much attention to this setting but it will be related to how normal maps are calculated in the shader.

- **Clear Coat**: Adds a second material layer that simulates a transparent and thin coating on top of the base material with maximum smoothness value.

- **Custom Editor GUI**: Sometimes you have a shader with some interesting data types that cannot be nicely represented using the built-in Unity material editor. Unity provides a way to override the default way shader properties are presented so that you can define your own.

Node Settings

The Node Settings tab will display editable information about a selected node in the Shader Graph Editor. Each node may have its own settings; for example, by left-clicking the color node we created we can see several settings, as in Figure 2-30.

Figure 2-30. *Node Settings tab*

- **Name**: Exposed name of the property

- **Reference**: The string that identifies that property if you want to access it from code.

- **Default**: The value that will take the property when a material with this shader is created.

- **Mode**: In this case, changing to HDR will allow you to set light intensity, useful for emissive materials.

- **Precision**: Inherited from the graph settings, but you can override it.

- **Exposed**: If toggled off it will no longer appear in the material inspector in Unity.

- **Override property declaration**: This toggle will allow the material shared by different objects to have this property overridden from the main material and allow you to change that property dynamically from one object to another, without creating new instances of the material.

Master Stack

The master stack in Unity Shader Graph is a collection of nodes and settings that define the overall behavior and output of a shader graph. It serves as the top-level node in the graph and determines how the various nodes and functions in the graph are combined and processed to create the final output.

The master stack (Figure 2-31) is where the **Vertex** and **Fragment** shaders will receive the outputs of every calculation performed in your shader graph. The master stack is divided into a **vertex block** and a **fragment block.**

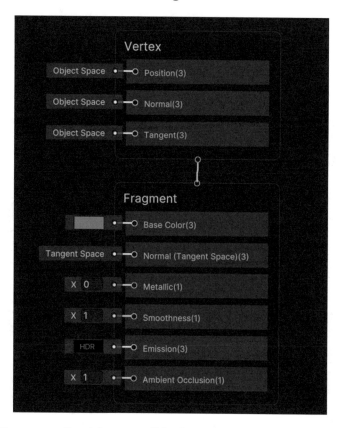

Figure 2-31. *Master stack with vertex block and fragment block*

Vertex Block

The vertex block will let you modify the following three main properties of every vertex in the surface of a mesh:

- Position node
- Normal node
- Tangent node

Position Node

Every vertex has a position in space and can be changed in real-time by modifying the **Position** node of the vertex block. Doing that will allow you to create different deformation effects (Figure 2-32), procedural animations, and other amazing effects.

Figure 2-32. *Deformation effect changing the vertex positions of a mesh*

Normal Node

As we saw previously in Chapter 1, the normal of a vertex indicates in which direction the vertex is looking based on the medium value of the normals of the triangles around that vertex. Changing the normals of a vertex will change how the object will interact with lighting. In Figure 2-33, you can see that the same object can be shown as smooth- or hard-faced depending on the values of the normals of each vertex.

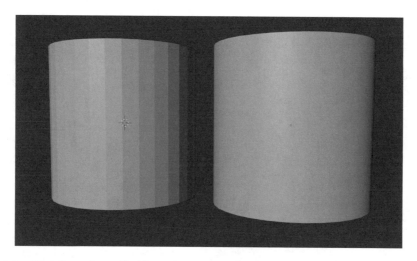

Figure 2-33. *Hard surface (left), soft surface (right) depending on the normal value of each vertex*

Tangent Node

The tangent value of a vertex is an important component of 3D graphics. It is used to define the direction of the surface of a model in relation to its texture space, and to enable a range of advanced texturing and shading techniques. It is perpendicular to the normal vector of the vertex. Normally, when the normal value of a vertex is modified, the tangent value should also be compensated to avoid aberrations in the surface of the object.

Fragment Block

The fragment block is a key component of the master stack, and is responsible for determining how the final output of the shader graph is generated. The fragment block contains a set of nodes and settings that define how the shader interacts with the pixels (or fragments) that make up the final output 2D image of a 3D object on screen.

Base Color

This node will give each pixel a determined color to be output on screen (Figure 2-34). You can assign here the output of a texture UV-mapped on the object, a plain color like in Figure 2-34, or even use the relative position of the pixel on the screen to change its color. We will use different techniques in this book to modify the colors of the pixels that represent our object on screen.

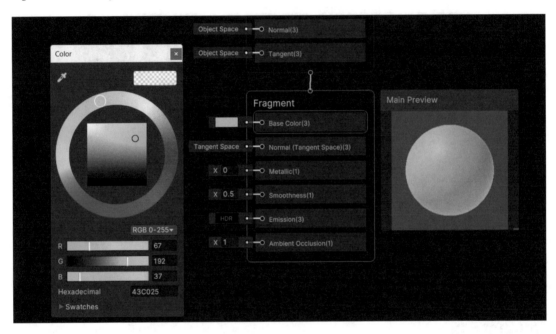

Figure 2-34. *Change color using Base Color node*

Normal

This node will change how the pixel will interact with lighting. We will use normal maps to assign different light interactions with the pixels (Figure 2-35). Normal maps encode surface normal information in the RGB channels of a texture map, with each pixel in the texture representing the direction that the surface is facing at that point. This gives a material the property of faking bumps or micro-deformations in the surface of the object without deforming the actual mesh.

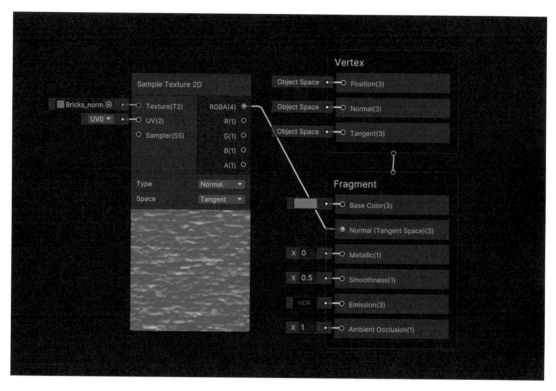

Figure 2-35. *Normal map assigned to Normal node in fragment block*

In Figure 2-36, you can see the same object without the normal map (left) and with the normal map assigned (right).

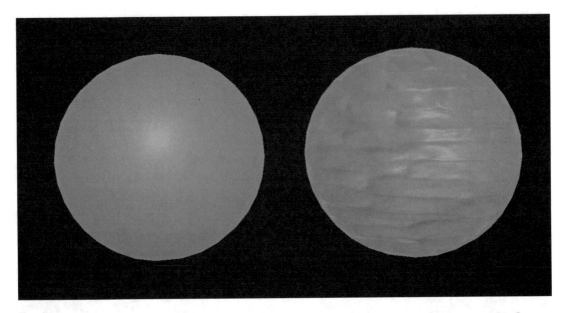

Figure 2-36. *Comparison between no normal map and normal map applied*

Metallic

In real life, a metallic object has free electrons in its surface that vibrate, absorbing the light energy and then reflecting it back. That is the reason metals have that reflective look, as you can see in Figure 2-37.

Figure 2-37. *Metallic objects in real life*

In video game graphics, the metallic property of a material determines how shiny and reflective its surface appears. A material with high metallic properties will appear highly reflective, like a mirror, while a material with low metallic properties will appear more diffuse.

Metallic is a property that will display when you select **Metallic Workflow** in **Graph Inspector**. This node expects a float from 0 to 1 which will determine how reflective the material will be (Figure 2-38). You can use reflection probes to let the material reflect the skybox of your scene and the object around that reflection probe. We will learn how to set reflection probes in later chapters.

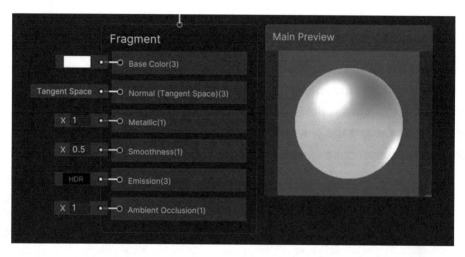

Figure 2-38. *Metallic of a material set to 1*

Smoothness

This property dictates how smooth a surface of an object is. A fully smooth surface could be the screen of your mobile phone, while a non-smooth sample could be the surface of an eraser or a clay figure. Non-smooth materials have little imperfections that trap and deviate light that bounces inside them. This phenomena can be replicated using the smoothness input.

This property takes a float value from 0 to 1 and determines if the material will absorb lighting (0) or will reflect it (1) (Figure 2-39).

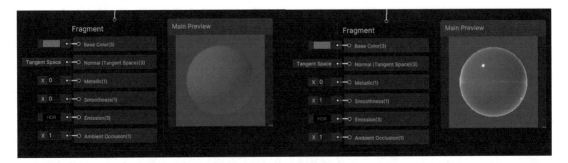

Figure 2-39. *Smoothness = 0 (left) vs. Smoothness = 1 (right)*

Emission

Emission is often used to create the appearance of glowing or illuminated surfaces in games. For example, the moon will have high emission values to create the appearance of a glowing effect. Similarly, the lights on a vehicle (Figure 2-40) can be made to glow. It could be used to attract the player's attention, glowing up important buttons in the interface that the player has to press.

Figure 2-40. *Different light sources with emissive materials in real life*

The Emission node will allow you to input a color that will determine how emissive the object will be (Figure 2-41), causing a bloom effect depending on the intensity parameter in the HDR color input and the threshold intensity value of your **post-processing volume**, because bloom is a post-processing effect.

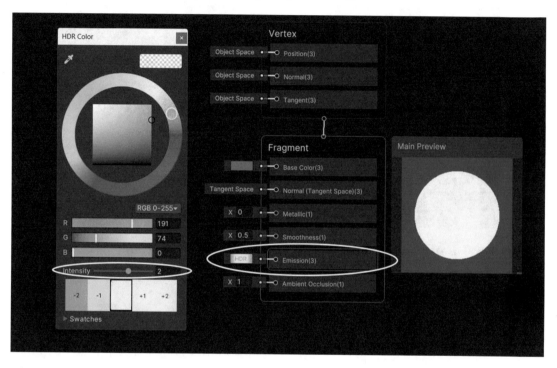

Figure 2-41. *Emission color applied to a material with intensity 2*

The emission effect will only work as expected if we have set up a post-processing volume inside our Unity Editor. In the next subsection we will explain a little bit more about post-processing effects and what they are useful for, like the emission or bloom effect we have just studied, and how to set up a post-processing volume object to make them pop up in our game.

Figure 2-42 shows a sphere running the previously created shader on its surface.

Figure 2-42. *Emissive material attached to an object in the scene*

Post-Processing Effects

Post processing refers to the application of visual effects to every rendered image of the scene (frame). In Figure 2-43, you can see the same scene split in two, with the top part showing some post-processing effects like (vignette, **bloom**, tone mapping, and color adjustments) and the bottom part having the post-processing disabled. Remember that this scene with these assets is available to download from the Unity Hub as "3D Sample Scene URP" template.

Figure 2-43. *Comparative between post processing enabled and disabled*

These effects are going to extract the color buffer of the last frame captured by the camera and apply visual operations on top of it to create another modified frame, which is the one that is going to be definitely rendered on the screen. Post-processing effects upgrade your game's visual quality a lot, but they are **expensive** in terms of **performance** of the GPU, so use them wisely in your games, especially if you want to create a game for mobile platforms.

In the template scene of the 3D URP Template project, you have a post-processing volume object that was created by default and contains a **Volume** component that is responsible for running and tweaking the post-processing effects (Figure 2-44).

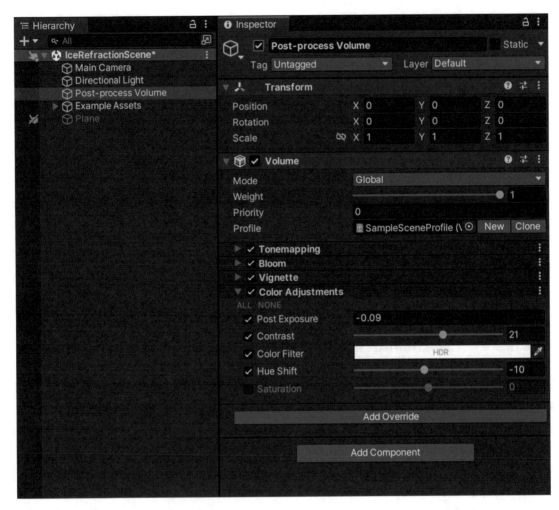

Figure 2-44. *Post-processing volume*

If this object and component don't exist in your Hierarchy tab, the post-processing effects will not trigger and some effects inside the shader, like the emission, will not behave as expected. Let's see a comparison between the same glowy shader of Figure 2-41 with the post-processing volume enabled and disabled (Figure 2-45).

Figure 2-45. *Comparative between post-processing volume enabled and disabled*

The post-processing volume will be created and set up by default in the template scene inside the URP 3D Template project. If you didn't use this template, you can add the **volume** component to any object in your hierarchy. I personally like to add it to the Camera object, since post processing is a rendering feature deeply associated with the camera. But you can create a new empty object into which to add the volume component.

To add a **volume** component to any game object, do the following:

- Select the game object that you want to host the volume component.

- Go to the Inspector tab with the game object still selected.

- At the very bottom of the Inspector tab, click the button **Add Component**.

- Search the name **Volume** and select the first one (Figure 2-46).

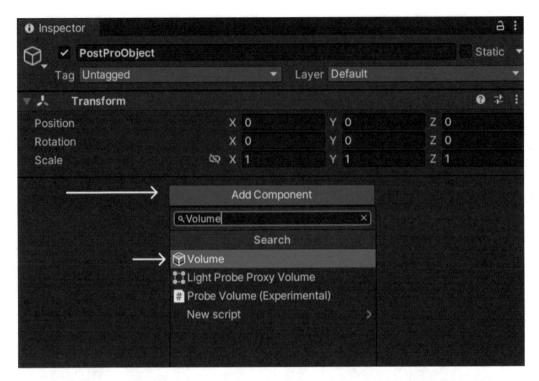

Figure 2-46. *Adding the post-processing volume to the post-processing object*

When it's added, you will find that the **Profile** setting is empty. You can load any profile existing in your project by dragging and dropping it from the Project tab, or you can click the **New** button to create a new profile that will automatically be referenced and stored in your project (Figure 2-47).

Figure 2-47. *Created and loaded Profile setting*

This profile is a special asset that will hold the post-processing effects and their internal settings. Let's add a bloom effect by clicking on the **Add Override** button and then select **Post Processing ➤ Bloom** (Figure 2-48).

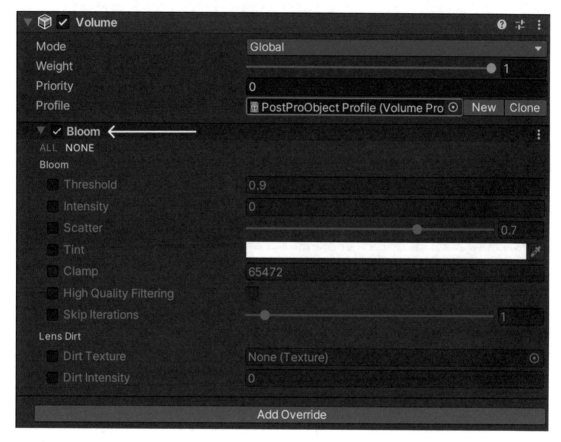

Figure 2-48. *Added bloom post-processing effect*

Nothing has changed, and our yellow ball is not glowing at all, because, by default, the **Threshold** and **Intensity** settings are disabled. To enable them, click the toggle box at the left side of the setting name. Then, crank up the Intensity value to 1 (Figure 2-49).

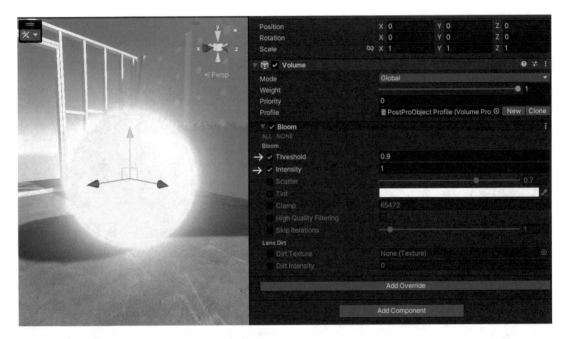

Figure 2-49. *Added bloom post-processing effect*

The effect is not similar to Figure 2-42, because we have overexposed values of the yellow color. To make this more subtle, we will add another post-processing effect called **tone mapping**. The purpose of tone mapping is to ensure that the final image appears visually appealing and avoids loss of detail or overexposure.

To add and set up the tone-mapping effect, do the following:

- Click on Add Override and select **Post Processing ➤ Tone Mapping.**

- Enable the **Mode** setting and select **ACES (Figure 2-50).**

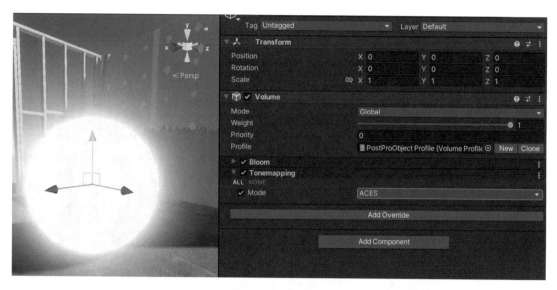

Figure 2-50. *Added bloom with tone mapping to the post-processing effect*

You can select between the following modes, taking into account the final look you want to achieve in your game:

- **None**: Use this option if you do not want to apply tone mapping.

- **Neutral**: Use this option if you only want range-remapping with minimal impact on color hue and saturation. It is generally a good starting point for extensive color grading.

- **ACES**: Use this option to apply a close approximation of the reference ACES tone mapper for a more cinematic look. It is more contrasted than Neutral, and has an effect on actual color hue and saturation. If you use this tone mapper, Unity does all the grading operations in the ACES color spaces for optimal precision and results.

I recommend you to keep these post-processing volume and settings every time you want to add a color input in HDR mode or you want to apply any emissive effects in your shaders.

Also, **make sure** that the Camera component in your Camera object has the setting **Post Processing enabled** (Figure 2-51). If not, the Game View will not display any post-processing effects and therefore your final game will NOT trigger post-processing effects.

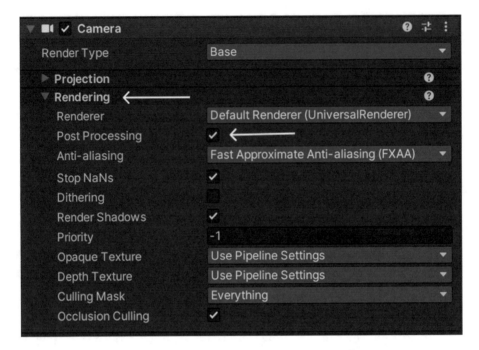

Figure 2-51. *Activate Post Processing setting in Camera object*

Post processing is a deep topic that we are not going to dive into further in this book, although there is a lot of documentation for Unity that describes the remaining post-processing effects in detail to enhance your game's visuals.

Ambient Occlusion

Ambient occlusion (AO) is a shading and lighting technique used in video-game graphics to simulate the way ambient light is blocked or scattered by nearby objects. It creates the illusion of depth and realism in a scene by darkening areas where objects are close together and lightening areas where there is more space, saving a lot of resources of real-time lighting/shading calculations.

Normally, ambient occlusion maps (Figure 2-52) are used to set up extra shading and sense of depth in objects without three-dimensional bumps, avoiding extra lighting calculations.

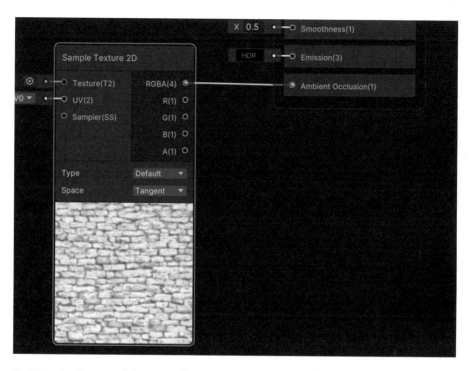

Figure 2-52. *Assign ambient occlusion map*

This value can be set up to establish how obscured a pixel is from light sources by other objects in the scene, such as walls. We can see in Figure 2-53 a comparison of two spheres, with and without an ambient occlusion map.

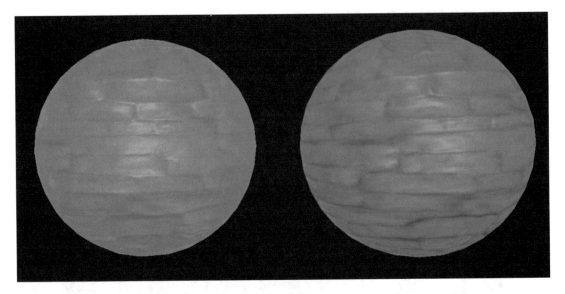

Figure 2-53. *Comparison between a material without ambient occlusion map (left) and a material with ambient occlusion map (right)*

Alpha

The alpha value of a pixel will determine how transparent that pixel is; in other words, how much the player will see through it. This node will accept values from 0 (fully transparent object) to 1 (fully opaque object).

If you change the Surface Type in the Graph Settings to Transparent, this output will appear in the Fragment Inspector, letting you introduce a value from 0 to 1 that will determine how transparent and opaque the material will be, respectively (Figure 2-54).

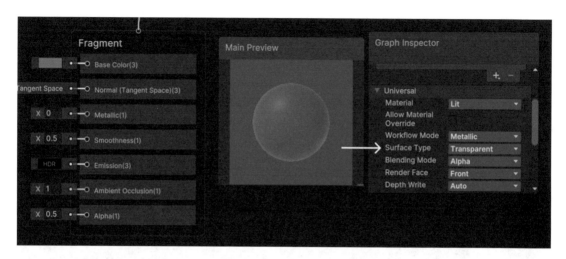

Figure 2-54. *Material set to transparent with a 0.5 alpha*

Figure 2-55 shows a translucent sphere with a 0.5 alpha, letting you see halfway through it, still identifying the object in the scene.

Figure 2-55. *Transparent material in the scene*

Specular Color

If you change the Workflow option in the Graph Settings from **Metallic** to **Specular** you can change the specular reflection's color in the surface of an object, as done in Figure 2-56.

Specular workflow and Metallic workflow are two different shading models used in Unity materials. The Metallic workflow defines a surface's reflectivity with a metallic parameter, which ranges from 0 (non-metallic) to 1 (fully metallic).

In the Specular workflow, the surface's reflectivity is defined by a Specular Color parameter, which determines the color of the specular highlight.

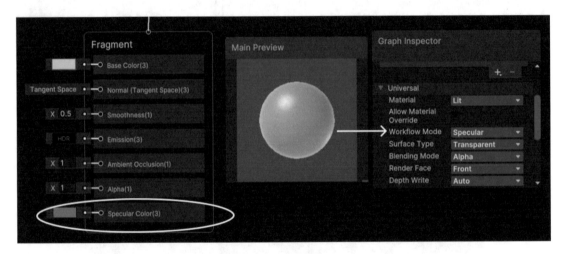

Figure 2-56. *Specular reflections color changed*

You can see in Figure 2-57 a spherical object running the previously created shader, creating custom color reflections when lighting hits its surface.

Figure 2-57. *Sphere with specular shader, with custom color reflections*

74

Shader Graph Elements

In this section we are going to cover the following main elements that can be used inside the Shader Graph Editor and how to use them:

- Nodes
    - Create nodes
    - Ports and connections
    - Node previews
    - Grouping nodes
- Properties
    - Properties settings
        - Reference
        - Exposed
        - Default
        - Modes
- Redirect elbows
- Sticky notes

Nodes

Nodes are the main element to be used inside the Shader Graph Editor. They are classified in different groups. They can be individual values that are input inside operation nodes, which perform different mathematical operations to achieve the result we want.

We will talk in this section about how to create nodes inside the Shader Graph Editor, but we will explain the different nodes we can use in the next chapter, which will cover some of the most important nodes we are going to use in this book.

Create Nodes

A node can be created, as we did at the beginning of this chapter, by just right-clicking in any empty space inside the Shader Graph Editor and then selecting the first option: **Create Node.**

This will pop up a series of dropdown categories, where every node is available. To select any one, just open the dropdown by left-clicking on top of it and left-clicking again on the name of the node. This will instantiate it inside the Shader Graph Editor. In Figure 2-58, you can see an example of creating a float input node.

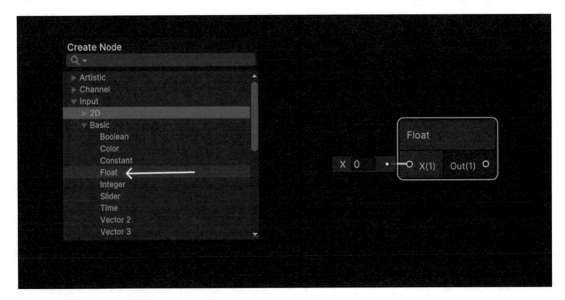

Figure 2-58. *Creating a float node*

Notice in the figure that the pop-up where you can select the node also includes a search bar to write the name of the specific node you are looking for.

Ports and Connections

Every node has inputs and outputs, shown as small circles, known as ports. Inputs are always on the left side of the node while outputs are on the right (Figure 2-59).

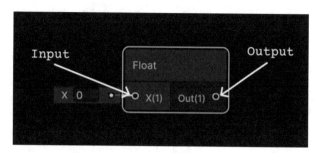

Figure 2-59. *Inputs and outputs*

You can create connections between nodes by clicking on the port. While still holding the mouse button, drag over to another port, and a connection will be made. You can only connect an output to an input. It's not possible to connect an input to another input, or an output to another output. Output ports can also have multiple connections to other nodes, but input ports must only have a single connection.

You can also delete a connection by selecting it and then right-clicking and selecting **Delete** or by just clicking the delete button of the keyboard while it is selected.

In Figure 2-60, you can check different connections between input nodes and an operational node that requires some inputs. In particular, we are inputting the UV coordinates and a texture asset to a texture sampler, which will output the RGBA color to the Base Color of the object in the Fragment Block.

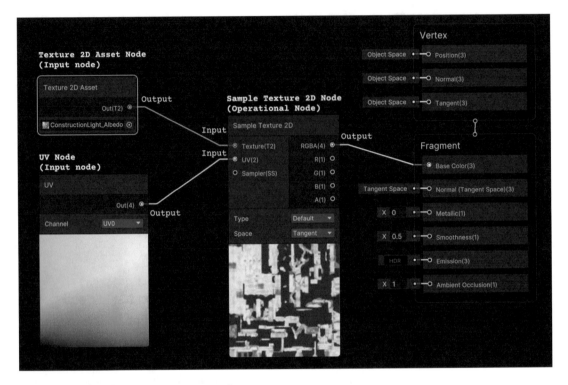

Figure 2-60. *Connections sample*

Ports always display a keycode value in parentheses next to the name of the port. This numeric value indicates the data type the node input is expecting, which is also indicated by the color of the connection. I will list here the different data types you can find and the key and color identification:

- Float (1), light blue

- Vector2 (2), green

- Vector3 (3), yellow

- Vector4 (4), pink

- Color (property only; converts to Vector4 in graph, so is also pink)

- Matrix (2x2, 3x3, or 4x4), blue

- Boolean (B), purple

- Texture2D (T2), red

- Texture2DArray (T2A), red

- Texture3D (T3), red

- Cubemap (C), red

- Virtual Texture (VT), gray

- SamplerState (SS), gray

- Gradient (G), gray

Unlike other data types, different-size vectors can be connected to other-sized vector ports. For example, a Vector3 or Vector4 can be connected to a Vector2 port (Figure 2-61).

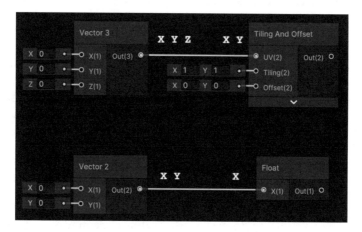

Figure 2-61. *Vector truncation*

This will cause the vector to be truncated. In the case of the Float input port, only the X/R component is used, while YZW/GBA is truncated. For a Vector2, the XY/RG components are used and ZW/BA is truncated, and for Vector3, XYZ/RGB are used, with W/A truncated.

As you can see in Figure 2-62, this flexibility is also used in some operational nodes that can modify their input type in order to operate with different data magnitudes (Add, Subtract, Divide, Multiply, and more).

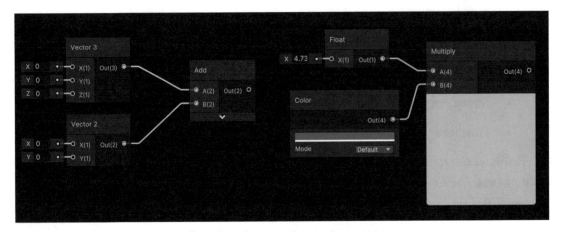

Figure 2-62. *Dynamic input ports in some operational nodes*

Node Previews

You may have noticed that some nodes include a small window at the bottom. This small square is called the **node preview** and shows the result of the operation being performed, depending on the input the node has been fed with.

It is really useful to see whether the steps you are performing during the development of the shader are implemented correctly.

In Figure 2-63, you can see that the sine is working as expected, creating a repetition pattern in a wave form, inputting an over-scaled polar coordinates output.

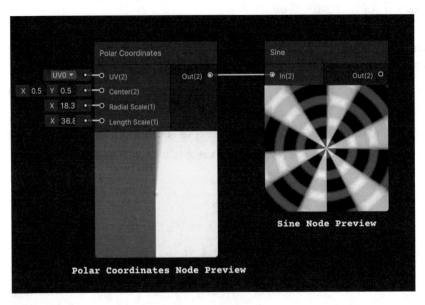

Figure 2-63. *Polar coordinates and Sine previews*

Group Nodes

You know what they say: *tidy house, tidy mind.* As your shader graph gets bigger and bigger, it is common to lose yourself inside a huge amount of nonsense connections. When this happens, it is recommended that you classify the nodes into small groups that define the whole functionality that they are performing. To do that, just select the number of nodes you want to group and then right-click on one of them and select **Create Group** (Figure 2-64).

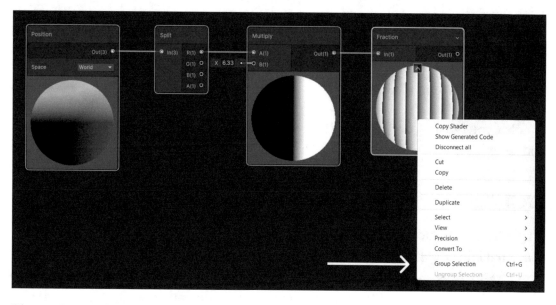

Figure 2-64. *Creating a group out of some nodes*

Then, you can name the group right away and rename it by just double-clicking on the group.

Now, you can select all the nodes at once, move them around, or delete them as if they were one single node (Figure 2-65).

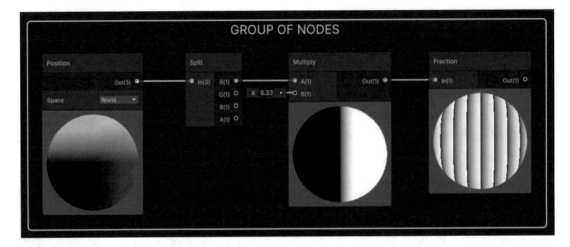

Figure 2-65. *Group of nodes*

Also, you can drag and drop any node inside the node group to include it inside that group.

Properties

Properties are the most useful and flexible tool Shader Graph has. They are input nodes converted into an exposed variable that you can tweak from outside the Shader Graph Editor. This will let you create unique materials with the same shader referenced, making your game unique without the need to recreate several shaders to achieve similar results

You can only convert variables of some data types, such as float, Vector2, Vector3, and Color.

To convert an input node into an exposed property you just need to right-click on the input node and then select **Convert To ➤ Property.** After that, the input node will become a small box with the name of the property and an output value. This new node will be visible inside the Blackboard, and some settings can be set inside Graph Inspector (Figure 2-66).

Figure 2-66. *Group of nodes*

When you create a material out of this shader graph, you can see in the Inspector tab that this property is exposed and modifiable in real-time (Figure 2-67).

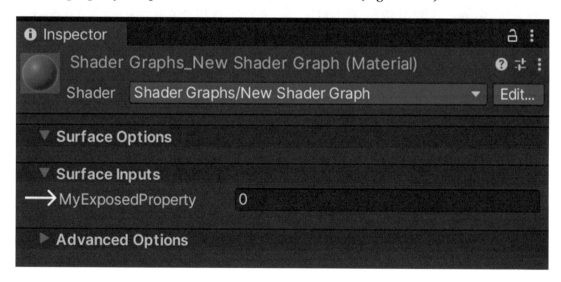

Figure 2-67. *Exposed property*

Properties Settings

Properties have a bunch of settings that change depending on the type of property. They can be set in the Graph Inspector to give the user a better shader-making experience.

Reference

The reference is the internal name of your property. It is used when you want to access or modify its value from a custom script. It usually starts with "_" and changes itself when you change the name of the variable to match it.

Exposed

If toggled off it will keep the property hidden in the Inspector tab when the material is selected.

Default

This is the default value that the property will have every time you create a new material with that Shader Graph referenced.

Modes

Depending on the property type there are different modes you can change between. For example, in a float property you can set the following:

- **Default**: Shows a regular float field in the Material Inspector.

- **Slider**: Equivalent of the "Range" property in shader code. Can set a **Minimum** and **Maximum** value. The property will appear with a slider in the Inspector (Figure 2-68).

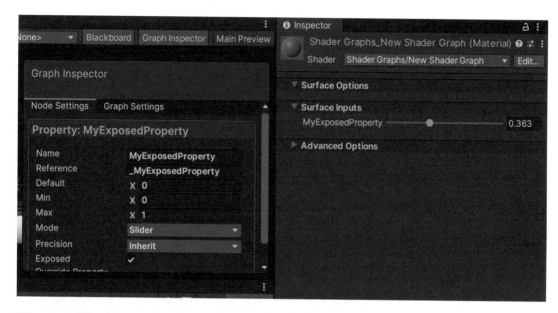

Figure 2-68. *Float property set in Slider mode*

The Color property has the following modes:

- **Default**: A regular color. From the Material Inspector it can only be set to values between 0 and 1 for each component.

- **HDR (High Dynamic Range)**: A color which components' value can be outside the 0–1 range. The Inspector shows this by having an Intensity slider added to the Color Picker UI (Figure 2-69).

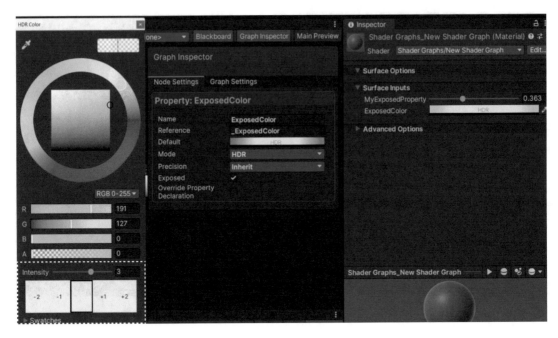

Figure 2-69. *Color in HDR mode*

Redirect Elbow

Sometimes, connections are overlapped by some nodes and it can be difficult to distinguish between them and to know exactly where they are connected (Figure 2-70).

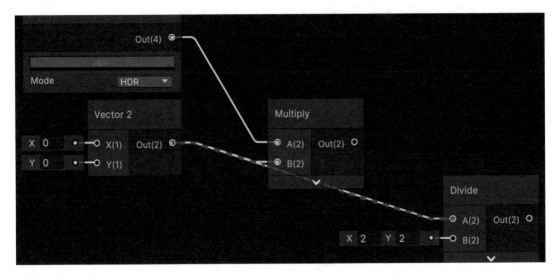

Figure 2-70. *Case of overlapped connection (bad legibility)*

To better organize connections, you can add redirect elbows. This tool allows you to create a bridge between different points of the same connection (Figure 2-71).

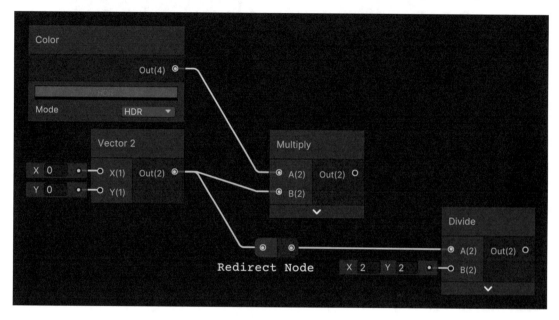

Figure 2-71. *Redirected connection (good legibility)*

You can create it by double-clicking along the connection wire (or right-clicking the connection and selecting it from the dropdown). It can be moved or deleted the same way as can common nodes.

Sticky Notes

These elements allow you to take important notes about anything inside your shader graph, serving the same purpose as comments do in scripting. They are useful when you want to clarify some default values, or explain why you are using a certain node to create that final result, or you can just write anything funny on them (Figure 2-72).

Figure 2-72. *Some samples of sticky notes*

You can create one by just right-clicking in any empty space inside the Shader Graph Editor and then selecting **Create Sticky Note.**

If you right-click on a sticky note you can change some parameters or perform some actions, like the following:

- Adjust the text size

- Change between light and dark themes.

- Fit the text to the size of the containing box.

Summary

In this chapter we have set up Unity, from creating our first project to creating our first shader graph in a new scene. We have also learned how to upgrade and set up any project in URP, which is going to be our primary render pipeline in this book.

We also learned about every Vertex and Fragment node that will deal with each property of the material, such as vertex position, base color, normal, and more.

We studied post-processing effects and how to set up our post-processing volume to achieve incredible glowy finishes in our games.

And, finally, we covered almost every element and interface available inside the Shader Graph Editor, which will be the main tool that we will use to create amazing effects.

In the next chapter, we are going to review the most important nodes that we are going to use in this book.

CHAPTER 3

Commonly Used Nodes

Shader Graph offers myriad nodes with which to create great shader effects. There are more than 200 nodes in the latest version of Shader Graph, but we will only study the ones that will help us in the projects in this book. Feel free to check out all the nodes in the Unity Manual page[1] dedicated to Shader Graph. Nodes are classified by their type of use and the nature of the calculations they perform, as follows:

- **Artistic**: These are nodes related to colors and mask representations.

- **Channel**: These ones are related to working with the different components of vectors and colors.

- **Inputs**: This huge group covers more than 100 nodes of different inputs, from colors or vectors to ambient texture samplers or even scene camera settings.

- **Math**: Every mathematical operation you can imagine is accessible inside this group, from the sine operation to the multiplication calculation.

- **Procedural**: These nodes use mathematics to generate procedural textures to use in your shaders: noise, checkboards, primitive shapes, etc.

- **Utility**: This group will make your life easier when creating effects. Inside we can find logic nodes to implement branches and different situations inside a shader, custom functions to write your own code, and subgraphs to reuse parts of the shaders you consider generic and reusable among different effects.

---

[1]https://docs.unity3d.com/Packages/com.unity.shadergraph@16.0/manual/Node-Library.html

© Álvaro Alda 2023
Á. Alda, *Beginner's Guide to Unity Shader Graph*, https://doi.org/10.1007/978-1-4842-9672-1_3

- **UV Nodes**: This group will give you access to the UV coordinates of your object, and some of them will even modify those values to create different effects.

- **Block Nodes**: These nodes are represented as outputs in the master nodes; some are present in the Fragment shader you are already familiar with: base color, normal, metallic, smoothness, alpha, etc.

In this chapter, we will create a new project. We will take advantage of a sample template Unity offers us, inside which we will find predefined assets that we can use to implement shaders. Feel free to create your own testing assets if you want.

To download that template, we will open Unity Hub and go to **Projects ➤ New Project** and scroll down until you see the template **3D Sample Scene (URP)**, shown in Figure 3-1. Then, download the template by clicking the highlighted button shown in the right bottom corner and then click the Create Project button. I called mine **Chapter3_Nodes.**

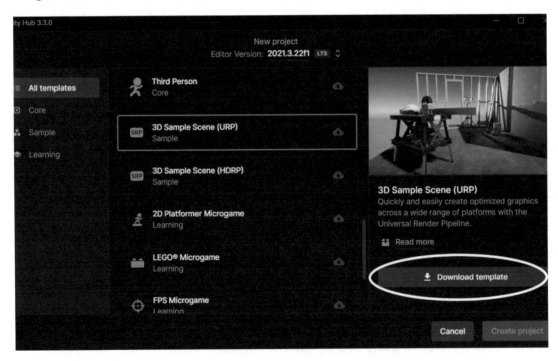

Figure 3-1. *Downloading the URP scene template*

After the loading process finishes you will find yourself looking at something similar to Figure 3-2.

Figure 3-2. *URP sample scene*

Every element in this scene has its own material with default shaders loaded to them. We will create our own shaders to experiment with different nodes.

Feel free to navigate through the folders of the Project tab to get familiar with the assets and reorganize everything as you please before continuing with the next section.

UV Node

Unity uses colors to represent axis directions, as shown in the **Gizmo** (Figure 3-3) at the top-right part of the Scene View tab. A Gizmo is a a visual representation or marker that is displayed in the Scene view or Game view, this Gizmo represents the coordinate system of the Unity world.

Figure 3-3. *Axis color correlation (x: red, z: blue, y: green)*

The UV node is going to access the UV coordinates mapped on the object mesh. The node will show the UV coordinates from (0,0) to (1,1). Using the color correlation we can see that 1,0 will be the maximum value in the x-coordinate, showing a red color, while the 0,1 will show a noticeable green value as we are in the highest value for the y-coordinate.

The value 1,1 will show a yellow color, which is the midpoint between red and green (Figure 3-4). Values equal to or below 0 will be represented as black.

Figure 3-4. *UV input node*

Now, we can create a shader to visually represent how the UVs are mapped in different objects. To do so, create a URP shader graph inside the Project tab, and then create a UV node connected with the Base Color block node of the fragment shader (Figure 3-5).

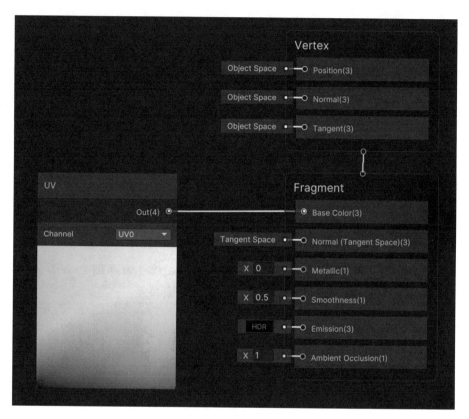

Figure 3-5. *UV representing shader*

Now, you can create a material out of the shader and drag and drop it to the element you want it on in the scene, or assign it to the corresponding MeshRenderer component of that object. Remember to click Save Asset at the top left part of the Shader Graph window.

Check the result in Figure 3-6 to see how those objects were UV mapped.

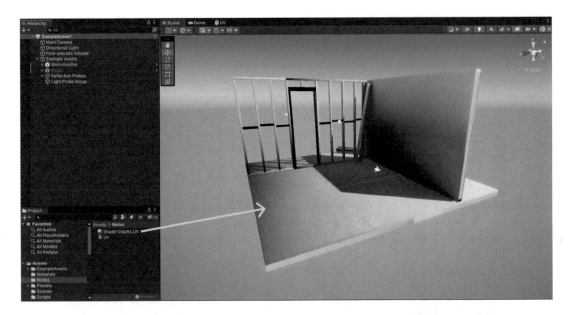

Figure 3-6. *Color correlation of the UV coordinates of the sample objects*

This is what the Sample Texture node will use to map textures in an object. You can modify the created shader as in Figure 3-7.

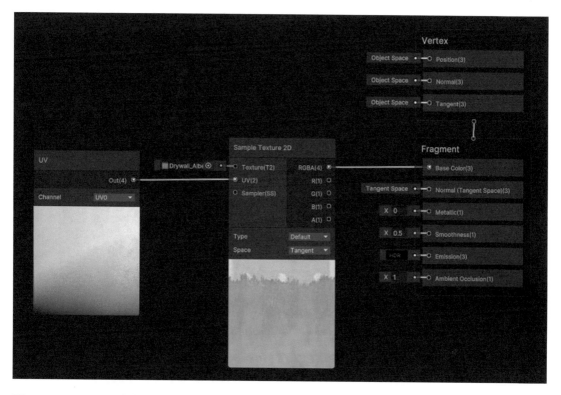

Figure 3-7. *Modify the shader to map a texture over the object*

You can select the texture by clicking in the **Texture (T2)** input in the **Sample Texture 2D** node. After saving the modifications, you will see the selected texture placed on every object that shares that material, like in Figure 3-8.

Figure 3-8. *Using the UV coordinates to sample a texture in an object*

One Minus Node

The **One Minus** node is a mathematical operation node that takes a single input value and outputs the result of subtracting that value from 1.

More specifically, for an input value x, the output of the **One Minus** node will be $1 - x$. This is useful in many shader effects, such as when you want to invert or reverse a value (Figure 3-9).

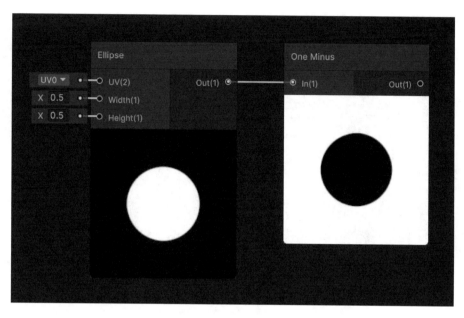

Figure 3-9. *One Minus node inverting colors*

Add Node

In Shader Graph, the **Add** node is a mathematical operation node that takes two input values and outputs the result of adding them together.

More specifically, for input values x and y, the output of the **Add** node will be x + y. This is useful in many shader effects, such as when you want to blend two textures (Figure 3-11) or colors together, or when you want to add a constant value to a parameter (Figure 3-10).

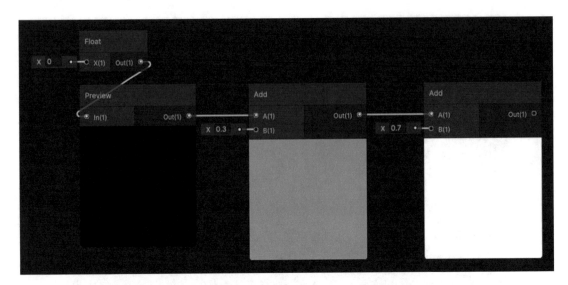

Figure 3-10. *Adding nodes to obtain 1 from 0*

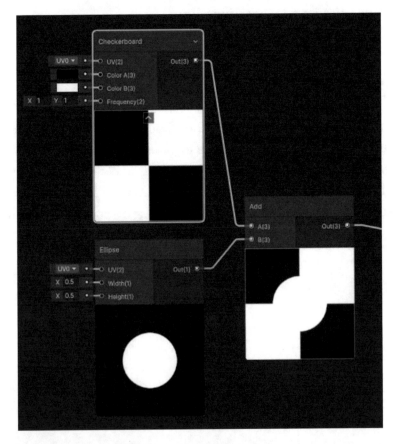

Figure 3-11. *Blending textures using the Add node*

Clamp Node

The Clamp node takes three input values: the input value to be clamped, the minimum value of the output range, and the maximum value of the output range. The output value of the Clamp node will always be within the specified range.

If the input value is greater than the maximum value, the output value will be the maximum value; if the input value is less than the minimum value, the output value will be the minimum value; otherwise, the output value will be the same as the input value.

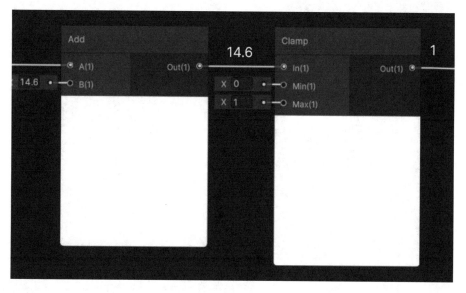

Figure 3-12. *Clamping an input value to 0 as minimum and 1 as maximum*

Note   The Saturation node works in a similar way, but the minimum and maximum values will always be 0 and 1, respectively.

Multiply Node

The **Multiply** node performs a mathematical operation that takes two input values and outputs the result of multiplying them together.

It is useful when you want to adjust the brightness or contrast of a texture or color, or when you want to create a mask or gradient effect by multiplying a texture (Figure 3-13) or a parameter with a gradient map.

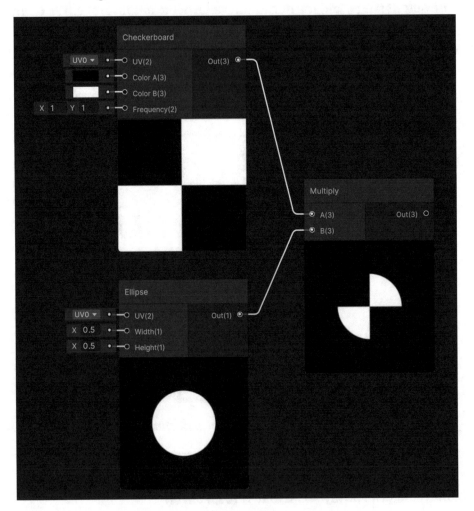

Figure 3-13. *Multiplying two textures to generate a new one*

Also, we can create a new shader using the UV node we already mentioned by multiplying the result by a two-dimensional vector, like in Figure 3-14.

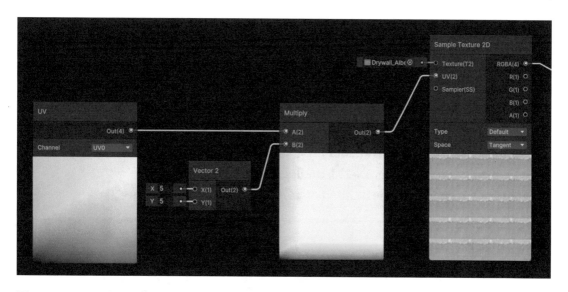

Figure 3-14. *Stretching a texture using the Multiply node*

As you can see in Figure 3-15, the Multiply node and the Vector 2 node will allow us to stretch the texture over our object.

Figure 3-15. *Stretched texture over the object*

Sine Node

The sine function is a periodic function with a period of 2π radians (or 360 degrees), which means that **it repeats itself every 2π radians**. The function has values that range from −1 to 1, with a maximum value of 1 at 90 degrees (π/2 radians) and a minimum value of −1 at 270 degrees (3π/2 radians).

In computer graphics and shader programming, the sine function is often used to create wave-like effects (Figure 3-17), oscillations, and animations.

Sine node responds to the mathematical operation shown in Figure 3-16.

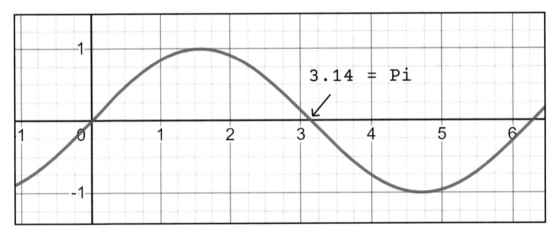

Figure 3-16. *Sine function*

The sine node will receive as input a floating value that represents the radians or degrees (*x* coordinate) in Figure 3-16.

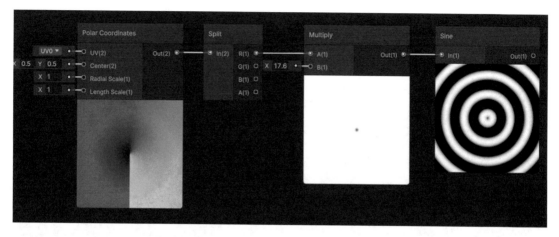

Figure 3-17. *Wave ripple effect using Sine node*

Time Node

The Time node is a special node that provides access to the current time in seconds since the game started. It is a really useful node that we will use to make animations, delays, and every effect that is dynamic in time and/or depends on time transitions.

The time node has the following outputs:

- **Time(1)**: This is the time that has passed since the shader or the level was loaded, in seconds. We will use it as the entry parameter of our Sine node, creating a smooth black-to-white animation in those objects with the material attached.

- **Sine Time(1)**: The output will give us the result of the operation Sine(Time(1)). Gives as output a transition in time of values between −1 and 1.

- **Cosine Time(1)**: This will give us the result of Cosine(Time(1)), which is the same function but with an offset of $\pi/2$.

- **Delta Time(1)**: This will give us the current frame value.

- **Smooth Delta(1)**: This will retrieve the same value as before but smoothed in time, instead of an instant value.

The two first outputs are used frequently, and we will focus on them when using this node.

For example, in Figure 3-18 we have connected the **Time(1)** output of the **Time** node to a **Sine** node input to generate a loopable animation between −1 and 1 (black to white).

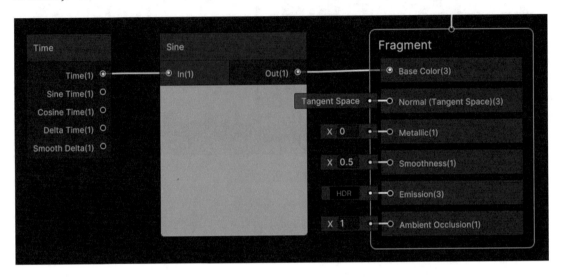

Figure 3-18. *Black-to-white loop transition using the Sine node*

In Figure 3-19, you can see the result of the transition, although I recommend that you replicate every dynamic shader we create in your project to understand it better.

Figure 3-19. *Black-to-white sine transition*

Remap Node

The **Remap** node takes three input values: the **input value** to be remapped, the **input range minimum and maximum value**. It also takes the **output range minimum and maximum value**. The node then scales and maps the input value from the input range to the output range using linear interpolation.

If you replicated the previous sample you may have noticed that the transition stopped with the black color's being longer than the white color. That happened because the sine function output goes from −1 to 1. Negative values will be represented with black, so we need to **remap** the output of the sine node to be from 0 to 1 instead (Figure 3-20).

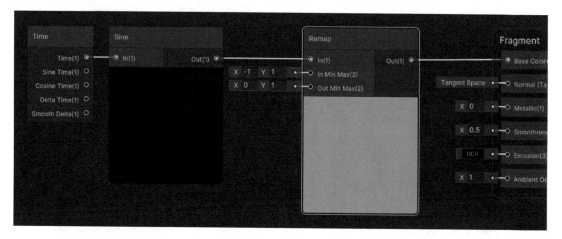

Figure 3-20. *Adding a Remap node*

Lerp Node

The Lerp node will calculate a linear interpolation between two inputs (*a* and *b*), using a third input (*t*) as the interpolator.

The output of the Lerp node is a linear interpolation between the first and second input values, based on the third input value. The third input value (*t*) is typically a value between 0 and 1, and it determines how much weight is given to each input value in the interpolation.

Linear interpolation responds to this formula: $a + (b - a) * t$.

- $t = 0$: Will output *a*.

- $t = 1$: Will output *b*.

- $t = 0.5$: Will output a value between *a* and *b*.

This node is really useful when you want to map different colors using a black-and-white texture as an interpolator, as shown in Figure 3-21.

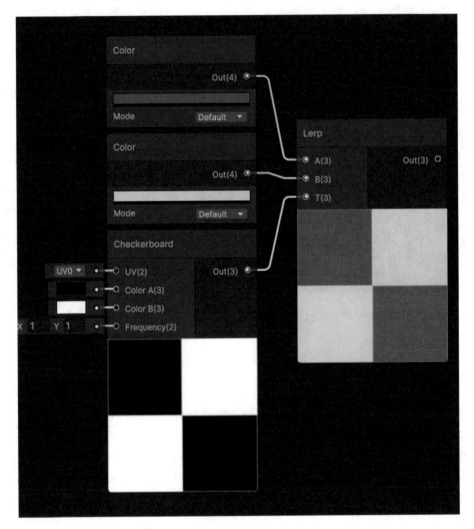

Figure 3-21. *Lerping colors in a chess-pattern texture*

You can also use it to generate a blending between textures using a floating number as an interpolator (*t*), like in Figure 3-22.

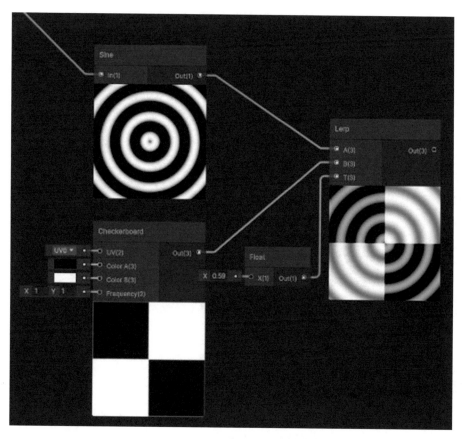

Figure 3-22. *Blending textures using the Lerp node*

We can see the example graph from Figure 3-22 implemented in a panel in a scene in Unity Editor in Figure 3-23.

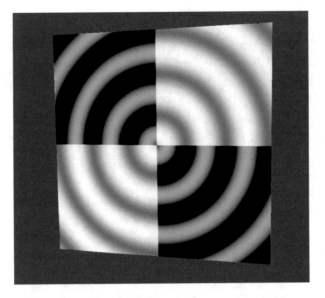

Figure 3-23. *Shader running on an object in the Scene view*

Fraction Node

The Fraction node will apply a fraction operation, which means that it will take the input value and just keep the fractional value. For example:

- Input = 1.5, Output = 0.5

- Input = 4.7, Output = 0.7

- Input = 3.2, Output = 0.2

The exact operation it will performs is:

$$Frac\big(In(1)\big) = In(1) - Floor\big(In(1)\big)$$

Floor(*In*(1)) gives as output the greatest integer less than or equal to *In*(1). For values like:

- Input = 0.3, Output = 0

- Input = 3.2, Output = 3

- **Input = −0.1, Output = −1**

Figure 3-24 shows the output of the Fraction node.

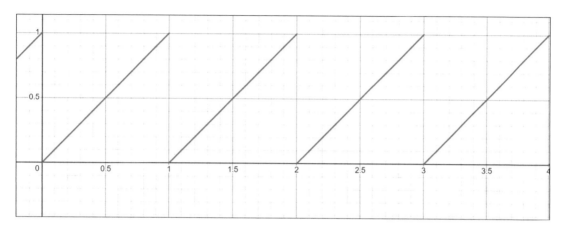

Figure 3-24. *Fraction node*

This allows us to create repetition pattern effects, as we can see in the Figure 3-25, where we take the value of the x UV coordinates, obtaining a horizontal gradient. If we multiply by 5 we will obtain a gradient from 0 to 5, and by passing through a Fraction node we will get five fractions from 0 to 1.

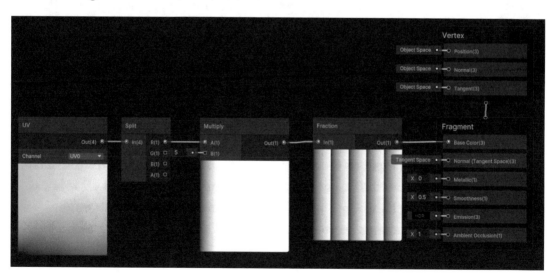

Figure 3-25. *Fraction pattern shader*

This will achieve a really nice pattern-like effect, as shown in Figure 3-26.

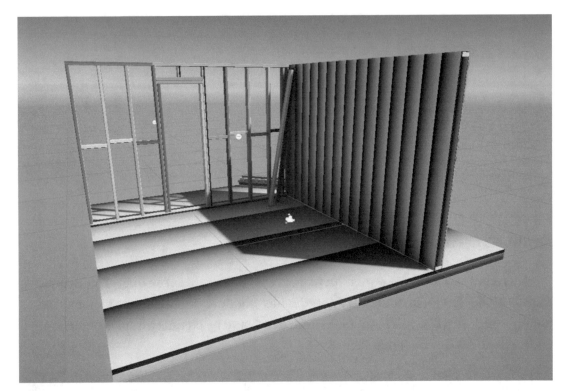

Figure 3-26. *Fraction pattern in sample objects*

Step Node

The **Step** node takes two input values: the input value to be compared to the threshold, and the threshold value itself. The output of the Step node is 0 if the input value is less than the threshold and 1 if the input value is greater than or equal to the threshold.

The **Step** node implements the function shown in Figure 3-27, taking x as the input and y as the output.

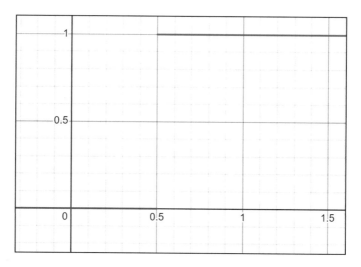

Figure 3-27. *Step function*

As you can see, we have a **Step** function with a threshold value of 0.5. If the input is 0.3, the output value of the Step node is 0, because the input value is less than the threshold value.

If we change the input value to 0.7, the output value of the **Step** node becomes 1 because the input value is now greater than or equal to the threshold value.

Implementing the Step node for the previous sample (Figure 3-28) can generate defined stripes, and the step value will determine the threshold value, translating into how thin or thick those lines are (Figure 3-29).

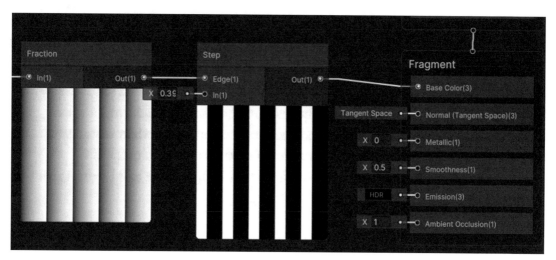

Figure 3-28. *Step node implemented in the previous sample shader graph*

Figure 3-29. *Defined stripes*

SmoothStep Node

The **SmoothStep** node takes three input values: the input value to be compared to the thresholds, and the two threshold values themselves. The output of the **SmoothStep** node is 0 if the input value is less than the first threshold value, 1 if the input value is greater than or equal to the second threshold value, and **a smooth interpolation between 0 and 1** if the input value is between the two threshold values.

In Figure 3-30 we can see the SmoothStep with Edge1(1) = 0.23 and Edge2(1) = 0.74.

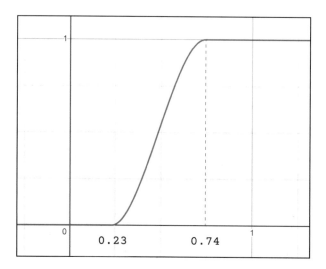

Figure 3-30. *SmoothStep plot*

In Figure 3-31 we can see the previously created stripes passed through a **SmoothStep** node, which defines a custom gradient on them.

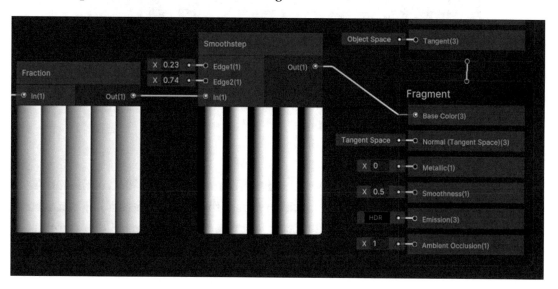

Figure 3-31. *Custom gradient stripes using the SmoothStep node*

113

Power Node

This mathematical node will implement the following formula: $Out = A^B$. This means that the input will exponentially increase or decrease its value. This node can be used, for example, to tighten gradients, like we can see in Figure 3-32.

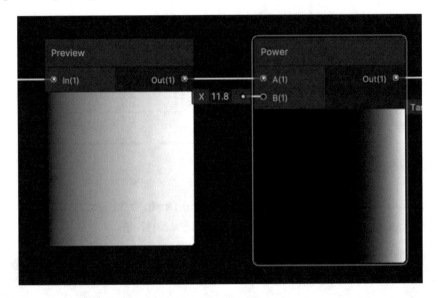

Figure 3-32. *Power node used to tighten gradients*

Position Node

The Position node will give you access to the three-dimensional position of the mesh vertex or the fragment, depending on to which part of the shader the result is connected.

In Figure 3-33 you can see a Position node is connected to the Base Color output, which will color the object surface depending on the distance of the vertices from the center, since we selected the space **Object.**

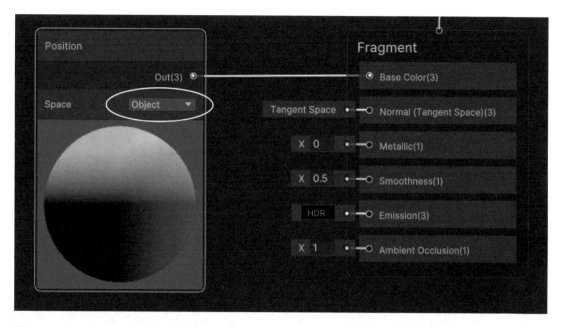

Figure 3-33. *Position node set to object space*

Remember that in object space the vertex position depends on the center of the object; therefore, when you move or rotate the object, nothing will happen.

If you change the coordinate space to **world space** in the dropdown, like in Figure 3-34, the object will be referenced to the origin of the scene and will change color when you move or rotate the object, indicating the distance from the center of the scene (Figure 3-35). This is very useful if you want to create fading particles, which will disappear when they are far away.

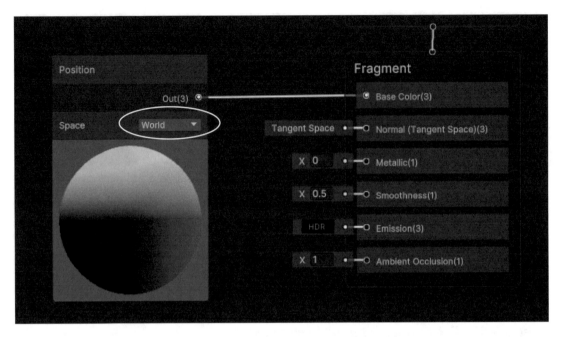

Figure 3-34. *Position node set to world space*

Figure 3-35. *Bucket surface color depending on the distance and orientation to the center*

Dot Product Node

The **Dot Product** node realizes the operation that we described in Chapter 1 when we talked about vectors.

This calculation will be very useful when you want to set directions to the effects (Figure 3-36) or when you want to establish correlations between vectors, like the normals of the vertices of our objects and the light direction.

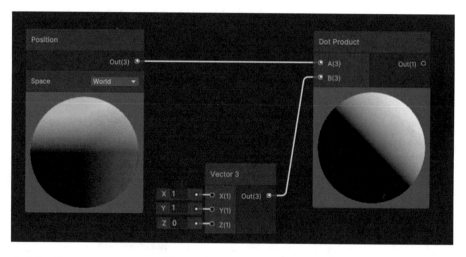

Figure 3-36. *Set a custom gradient direction using the Dot Product node*

If we attach this shader to an object, we can see that we have a custom three-dimensional gradient along it that we can use—for example, to mask effects (Figure 3-37).

Figure 3-37. *Attach the custom gradient direction shader to an object in the scene*

117

Posterize Node

The Posterize node takes an input value, such as a color or grayscale value, and maps it to a specified number of output levels or samples. This can be useful for creating stylized or cartoon-like effects.

For instance, if you set the posterize node to have four levels, any input value between 0 and 0.25 would be mapped to 0, any value between 0.25 and 0.5 would be mapped to 0.5, any value between 0.5 and 0.75 would be mapped to 0.75, and any value between 0.75 and 1.0 would be mapped to 1.0. This results in a posterized or "chunky" appearance of the image. We can see a sample working with the UV node output in Figure 3-38, sampling the U (horizontal) component five times and the V (vertical) component four times.

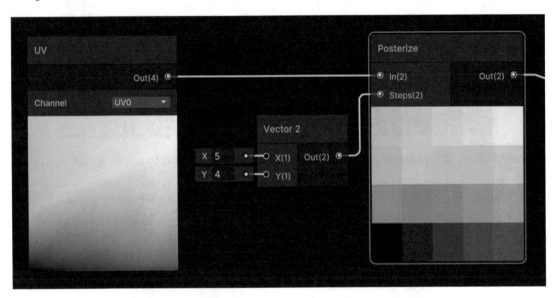

Figure 3-38. *Posterizing the UV output*

This node is really useful if you want to sample a gradient into discrete parts (Figure 3-39).

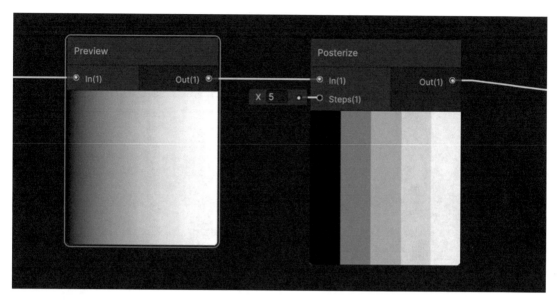

Figure 3-39. *Sampling a gradient*

It is also really nice if you want to create retro textures (Figure 3-40) or retro particles.

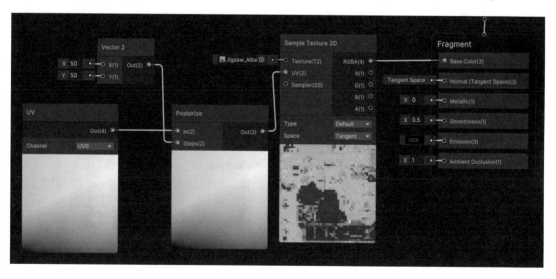

Figure 3-40. *Posterizing a texture to create a retro mosaic version of it*

If we apply the resulting texture to the original object, we will have a pixelated version of it that really looks good in any retro-themed game (Figure 3-41).

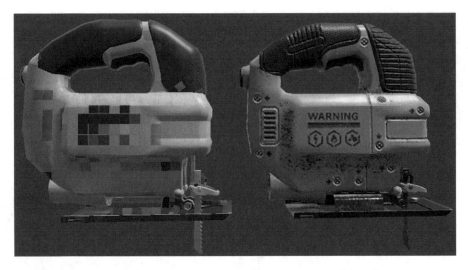

Figure 3-41. *Posterized texture (left) and original object (right)*

Procedural Noise Nodes

Noise can be more than a strong and unpleasant sound. Noise is present in every natural phenomena: in the air, in the water, in the clouds, in the rocks' shapes and colors, or in the disposition of trees in the forest. This randomness and chaos in nature is what makes it beautiful (Figure 3-42).

Noise can be generated in a variety of ways, such as using mathematical functions or sampling from a predefined set of values. In computer graphics and image processing, noise is commonly used to add texture and realism to synthetic images, as well as to simulate natural phenomena like fire, clouds, and water.

Figure 3-42. *Noise in nature*

Noise can achieve the most beautiful and unique results in your shaders. In this book, we are going to take advantage of three of my personal favorite nodes in Shader Graph, the **noise nodes:**

- **Simple Noise**

- **Gradient Noise**

- **Voronoi Noise**

These nodes generate **procedural**[2] black-and-white textures based on the input UV and unique variables each node receives as inputs.

Simple Noise

This node uses a type of noise called "value noise" that displays something very similar to what we saw when old TV screens showed white noise. It has a UV input, selected by default, and a scale value that will rescale the texture, zooming it in and out depending on the value (Figure 3-43).

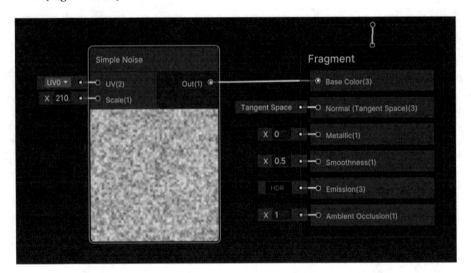

Figure 3-43. *Simple noise node*

---

[2] A procedural asset is one that will be created by a program during execution in real-time, instead of being a preloaded and precreated asset.

We can reduce the scale to zoom and obtain results that we will use to achieve shaders like clouds or snow. For example, in Figure 3-44 I have assigned the noise as a black-and-white texture to the Base Color of the Fragment shader block to obtain a nice marble effect.

Figure 3-44. *Marble effect*

This type of noise can also achieve volatile phenomena effects like fire particles (Figure 3-45).

Figure 3-45. *Fire particles effect with simple noise*

Gradient Noise

The **Gradient Noise** node outputs the result of a Perlin noise function. Perlin noise is a type of gradient noise that was invented by Ken Perlin in the 1980s and is widely used in computer graphics and procedural content generation.

Gradient noise is generated by sampling a grid of pseudo-random values and then interpolating those values using smooth interpolation functions, such as cubic or quintic interpolation. The key idea behind gradient noise is to create smoothly changing values that mimic the appearance of natural phenomena, such as the unevenness of terrain or the irregular patterns found in natural textures like marble or wood.

We can check the difference between the previous noise nodes in Figure 3-46.

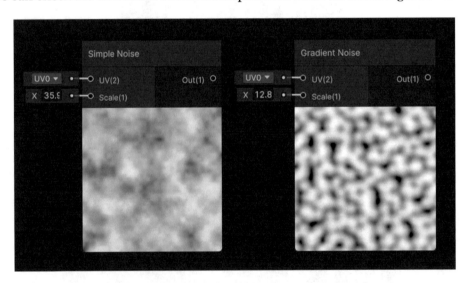

Figure 3-46. *Comparison of simple and gradient nodes*

We will use this node to create a dissolving effect (Figure 3-47), since this noise node suits perfectly when you want to apply connected flow effects like lava lamps, ink drops, and more.

Figure 3-47. *Dissolving effect using Perlin Noise*

Voronoi Noise Node

The **Voronoi Noise node** outputs the result of the calculation of the Voronoi noise (Figure 3-48).

The Voronoi noise (also known as Worley noise or cellular noise) is a type of noise function that generates patterns based on the distances between random points in space. Voronoi noise is named after Georgy Voronoy, a Russian mathematician who studied the properties of geometric tessellations.

Voronoi noise works by dividing space into cells based on the proximity to randomly placed "seed points." Each point in space is assigned to the cell corresponding to the closest seed point, and the value of the noise at that point is determined by some function of the distance between that point and its nearest seed point.

The resulting pattern of cells and noise values has a distinctive "cellular" appearance, with sharp edges and clearly defined regions of high and low values.

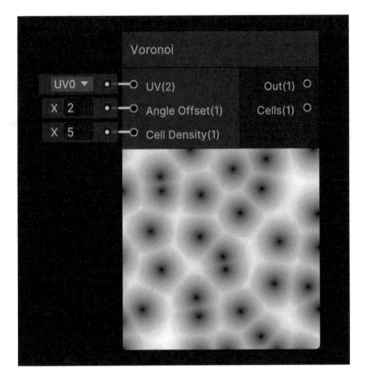

Figure 3-48.   *Voronoi Noise node*

This noise node introduces an input called **Angle Offset**. If you play with it you may see the cells moving around, which is really useful to create animated textures. The **cell density** input works the same as **scale** input in the other noise nodes, zooming the texture in and out. This noise is very present in nature: muscle fibers' disposition, insect wings (Figure 3-49), and water caustics (Figure 3-50). Also, it is really useful to create stained glass or mosaic patterns (Figure 3-51).

Figure 3-49. *Dragonfly wings with a voronoi pattern*

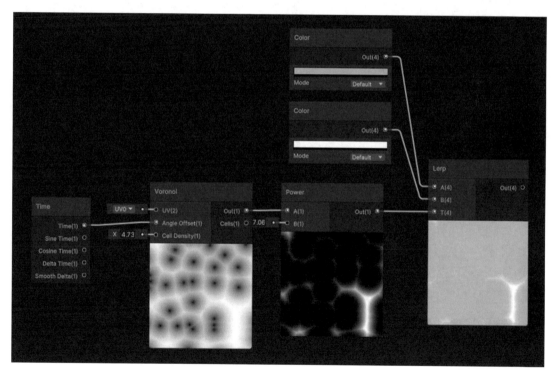

Figure 3-50. *Water caustics shader effect*

Figure 3-50 shows a sample of a really simple dynamic caustics effect of a water surface. We will dig more into this type of shader in further chapters.

The Voronoi Noise node has another output where you can have the cells' disposition, which is really useful to achieve mosaic or stained glass effects (Figure 3-51, Figure 3-52).

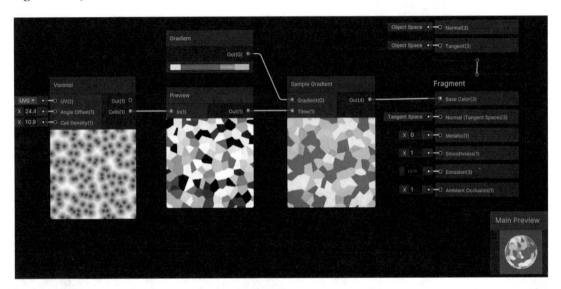

Figure 3-51. *Stained glass shader using the output cells*

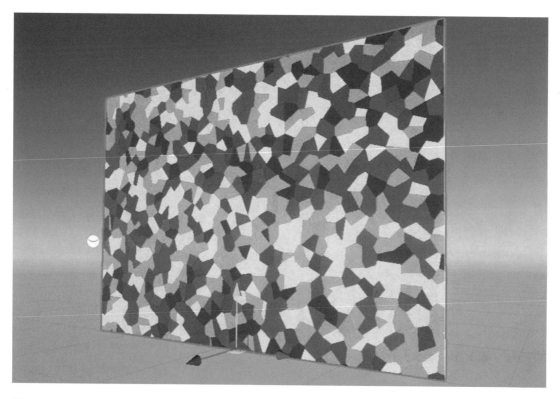

Figure 3-52. *Stained Glass material on an object*

Fresnel Node

The **Fresnel** effect, also known as **Rim Lighting**, is a special calculation that will perform an inverse dot product between the **View Direction** and the **Normal** of the surface. The result will be passed through a **power** calculation to adjust the **rim** thickness. You can check the node in Figure 3-53.

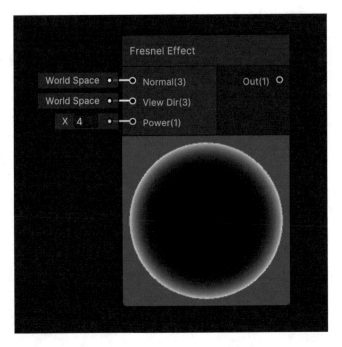

Figure 3-53. *Fresnel Effect node*

Let's go through each input:

- **Normal**: This input defines the surface normal of the object. It should be connected to the normal output of the desired material or geometry.

- **View Direction**: This input represents the direction from which the object is being viewed. Typically, it is connected to the view direction output of the camera or a vertex Position node.

- **Power:** The power input controls the strength of the effect. Higher values increase the contrast between the reflective and non-reflective areas of the object.

This effect will display a **rim** lighting effect along the surface of the object, as shown in Figure 3-54, that will depend on the view angle.

Figure 3-54. *Rim lighting example*

It is really useful to create shaders like glass, singularities, bubble reflections (Figure 3-55), and more.

Figure 3-55. *Iridescent bubble effect using Fresnel node*

Summary

We have reviewed almost all of the nodes we will use and the mathematical operations behind them from a user-friendly perspective by creating samples in the Unity Editor scene view. Now we are prepared to start with the recipes to develop outstanding shaders that you can use in your projects.

This chapter will serve you as a cheat sheet whenever you want to remember what each node does when you are creating effects in Shader Graph.

In the next chapter, we are going to start making our first type of shader: dynamic shaders using the Time node. These shaders will create amazing and dynamic effects in time when clicking the Play button in the Editor. I will also teach you how to create gradients and repetition patterns using the Fraction node to achieve final effects like **scanlines**, **holograms**, and more.

CHAPTER 4

Dynamic Shaders

Congratulations! If you've made it all the way through to this chapter you are ready to start making shaders step by step. Remember that the whole project will be available in the github repository[1] so you can access the shaders, materials, models, scenes, and scripts used in the next sections of this book.

For the effects in this book I am going to use a huge variety of meshes, some of them primitive shapes (sphere, cube, capsule), which are included in the default Unity project, as are the props provided by the template **3D Sample Scene (URP)** that I showed in the introduction of Chapter 3. I will also download assets from C00 license web pages, and sometimes I will use the little bunny shown in Figure 4-1, which I created in Blender. You can access it inside the github project under **Assets ➤ Shared Assets ➤ Prefabs.** I will also teach you how to import custom meshes inside your Unity Project.

Figure 4-1. *Bunny object*

---

[1] https://github.com/AlvaroAlda/ShaderGraphCookBook.git

© Álvaro Alda 2023
Á. Alda, *Beginner's Guide to Unity Shader Graph*, https://doi.org/10.1007/978-1-4842-9672-1_4

In this chapter we will study how to use different nodes like **Time node**, **UV node**, **Power node**, and more to create the following amazing visual effects:

- **Scanline 3D**: Basic but eye-catching effect that will display scan lines along the objects in your scene following a custom orientation (Figure 4-2).

Figure 4-2. *Scanline 3D shader*

- **Arrow Pattern**: We will take advantage of the Line Renderer component in Unity to implement a procedural arrow pattern shader that can be used to create direction indicators, track boosts in a racing game, and more (Figure 4-3).

Figure 4-3. *Arrow pattern in line objects*

- **Dissolve Effect**: Do you want to make things disappear with style in your game? Use this shader to dissolve enemies that have died or to make a special item appear when getting closer to it (Figure 4-4).

Figure 4-4. *Dissolve shader*

- **Hologram Shader**: Last but not least, we are going to create a simple, yet very impressive, shader that can be used in any of your sci-fi themed games—the hologram shader (Figure 4-5).

Figure 4-5. *Hologram shader*

In addition to all of that, at the end of the chapter we will study how to improve and reorganize our shaders to keep them as tidy and readable as possible.

Scanline 3D

This dynamic effect is used in games when you have to scan the place to detect enemies or use a certain tool to discover hidden objects or secret passageways. To achieve this effect, perform the following steps:

- Display object coordinates with Position node.

- Define vertical gradient using Split node.

- Use Multiply and Fraction nodes for repetition.

- Add dynamic effect with Time and Add nodes.

- Adjust contrast with Power node.

- Add custom color.

- Use Dot Product node to set a custom orientation.

- Expose properties.

Display Object Coordinates with Position Node

Let's start by creating a **URP Lit Shader Graph** and attaching it to a material that you can use on any object you want in your scene, as we learned in previous chapters. To do so, do the following:

- Create a new URP Lit Shader Graph by right-clicking inside the Project tab in the Unity Editor and then choose **Create ➤ Shader Graph ➤ Lit Shader Graph**. I called it **Scanline**.

- Create a new material asset with that shader graph attached to it by right-clicking on the recently created shader graph asset and selecting **Create ➤ Material.**

- Create any 3D object in the scene by right-clicking in the Hierarchy tab and then **3D Object** and choose the object you want to be affected by the shader. In my case, I imported a custom mesh created in Blender.

- Drag and drop the material asset from the Project tab to the 3D object in the scene to assign the material to it.

Double-click the **Scanline** shader graph asset to open the Shader Graph Editor and then do the following:

- Create a **Position node** and set it in **Object Space** in the node dropdown setting.

- Connect the output of the **Position node** to the **Base Color** input in the **Fragment block**, as I am showing in Figure 4-6.

- Remember to **always** save the asset at the top-left corner of the Shader Graph Editor to see the result in the scene (Figure 4-6).

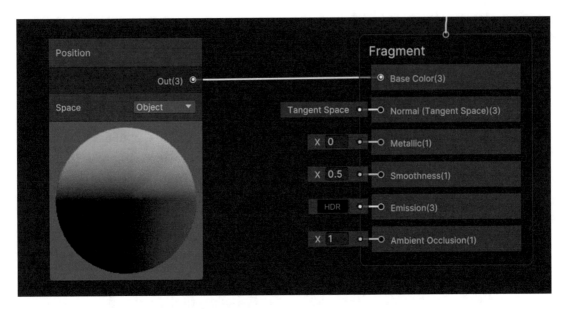

Figure 4-6. *Scanline final effect on bunny*

You can see in Figure 4-7 that the object with the material attached now shows the colors corresponding to its local coordinates. For the moment, we just want to extract the Y orientation, also defined by the **Green** color. This will be used as reference to know which local coordinate we want to access to create vertical scanlines across the mesh.

In this book we will use the terminology **X/R** to refer to the *x* coordinate or **red color** component, **Y/G** as *y* coordinate or green color component, and **Z/B** as the *z* coordinate or blue color component.

Figure 4-7. *Bunny showing the local coordinates' colors*

In the next subsection we are going to extract one of the coordinates to create gradients in a desired direction, which are going to be transformed into our scanlines.

Define Vertical Gradient Using the Split Node

In this step, we will access one of the three coordinates we displayed before to create a gradient that will represent one of our scanlines, pointing in a desired direction. The **Split node** performs the operation of extracting individual coordinates or components from a vector/color. Do the following:

- Create a new **Split node** and connect the output of the **Position node** we just created to its input. Extract the **Y/G** component by **accessing the G(1) output of the Split node**.

  The Split node is going to let you access the individual components of the input; therefore, we can access ONLY the Y/G coordinate from the G(1) output as a floating value instead of using a Vector3.

- Connect the output of the **Split node** G(1) to the **Base Color input of the Fragment block**, as seen in Figure 4-8.

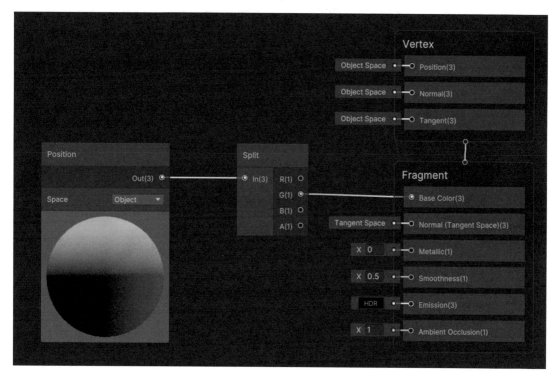

Figure 4-8. *Using Split node to obtain the Y/G coordinate*

You can check in Figure 4-9 that there is a gradient along the bunny's **local** vertical axis. This is our first scanline, but we need way more of them displaying along the Y/G axis of the object.

Figure 4-9. *Gradient in the local vertical axis of bunny*

Use Multiply and Fraction Nodes for Repetition

We have one really wide and static scanline represented as a gradient. To achieve the effect of lots of scanlines running through an object, we need to generate more than one gradient in the same direction. We now want this gradient to be repeated. To achieve that, do the following:

- Connect the **output** of the **Split node G(1)** to the **input A(1) of a new Multiply node input**.

- Increase the default value of the **input B(1)** of the **Multiply node up to 3**.

  The Multiply node will increase the value of the output G(1). So the gradient, instead of going from 0 to 1, will go from 0 to 3. This will increment the white intensity of the gradient.

- Connect the output of the **Multiply node** to the input of the **Fraction node**.

In Chapter 2, we saw that the Fraction node will output only the decimal part of the input. The gradient values extracted from the G(1) output of the Split node are from 0 to 3; therefore, we will have as a result at the output of the Fraction node three gradients from 0 to 1. If we increase the Multiply node input B(1), we will increase the number of gradients. This is a really common setup to create repetition patterns in a desired direction.

- Then, connect the **Fraction node output** to the **Base Color input of the Fragment block** to see the result.

Increasing the default floating value of the Multiply node input B(1) will increase the number of repetitions of the gradient that will output from the Fraction node. For example, when the input is 8, the fraction node will create eight gradients from 0 to 0.999 (Figure 4-10).

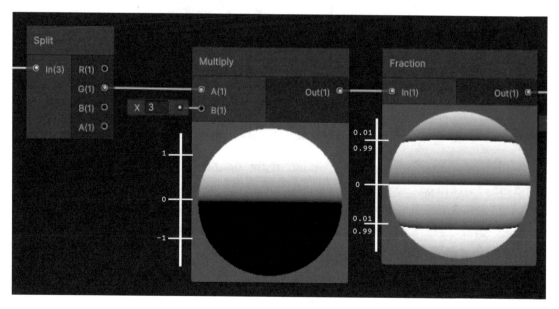

Figure 4-10. *Obtaining a repetition of the gradient pattern using Multiply and Fraction nodes*

After saving these changes, we can appreciate that the vertical gradient we have calculated is repeated along the vertical local axis of the object in the scene. (Figure 4-11).

But, the effect is not scanning the object. In fact, the lines are static and not moving along the surface of the object, so let's add some movement to the effect using the **Time node**.

Figure 4-11. *Repeated gradient on bunny*

Dynamic Effect with Time and Add Nodes

Currently, the wide scanlines we have created are not moving at all, resulting in a really bland effect. We need the gradients to move along the vertical axis with a desired speed so the effect is dynamic and changes over time, simulating that the object is being scanned. To achieve that, we will create a series of interconnected nodes between the Split node and the Multiply node (Figure 4-12), as follows:

- Create a **Time node** and connect its Time(1) output to a new **Multiply node input A(1)**.

    The Time(1) output of the Time node represents the seconds that have passed since the beginning of the game, so, each frame, this value will increase. This node's output is the base for every dynamic effect since it represents the passing of time.

- Set the **input B(1)** of the previously created **Multiply node** to **0.5**.

  This value will determine the **scrolling speed** of the scanlines along the object. Multiplying the Time(1) output by 0.5 will slow down the scrolling speed by half. For instance, when the Time(1) is 10, meaning that 10 seconds have passed since the beginning of the game, the output of the Multiply node will be 5.

- The output of that **Multiply** node will go to one input of a new **Add** node, and the other input will be fed by the previously created **Split** node output G(1).

- The **Add node output** will connect to the **input A(1)** of the **Multiply node** we created in the previous subsection.

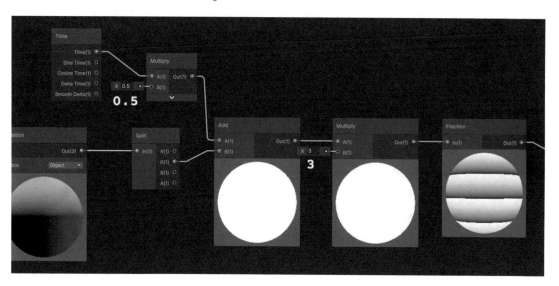

Figure 4-12. *Repeated gradient on bunny*

You can see the dynamic scrolling effect right away in the **Fraction** node preview. After you save the resulting shader, it will be applied to the object with the material attached.

Let's take a deeper look at what is really happening with this operation, as follows:

- Thanks to the Multiply node, there are values greater than 1 entering the Fraction node.

- The Fraction node is extracting only the decimal part, so an input value of 1 is translated as an output value of 0; an input of 1.5 as an output of 0.5, and so on, causing a repetition pattern, because every time the input value gets equal to or bigger than 1, the output resets its value to 0 plus the decimal parts.

- If we add to the input value a certain amount, let's say 0.2, that repetition pattern is going to be offset 0.2 units. A previous input of 1.5 now is 1.7, outputting 0.7. If we are constantly adding using the Time node, we are creating a constant offset, translated into a scrolling effect of the repetition pattern.

At this moment, you may have noticed one **important thing**. We never clicked Play to see the shaders running. This is because Unity can run shaders in Edit mode, which is really helpful for debugging and tweaking shaders without constantly changing to Play mode.

But it is important to note that, while shaders can run in Edit mode, they might not have the same level of optimization and performance as when running in Play mode. This is highly noticeable when using dynamic shaders, like the one we are creating. In Edit mode, the **Time(1) output** of the **Time** node is updated every time the user interacts with the Unity interface, showing us a non-realistic dynamic behavior of the shader. I recommend that, once you add a dynamic behavior to your shader, you try it in Play mode, since it will provide a more accurate representation of the final runtime performance and behavior of the shader.

Adjust Contrast with Power Node

The gradients are too wide and are not looking like the thin scanlines we want to achieve. We want the lines to be thin and subtle, like any sonar or sci-fi tracker would display. To achieve that, do the following:

- Connect the **Fraction** node output to a new **Power node** input (**A**), then set a default **B(1) value between 1 and 9.** The input value **A(1) will be powered to the exponent value in the input B(1).** The Fraction node ensures that the value entering the A input of the Power node will always be between **0 and 1** (Figure 4-13).

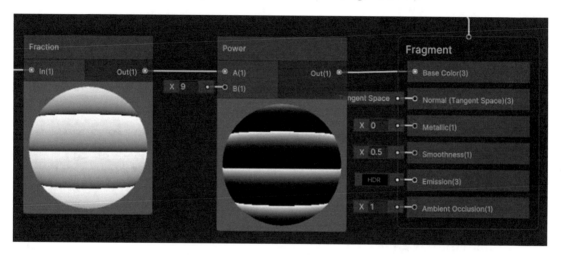

Figure 4-13. *Narrowing the scanlines using the Power node*

Notice that increasing the float value of the input **B** of the **Power** node will narrow the scanlines' gradient, as we can see in Figure 4-13.

But why are lines getting narrower? What happens if the input value B(1) is negative? The answer resides in math.

If we take, for example, 2^2, we are getting 2 times 2 equals 4 as a result. If we increase the exponent, the resulting value is bigger and bigger, but this is not our case. Thanks to the Fraction node, the input values going inside the Power node are between 0 and 1 (not included). If you now make this calculation, 0.5^2, you will get 0.25. Therefore, if the base in a power calculation is between 0 and 1, and the exponent is greater than 1, the result is smaller than the base. In fact, the closer the value of the base is to 0 the more it will be affected by the exponent. That is why, in our case, increasing the exponent B(1) of the Power node will make the darker parts of the gradient collapse to the white parts. Numbers really close to 1 (whiter) are barely affected by the exponent. For instance, $1 = 1^{10} = 1^{1000} = 1^{10000}$.

Add Custom Color

Let's customize the scanlines a little bit by adding some color to them. This is useful, for example, when you want to set up red scanlines when enemies have detected you in the map or blue scanlines when the player is using a scanner to detect hidden elements in the scene. Do the following:

- Add a **Multiply node** with the **input B(4)** connected to the previously created **Power node** output.

    Normally, I work on creating the procedural texture I need for the effect, and, when I am happy with the result, I apply color that will be multiplied with the texture created. This is really nice for performance because we are always working with single floating values instead of working with two or more components of a vector, like a color.

- Create a new **Color input node** and connect it to the **A(1) input** of the **Multiply node**.

- Let's now remove the connection with the Base Color input and connect the output of the **Multiply** node to the **Emission** node of the **Fragment** block to create an emissive effect (Figure 4-14). This will output a glowy emission effect, as a real sci-fi scanline should look (Figure 4-15).

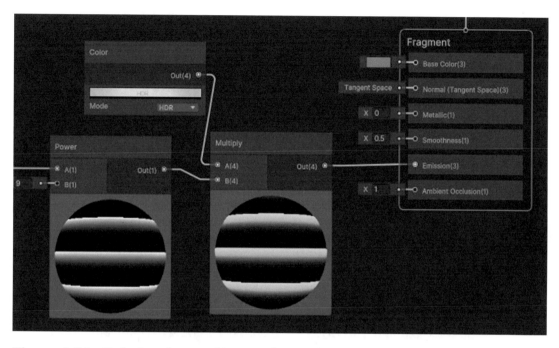

Figure 4-14. *Coloring the scanlines and setting as emissive*

Remember that you can set the **Color** node as **HDR** in the dropdown setting. This will allow you to select a glow intensity, as we saw in Chapter 2. This will be a nice touch for the scanlines effect. An intensity value between 1 and 2 should be enough. The color values shown in Figure 4-15 are **R =29, G=191, B=0, with intensity value of 2**.

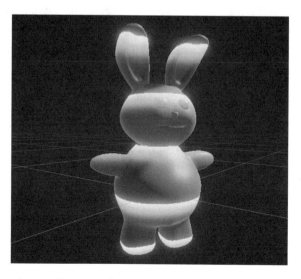

Figure 4-15. *Colored scanlines on bunny*

The intensity value of 2 is going to be captured by the post-process volume to create the bloom effect.

Remember that emission is a post-processing effect. Therefore, if you want to see emissive colors behaving properly in your game, you have to have the post-processing volume set up correctly in your Unity Project, as described in Chapter 2 and here:

- Create a **volume component** attached to any game object in your hierarchy.

- Create a new **profile** by clicking the **New button**, or use an existing profile in your project.

- Then, click **Add Override** and add a **Bloom** post-processing effect with **Threshold** and **Intensity** values **enabled**, and set the Intensity value to **1**.

- Also, add a **Tone Mapping** post-processing effect with the setting Mode enabled and with **ACES** selected. This is going to create an appealing final look to the glow effect.

- Finally, set your camera **Post Processing** option to **True**.

Dot Product Node to Set a Custom Orientation

This effect will be more flexible if you can determine the direction in which the scanlines are traveling. For example, when using a moving sonar, the lines may move with the same orientation as the direction the device is pointing. As we reviewed in previous chapters, the output of a **Dot Product** node will be the maximum when the two vectors that feed the inputs of the node are parallel, so with this operation we can create a gradient—this time, in a desired direction (Figure 4-16). Do the following:

- Create a new **Dot Product node** and connect the **input A(3)** to the **output** of the first **Position node** we created to set the direction in which the scanlines will scroll.

- Create a **Vector3 input node** and connect it to the **B(3) input** of the **Dot Product node**. This will give us our desired scanline movement direction. As I want the scanlines to move along the **X/R axis** I set the **Vector3 input node** to **(1, 0, 0)**.

- Remove the **Split node** and connect the output of the **Dot Product node** to the input of the **Add node**, which was fed by the Split node.

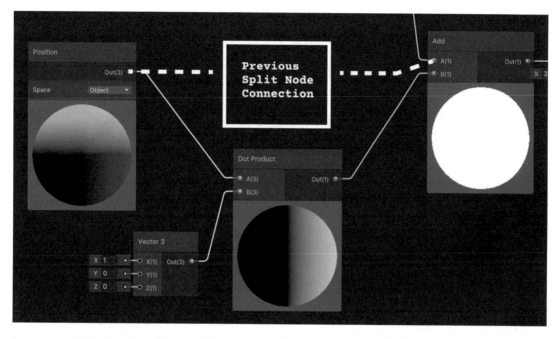

Figure 4-16. *Dot Product node to set up the scanlines direction*

You may notice that setting the input **Vector3** node as **(1, 0, 0)** will orient the scanlines on the positive **X/R** axis (Figure 4-17).

Figure 4-17. *Scanlines oriented horizontally*

149

The effect is now completed, but we can take it to a whole new level by exposing some properties to make unique effects with the same shader graph.

Expose Properties

If you want your shaders to be flexible and reusable, it is recommended that you expose input nodes as properties so they can be changed inside the Inspector tab in Unity Editor when the material is selected in the Project tab.

You can expose an input node as a property by right-clicking on any input node and selecting **Convert to ➤ Property** as in Figure 4-18. Then, it will be automatically added to the **Blackboard** and exposed in the **Unity Editor Inspector tab** when the material is selected.

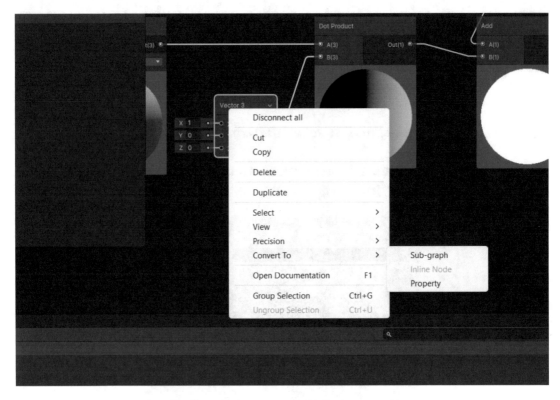

Figure 4-18. *Exposing the direction vector property*

You can change the name and the default value of the property you exposed. I will do it with the **Color, Direction, ScanLines Amount,** and **Scroll Speed** (Figure 4-19).

Note   Only input nodes can be exposed, although there are some that cannot be exposed yet, like the Gradient node. Maybe in future Unity updates we will be able to do so.

Figure 4-19. *Exposed properties in Blackboard*

You can create duplicates of the material by selecting the material asset in the Project tab and then clicking Ctrl +D. Each material asset from the same shader can have unique values for the exposed properties, as you can see in Figure 4-20.

Throughout this book I recommend that you expose as many properties as you want so as to make your shaders unique and flexible for use within different materials.

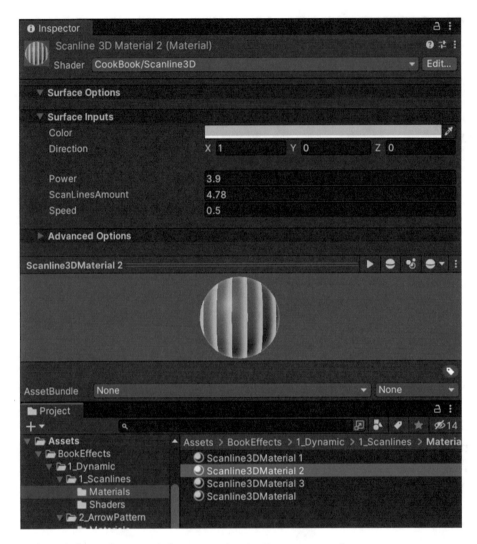

Figure 4-20. *Selected material properties in Inspector tab*

Congratulations! The shader is completed, and you can see the whole shader in Figure 4-21.

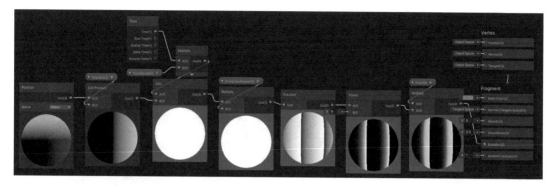

Figure 4-21. Entire displayed scanlines shader graph

Wow, that was a lot of new information! I encourage you to take your time reviewing the shader graph and playing with different values to understand everything we did before continuing with the next effect.

Arrow Pattern

The arrow effect will be useful in any racing game where it can be used to show track boosts or curve indicators to the player. You should follow these steps:

- Create and set up a line renderer.

- Create a diagonal line pattern with the Subtract node.

- Create a vertical symmetry with the Absolute node.

- Define an arrow pattern with Fraction and Step nodes.

- Move the arrow along the line renderer.

- Customize the arrow color.

Create and Set Up a Line Renderer

The first thing you want to do is to create a **line renderer** component attached to a **game object** in our Unity Scene. To do so, right-click anywhere inside the **Hierarchy** tab and then select **Effects ➤ Line** as in Figure 4-22.

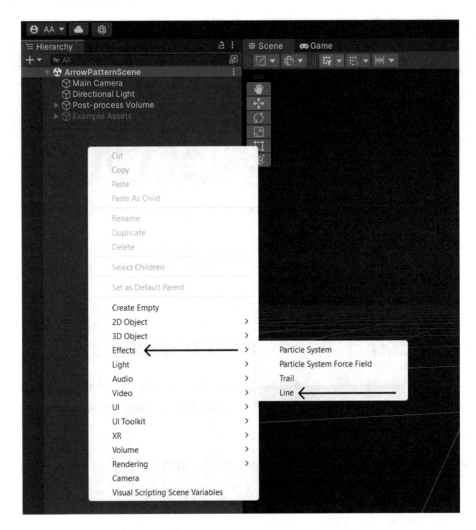

Figure 4-22. *Create a line renderer*

You will now have a new game object with a line renderer component attached to it (Figure 4-23).

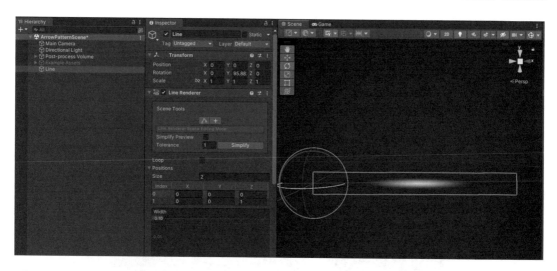

Figure 4-23. *Instantiated line object*

Now, click inside the Width setting in the line renderer component and set the value to something between 0.1 and 1.0, as in Figure 4-24.

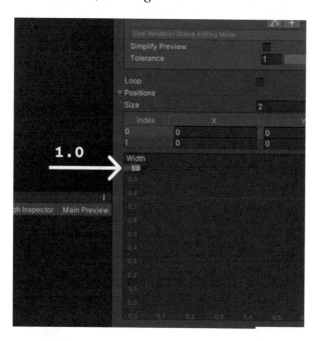

Figure 4-24. *Change width value to something between 0 and 1*

You will see that the line renderer turned into a square shape, as in Figure 4-25.

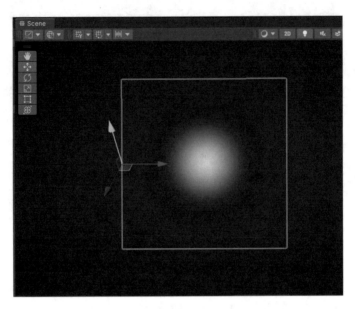

Figure 4-25. *Default line renderer with width value of 1.0*

If you scroll down in the line renderer component you will find a variable called **Materials**. Inside it you will find a default **ParticlesUnlit** material, which you are going to substitute with the new material you are going to create. You can always assign a material by dragging the asset from the **Project** tab to the destiny **game object** (Figure 4-26).

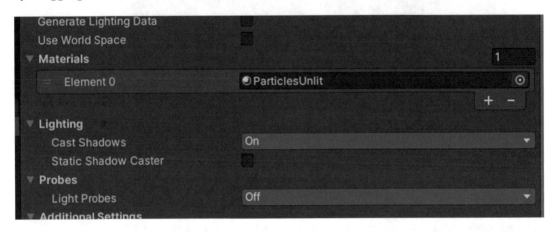

Figure 4-26. *Default ParticlesUnlit material to be swapped with brand-new material*

There is also the Texture Mode property in the line renderer. For our effect, we need to change this from "Stretch" to "Tile" (Figure 4-27).

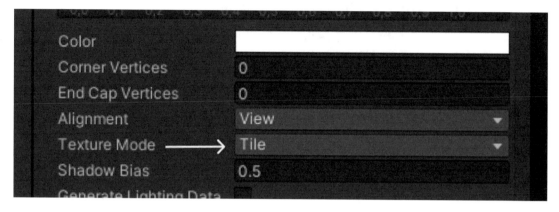

Figure 4-27. *Set line renderer Texture Mode to Tile*

This setting will create a tiling or repetition in the UVs of the line renderer object instead of stretching it when we scale the object. This will naturally create a repetition in our arrow pattern and will avoid ugly and uncontrolled stretching of the effect along the object. In the next figure you will find a comparison between both texture mode options as they are applied to identical line renderers stretched three units in their local X/R direction (Figure 4-28).

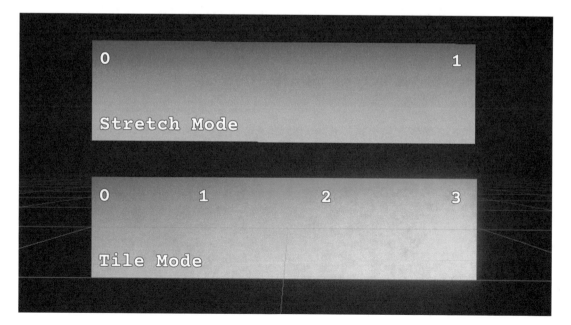

Figure 4-28. *Comparing the UVs using **Stretch Mode** versus using **Tile Mode***

Create a Diagonal Line Pattern

Perform the following starting steps to create a shader:

- Create a new **unlit** shader graph by right-clicking in the Project tab
  and then selecting **Create ➤ Shader Graph ➤ URP ➤ Unlit Shader
  Graph**. I called it **ArrowPattern**. We are creating an unlit shader
  graph since we don't need the light to interact with our shader.
  Avoiding light calculations will save a lot of performance in our game,
  albeit sacrificing light and shadow realism.

- Create a new material by right-clicking the recently created unlit
  shader graph asset in the Project tab and then choose **Create ➤
  Material**.

- Drag and drop the material asset from the Project tab to the line
  renderer object in the Scene view.

Double-click the shader graph asset to open the editor, and inside of it follow
these steps:

- Create a **UV node** and connect its output to the input of a new
  Split node.

- Then connect the **R(1)** output of the **Split node** to the **A(1)** input of
  a **Subtract node**. Finally, feed the **B(1) input** of the **Subtract node**
  with the **G(1)** output of the **Split node** (Figure 4-29).

- Connect the **Subtract node** to the Base Color input in the
  Fragment block.

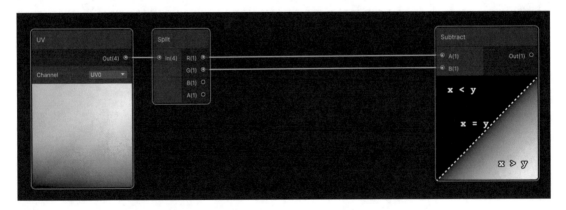

Figure 4-29. *Diagonal gradient pattern*

Every procedural texture, every effect, every pattern is made out of mathematical functions. What we did here is replicate the function $X - Y = 0$. Notice a diagonal gradient that is positive when A(1) is greater than B(1), zero when the values are equal, and less than 0 when B(1) is greater than A(1).

Create Vertical Symmetry with Absolute Node

We need to add **symmetry** to our previously created gradient to achieve a pointy, arrow-like end. We want to get the other side of the triangle that will form an arrow, and to achieve that we will use the **Absolute** node. This node will output the absolute value of the input, removing the negative sign, if any. For example:

- Input = 3, Output = 3

- Input = −5, Output = 5

- Input = −0.5, Output = 0.5

Let's now add new calculations between the G(1) input of the Split node and the B(1) input of the Subtract node, as follows:

- Create a new **Subtract** node and connect its **input A(1)** to the **output G(1)** of the previously created **Split node** and set a value of 0.5 in the **default input B(1)** of that **Subtract node**.

  This calculation will center the y = 0 line to the center of the texture we are generating.

- The output of the last mentioned **Subtract node** now will be connected to the input of a new **Absolute node**. We are creating symmetry between the upper and lower parts of the texture.

  We want to achieve the same result as in the last subsection, but with the origin displaced 0.5 to the center of the texture and symmetrical on that axis.

- Connect the output of the Absolute node to the input of the first created Subtract node (Figure 4-30).

- Finally, to see the result in the Scene view, connect the output of the first created Subtract node to the input Base Color of the Fragment block and save the asset.

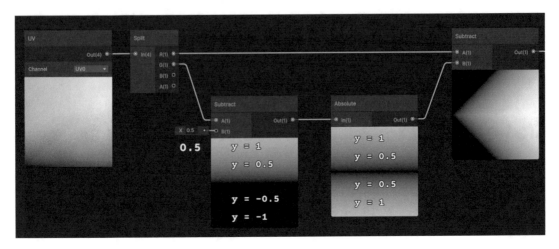

Figure 4-30. *Absolute node to get a symmetry pattern*

Hard-Edged Arrow Pattern with Fraction and Step Nodes

We have achieved a pointy end for our arrow pattern. But we want the pattern to be sharper and with defined corners and edges, as in the sample Figure 4-3. Now, if we take a look at the line renderer in Figure 4-31, we can see how it looks after saving the shader graph asset.

Figure 4-31. *Current arrow pattern*

Let's modify our shader by adding some nodes after the output of the first created Subtract node. These nodes should be placed at the rightmost part of the shader graph, connected to the Base Color input of the Fragment block.

- Create a **Fraction node** and feed it with the output of the mentioned **Subtract node**. This will define a border of the arrow pattern. But it still looks like a gradient, and we want hard edges.

- The output of the **Fraction node** will be connected to the input **In(1)** of a **Step** node and set a float value of **0.5** to the input **Edge(1)** of that **Step** node, resulting in what is shown in Figure 4-32.

    The step and smoothstep nodes are perfect when we want to achieve hard edges without gradients (synthetic finishes, cartoon effects, geometry patterns).

- Finally, connect the Step node's output to the Base Color input of the Fragment block.

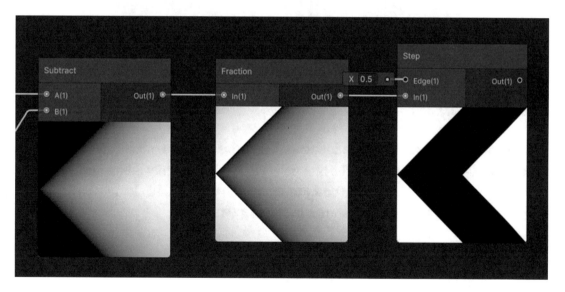

Figure 4-32. *Fraction and step nodes to achieve hard-edge arrow pattern*

The Fraction node will take values less than 0 and invert them. Remember that the Fraction node will perform this operation: **Frac(In(1)) = In(1) - Floor(In(1))**.

If In(1) is a negative value, for example, the floor of (−0.1) will result in the greatest integer's being less than or equal to −0.1, which is −1. So the Frac of −0.1 results in −0.1 − (−1) = −0.1 + 1 = 0.9. This is what makes the Fraction node really powerful, since the repetition patterns work the same with positive or negative values of the input.

Finally, the Step node will threshold the input gradient to 0.5, meaning that values below 0.5 will be 0 (black) and values greater than 0.5 will be 1 (white).

After saving the asset in the Shader Graph Editor, you will now see your line renderer as a beautiful, hard-edged arrow (Figure 4-33).

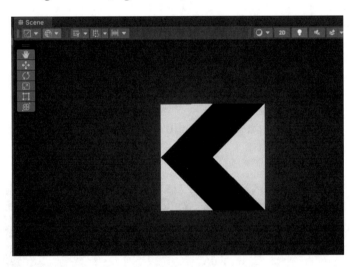

Figure 4-33. *Defined arrow*

You can now stretch the line renderer and have this pattern repeated along its surface. Select the **Line object** in the hierarchy tab inside the Unity Editor and, in the Inspector tab, go to the **Transform component** at the very top and change the **Scale** vector from (1, 1, **1**) to (1, 1, **3**), as shown in Figure 4-34.

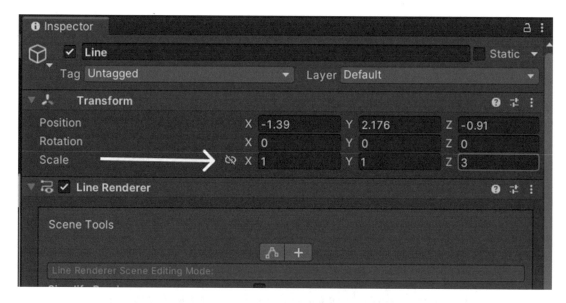

Figure 4-34. *Scaling the arrow 3 units on the z-axis*

This will stretch the line renderer on its local *z*-axis by 3, but, as you previously changed the texture mode from Stretch mode to Tile mode, you can see the arrow pattern repeated successfully three times along the scaled surface of our line, as shown in Figure 4-35.

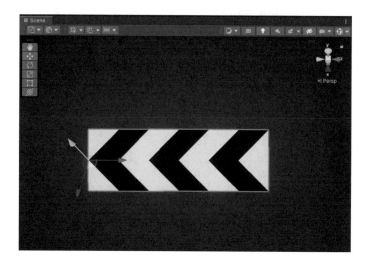

Figure 4-35. *Defined arrow*

Move the Arrow Along the Line Renderer

As we are making dynamic effects in this section, we need these arrows to scroll across the surface of the line renderer object. This effect will make the surface of the line object alive and vibrant, emphasizing to the player that stepping on top of it is going to accelerate them. To achieve that scrolling movement, do the following:

- Create a new **Multiply node** that will receive the output **Time(1)** of a newly created **Time node** in the **A(1) input**. The Multiply node also receives a float value input connected to its **B(1) input**.

  I exposed the float input as a property and called it Scroll Speed with a default value of 0.5. This value will adjust how fast the arrow pattern is scrolling along the line renderer object surface.

- Create an **Add node** whose **input B(1)** will be connected to the **Subtract node output** that was previously connected to the Fraction node.

  As we did previously with the scanlines effect, using the Add node and the Fraction node together will end up in a scrolling effect. Furthermore, using the Time node will include a scrolling effect in time, achieving dynamism.

- The **input A(1)** of the **Add node** will receive the previously created **Multiply node**, which is controlling the **scroll speed** (Figure 4-36).

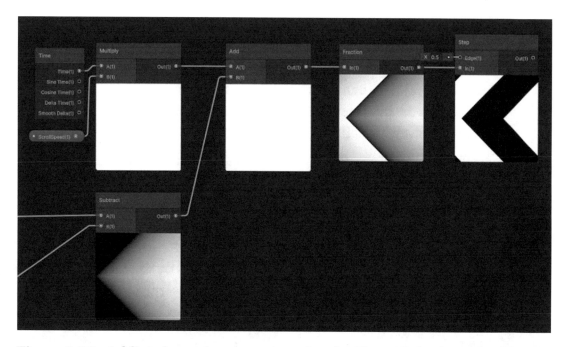

Figure 4-36. *Adding dynamic movement using the Time, Multiply, and Add nodes*

If you save the asset and go back to the Scene view you will see that the arrow pattern is scrolling along the surface. You can change the scrolling speed by tweaking the property Scroll Speed. If you set negative values for that property, the scroll orientation will be inverted.

Customize the Arrow Pattern Color

The effect is almost done, but we normally don't want things in black and white unless we are creating a dark-themed game. Let's add some color using the Lerp node, as follows:

- Create a **Lerp node** and feed the interpolator **T(1) input** with the output of the previously created **Step node**.

- Create two **Color Input nodes**, which will define the two colors of the arrow pattern. Connect them to the inputs **A(1)** and **B(1)** of the **Lerp node**. You can **expose** those **Color Input nodes** as properties to achieve different materials from the same shader. Change both color properties to any color you want; for example, blue and pink.

The **Lerp node** will create an interpolation from **A(4)** when **T(1)** is 0 to **B(4)** when **T(1)** is 1. Since the output of the Step node will be 0 or 1, what you are doing is setting the dark parts of the arrow texture as **B(4)** color and the white parts of the arrow texture as **A(4)**. This is the most common way of coloring black-and-white textures in Shader Graph.

- Finally, connect the **output** of the **Lerp node** to the **Base Color input** of the **Fragment block** (Figure 4-37).

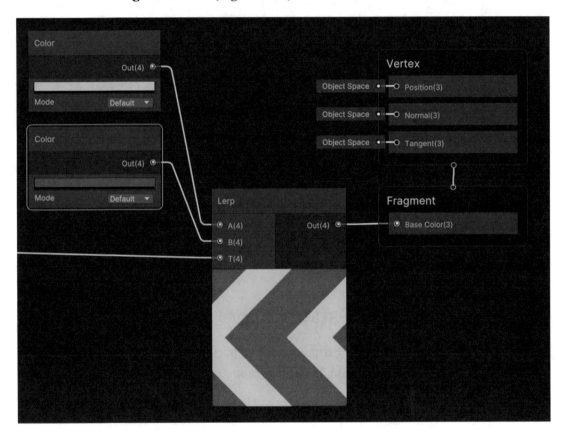

Figure 4-37. *Colored arrow pattern*

Save the asset and check the final result in the Scene view, shown in Figure 4-38.

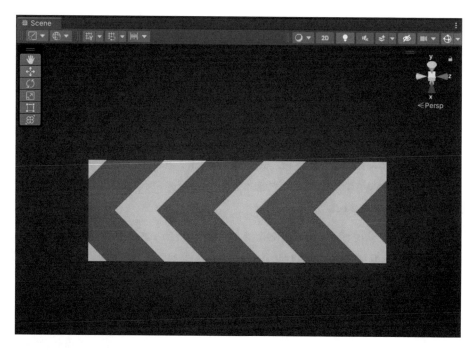

Figure 4-38. *Line renderer with colorful, defined, scrolling arrow pattern*

Nicely done! Play with the arrow velocity and with the input colors to achieve different results.

Dissolve Effect

This effect is perfect when you want to get rid of a dead enemy in the scene or you want to make an object magically appear from cosmic dust. Following these next steps will allow you to make your own dissolve effect:

- Noisy texture using the Gradient **Noise** node
- Gradual dissolve effect using **Add** node
- Dynamic ping-pong dissolving effect
- Create a colored dissolving edge
- Create a colored edge

Noisy Texture Using the Gradient Noise Node

We are going to start as usual, with the following:

- Create a new URP Lit Shader Graph by right-clicking inside the Project tab in the Unity Editor and then selecting **Create ➤ Shader Graph ➤ Lit Shader Graph**. Then, call it Dissolve.

- Create a new material asset with that shader graph attached to it by right-clicking on the recently created shader graph asset and select **Create ➤ Material.**

- Create any 3D object in the scene by right-clicking in the Hierarchy tab and then selecting **3D Object**; choose the object you want to be affected by the shader.

- Drag and drop the material asset from the Project tab to the 3D object in the scene to assign the material to it.

You want your object to dissolve, such that some parts will gradually become invisible. You need to set the object as transparent, as follows:

- Open the shader graph by double-clicking the asset in the Project tab.

- Open the **Graph Inspector** and select the **Graph Settings tab**.

- Go to the **Surface Type** setting and change it from Opaque to **Transparent** (Figure 4-39).

- You will see an **Alpha input** appear in the **Fragment block**. Now your shader is set as transparent, and the alpha value will change the opacity of the object in the scene.

Figure 4-39. *Setting the object as transparent*

Let's add a noisy texture to the Alpha input, so the object will be dissolved following a noisy pattern. Do the following:

- Create a new **Gradient Noise node** and feed the input **Scale(1)** with a **float input** value between 5 and 10.

  Remember that the scale input will define how "zoomed in" we see that texture. The bigger it is, the higher the resolution of the noise texture. You can expose that value as a property to change it in the Material Inspector.

- Connect the **Gradient Noise** node output to a new **Step** node input **In(1)**, and set the other input **Edge(1)** with a value of 0.5 to set a hard-edged gradient texture. Connect the output of the Step node to the **Alpha** input of the **Fragment** block (Figure 4-40).

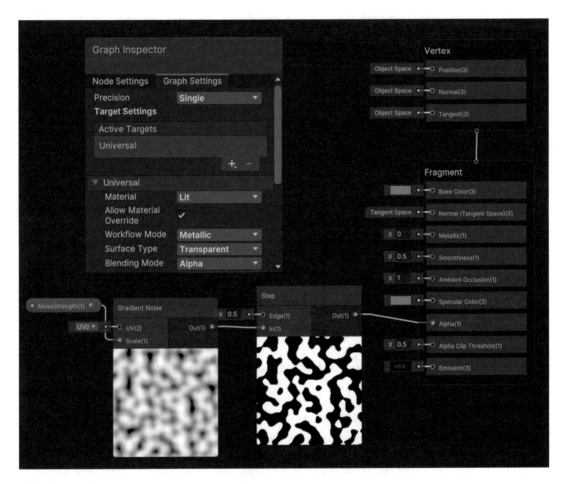

Figure 4-40. *Setting up an alpha noisy texture*

Textures and colors you achieved in the Shader Graph Editor can be connected to almost every input node of the different blocks in the master stack, achieving different results, mapping their behavior. We see in Figure 4-41 that the object is transparent in the dark spots of the noisy texture and is opaque where the noise texture is white.

Figure 4-41. *Current material applied to the bunny*

Gradual Dissolve Effect Using Add Node

Now we want to control how transparent our object is in the scene. We want to gradually dissolve our object depending on custom values. To gradually dissolve the bunny you need to do the following:

- Create a new **Add node** between the **Gradient Noise** node and the **Step** node we just created.

- Connect the **input B(1)** of the **Add node** to the **output** of the **Gradient Noise node** and connect the **output** of the **Add node** to the **input** of the **Step node In(1)**.

Try changing the default float value in the input A(1) of the Add node to achieve different dissolve states. A positive value in A(1) will add white color to the texture of the gradient noise, opaquing the object, while introducing negative values will increase the black part in the texture, translucing the object (Figure 4-42). The Step node threshold value will set values above 0.5 as totally white and values below 0.5 as totally black.

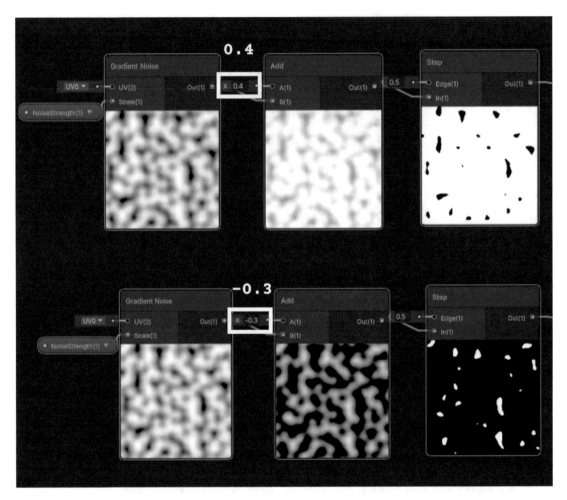

Figure 4-42. *Different "dissolve" states depending on the default value of the Add node A(1)*

You can see in Figure 4-43 the impact of different A(1) float input values on the opacity of the object.

Figure 4-43. Different "dissolve" states applied to bunny

Dynamic Ping-Pong Dissolving Effect

We will create a "ping-pong"[2] loop animation that transitions the object in the scene from a completely opaque state to a totally "dissolved" state. To do so, do the following:

- Create a **Time node** and connect the output **Sine Time (1)** to the input **In(1)** of a new **Remap** node.

  The Sine Time (1) will output floating numbers between −1 and 1, following a sine function in time. This output is very useful when you want to achieve loop animations like the ping-pong one.

- Leave the **In Min Max (1)** values with the default values (−1, 1) since these are the sine limit output values.

---

[2] A ping-pong animation is an animation that loops back and forth between two states, like a ping-pong ball bouncing between two paddles.

- Set the **Out Min Max(1)** input of the **Remap node** to (−1.5, 1) to ensure that the object goes from fully transparent to fully opaque.

- Finally, connect the **Remap node** output to the previously created **Add node input A(1)** (Figure 4-44).

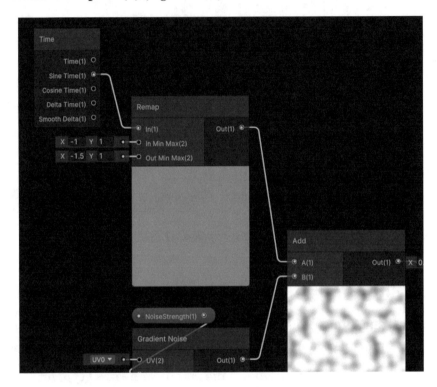

Figure 4-44. *Loop animation of the dissolve effect*

After saving the shader, you will see the object in the Scene view going from transparent to opaque in a rather cool time transition.

Dissolve Effect Along Custom Direction

We have already made something similar in the **scanlines effect**. We want to make this effect occur in a specific direction; for example, an object receives a shot from a plasma gun, so it will disintegrate that object starting from the shooting direction. To do that, do the following:

- Create a **Position** node and set the **Coordinate Space** dropdown to **Object**. Then, connect its output to **Dot Product** node input B(3).

- Connect a **Vector3** input node to the other **Dot Product** input. I exposed that node as a property and called it DissolveDirection with a default value of (1, 1, 0), which translates into a diagonal pattern.

- Finally, connect the **Dot Product** node output to the **Step** node input **Edge(1)** (Figure 4-45).

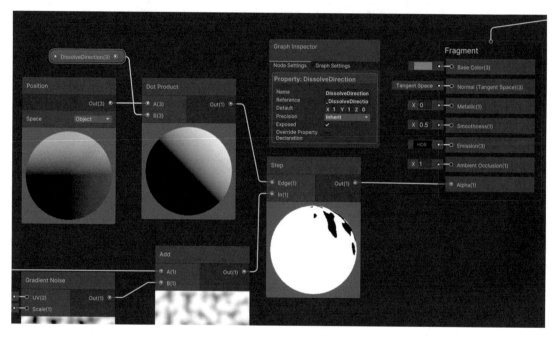

Figure 4-45. *Setting direction of the dissolve effect*

By connecting the gradient texture to the Edge(1) input of the Step node, you are effectively using the gradient texture as the threshold for the step function. The Step node will compare the values of the gradient texture with the threshold set by the Edge(1) input. The Step node will output a value of 0 for any input value in the gradient texture that is below the threshold, and a value of 1 for any input value that is equal to or above the threshold. This creates a distinct transition effect between the two states defined by the Step node and by the noisy texture.

You can see in Figure 4-46 that the object is gradually affected by the noise texture in a determined direction.

Figure 4-46. *The object in the scene is affected by the noise gradually, following a gradient direction*

Create a Dissolving Edge with Color

Now comes the tricky part. The final step is to create a border that will emphasize the dissolve effect so the player will know exactly what is really happening; for example, if the plasma gun you use to shoot an enemy has green bullets, it makes sense that the dissolve effect would create a colorful green border when destroying the enemy. To achieve that, do the following:

- First, connect the lastly created **Dot Product node** output to the input A(1) of a new **Add node**. Then feed the Add node B(1) input with a **float input node** that you can expose as **Edge Width**.

    The edge width value should always be positive, creating an offset between the gradient used to change the alpha value. Set a small value of 0.23 as the default (Figure 4-47).

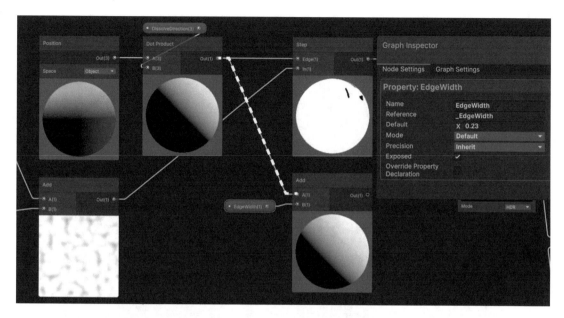

Figure 4-47. *Creating a gradient offset with Add node*

- Take the output of the last created **Add node** and connect it to a new **Step node In(1) input**. Also feed the **Edge(1) input** with the **output** of the first **Add node** we created that outputs the noise pattern texture (Figure 4-48).

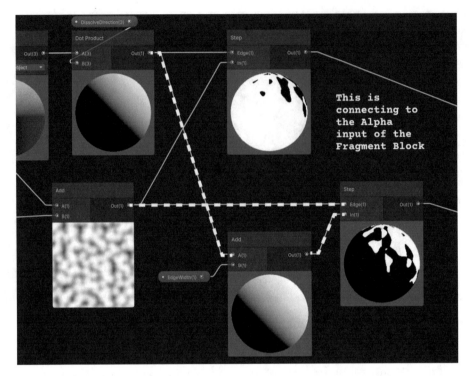

Figure 4-48. *Created a defined edge of the dissolve effect with the Step node*

- Create a **Multiply node** and connect the last created **Step node** output to the input **B(1)** of the **Multiply node**.

- Create a new **Color input node** that you can expose as **Edge Color** and connect it to the A(1) input of the **Multiply node**.

- Finally, connect the **Multiply node** output to the **Emission input** of the **Fragment block** (Figure 4-49).

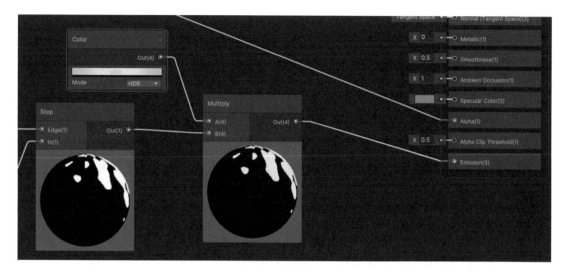

Figure 4-49. *Creating a colored edge*

Save the asset and come back to the Scene view, where you will find your object appearing and disappearing in a ping-pong animation following a noisy pattern. See Figure 4-50.

Figure 4-50. *Dissolve effect*

You can use another noise pattern to achieve different effects or play with the edge width and color until you achieve the effect you want. Check out the github project, where you can change between different noise textures.

Hologram Shader

The hologram shader is very useful when you want to give your game a sci-fi theme and create futuristic holograms. Do the following:

- Set a vertical gradient with **Screen Position** node.

- Repeat the pattern using a **Fraction** node.

- Randomize the pattern using the **Noise** node.

- Create a moving pattern using Add and Time nodes.

- Add color to the gradient hologram lines.

- Emphasize the effect with a **Fresnel** node.

- Create blink effect using logic and random nodes.

Set a Vertical Gradient with Screen Position Node

Create a new unlit shader graph by right-clicking in the Project tab and then selecting **Create ➤ Shader Graph ➤ URP ➤ Unlit Shader Graph**; I called mine **Hologram.** Then, create a new material by right-clicking the recently created unlit shader graph asset in the Project tab and then select **Create ➤ Material**. Create a new 3D object in the hierarchy as we usually do and then drag and drop the material to that object in the hierarchy or Scene view.

Then, set the surface type of the shader **Hologram** to **Transparent** as we did in the previous effect, as follows:

- Open the shader graph by double-clicking the asset in the Project tab.

- Open the Graph Inspector and select the Graph Settings tab.

- Go to the Surface Type setting and change from Opaque to Transparent.

When you see holograms in movies or video games, they are projections made by a sci-fi device into the air. They have moving lines across the surface that define the resolution of the projector device. These line orientations don't depend on the projecting object's orientation or size. Since that is the case here, as a reference for the orientation of those scrolling lines, we are going to use the **Screen Position node**.

Normally, we use the **Screen Position node** in **default mode.** This mode will divide the screen pixels by the **clip space position**, returning normalized screen coordinates from **(0,0) to (1,1)**. Unlike raw mode, which provides direct access to the untransformed screen position of the pixel, the default mode output is transformed and adjusted by the camera's projection matrix. See a full schema of this coordinate system in Figure 4-51.

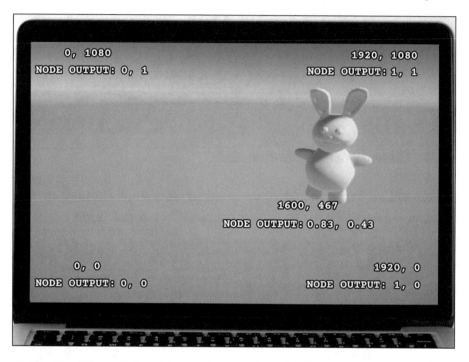

Figure 4-51. *Position of the object referenced to the Screen Position node in default mode*

- Create a **Screen Position node** in **default** mode. This node will output the current position of the pixel on the screen. This node will display a constant texture along the object, independent from the object position and UV mapping, creating a holographic effect that will depend on the position the object is in on the screen.

- Connect the **Screen Position** node output to a **Split** node and connect the **G(1)** output to the **Alpha** input of the **Fragment** block.

This will make the object gradiently transparent depending on the vertical position of that object on the screen, like in Figure 4-52, from 0 (transparent) at the bottom of the screen to 1 (opaque) at the top of the screen.

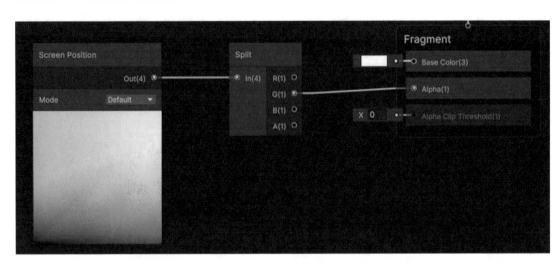

Figure 4-52. *Using the Screen Position node*

The object will become transparent or opaque depending on its position on the screen. You can see the result in Game view inside Unity Editor (Figure 4-53).

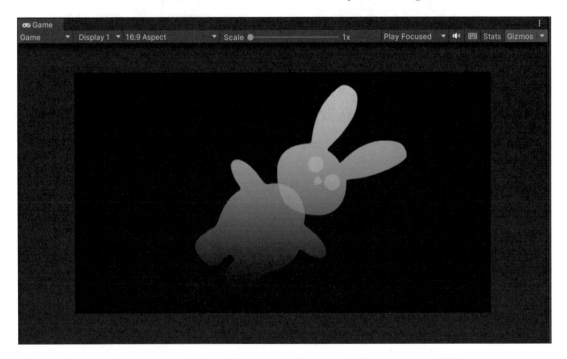

Figure 4-53. *Fragments of the object near the top of the screen will be more opaque than the ones at the bottom*

Repeat the Pattern Using Fraction Node

We now want this behavior to happen with a certain frequency along the object, simulating the resolution of the projection of the sci-fi device that is creating the hologram. To achieve that result, do the following:

- Take the **Split node G(1)** output and connect it to a **Multiply node** input **A(1)**.

- The B(1) input of the Multiply node will be fed with an exposed float input we could call *Resolution* with a **default value of 5.** As we saw before, this node will set values above 1 as output, and the Fraction node will extract only the decimal values of them, creating a repeating pattern.

- The output of the **Multiply** node will be connected to the input of a **Fraction** node, creating a pattern of horizontal gradient lines (Figure 4-54).

- Connect the Fraction node output to the Alpha input of the Fragment block to check the result in the scene after saving the asset.

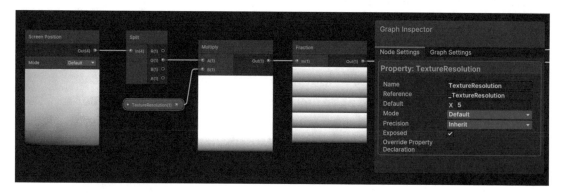

Figure 4-54. *Repeating horizontal lines pattern*

You can see that the object's surface in the scene is now showing a repeating pattern in the vertical direction of the screen. It doesn't matter if we rotate the object—the vertical lines are going to be displayed in the same direction because we are using the screen coordinates as a reference (Figure 4-55).

Figure 4-55. *Bunny with the horizontal pattern effect*

Randomize the Pattern Using the Noise Node

Our hologram shader is quite bland currently, as it lacks details. In hologram effects in video games or films, the effect is *glitchy* and irregular, simulating an imperfect three-dimensional projection in space that is affected by ambient and light noises. To create an imperfect line pattern, do the following:

- Create a **Simple Noise node** whose input **UV(2)** will be fed by the **Fraction node** output.

- Create a **float input node** with value between **30** and **60** and connect it to the **Simple Noise node** input **Scale(1)**. I exposed it and named it **Noise Resolution**. Keeping this value low will make the irregular pattern have a lower resolution and be better looking.

- Connect the output of the **Simple Noise node** to the **Alpha input** of the **Fragment block**.

The output of the Fraction node feeding the UV(2) input will distort the noise calculation into the line pattern, creating an irregular and noisy gradient lines texture, like a glitchy sci-fi projector would reproduce, as shown in Figure 4-56.

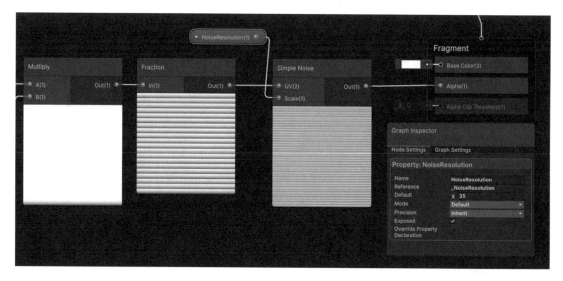

Figure 4-56. *Simple noise to randomize the line pattern*

We are getting closer to the desired sci-fi effect, as you can see in Figure 4-57.

Figure 4-57. *Randomized line pattern applied to bunny*

Create a Moving Pattern Using Add and Time Nodes

These lines need to scroll along the surface of the object, simulating that the object is being rendered in space by the projector.

As we did in all the effects in this chapter, we are going to include movement in our effect. We want to simulate the projection waves rendering the object in three-dimensional space. To achieve that, do the following:

- We are going to create a **Time node** whose output **Time(1)** is going to connect to the input of a **Multiply node A(1)**.

- The **B(2) input** of the **Multiply** node is going to be fed by a **new float value input node** that I exposed as **Scroll Speed** with a default value of **0.1**.

- The output of the **Multiply node** will be connected to a new **Add node** input **B(2)**.

- This **Add node** will be placed **between** the **Split** and **Multiply nodes** we created in the previous subsections of this effect. The **input A(1)** of the **Add node** will be connected to the **output G(1)** of the **Split node**, and the **output of the Add node** will be connected to the **input A(1)** of the **first Multiply node** we created that is managing the texture resolution (Figure 4-58).

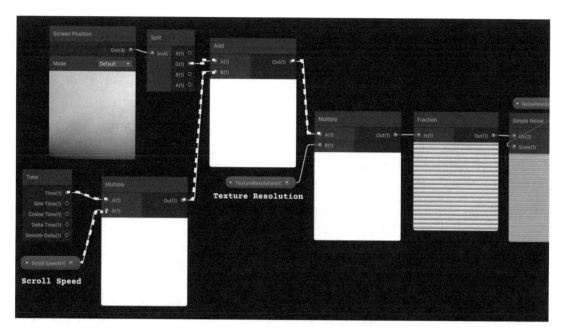

Figure 4-58. *Scrolling animation applied to the pattern*

After saving these changes, your pattern will scroll on the vertical axis of the screen at a custom speed. Set the scrolling speed at low values to create a nicer effect (0.1–0.5). Setting negative values for the Scroll Speed will invert the scrolling direction.

Add Color to the Gradient Hologram Lines

This effect in black and white is not very good looking. In sci-fi movies or video games, the holograms are displayed in stunning and glowy colors. Let's add some, as follows:

- Create a new **Multiply node** and connect the **B(4) input** with the **Simple Noise node output.**

- Create a **Color input node** set up as **HDR** and exposed as **Base Color**, then connect it to the **A(4)** input of the recently created **Multiply node.**

- Connect the output of that **Multiply node** to the **Base Color** input of the **Fragment block** (Figure 4-59).

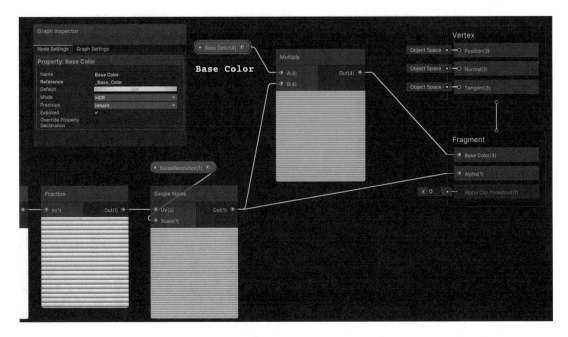

Figure 4-59. *Adding color to the Hologram pattern*

In Figure 4-60 you can see the resulting shader, but it lacks a volume sensation. Holograms are a 3D representation of a virtual object projected in space.

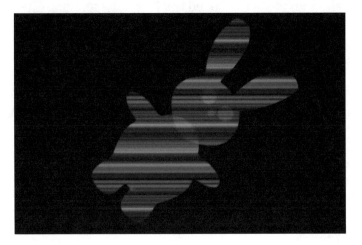

Figure 4-60. *Colored hologram*

The effect is too planar, as it is an unlit shader graph effect. We are lacking the 3D feeling. Using the fresnel effect, we will add a volumetric light effect around the edges of the object, which will change depending on the point of the view of the user.

Emphasize the Effect with Fresnel Node

To add virtual volume to the object without external lighting interfering with the object, add a fresnel effect to the object, as follows:

- Create a **Fresnel Effect node** and set the **Power(1)** default value to **3**. You can expose that property if you want to adjust the width of the light rim of the edges.

- Connect the output of the **Fresnel Effect node** to a **Multiply node** **A(1) input** and **feed the B(2) input** with a **Color** input node set to **HDR** and exposed as a property. I called it **FresnelColor**.

The implementation is shown in Figure 4-61.

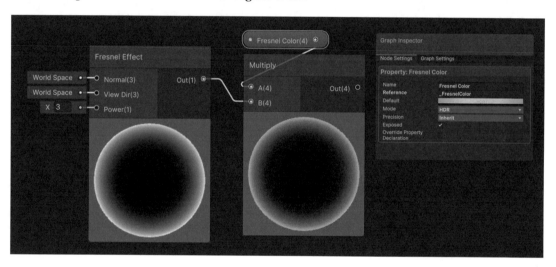

Figure 4-61. *Colored fresnel effect*

Let's now connect the Fresnel nodes group to our previously created Hologram effect nodes:

- Create an **Add node** and connect the output of the recently created **Multiply node** to its A(4) input.

- The **input B(4)** of the **Add node** will be fed with the **Multiply node** created in the previous subsection in charge of applying the **Base Color** property to the shader.

- Finally, connect the output of the **Add node** to the **Base Color** input of the **Fragment block** (Figure 4-62).

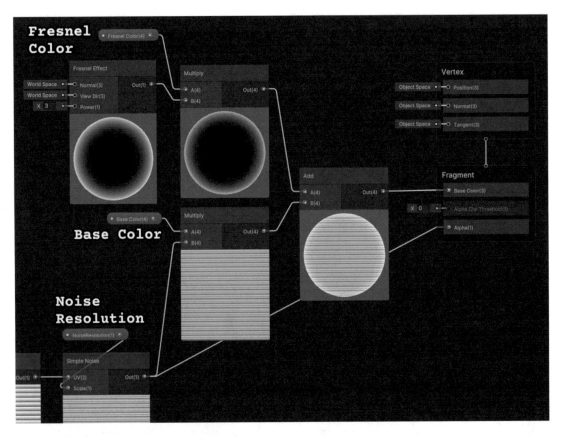

Figure 4-62. *Added fresnel effect*

The Fresnel Effect node will pop up the edges of the mesh in a gradient and glowy color, creating a light illusion and livening up the 3D mesh without interacting with the real-time directional light. You can check the final result in Figure 4-63.

Figure 4-63. *Fresnel effect completing the shader effect*

In Figure 4-64, you can see the property values set in the Inspector tab in the selected material.

Figure 4-64. *Exposed property values in Inspector tab*

Create Blink Effect Using Logic and Random Nodes

Let's add a bonus touch to the final hologram shader. We want to make a glitching effect, a random blink that will create a real and natural sensation that the hologram projector is struggling with light intensity spikes. Do so as follows:

- Start by creating a **Time node** whose output **Time(1)** will be connected to a **Random Range node**. Set the **Min(1)** and **Max(1)** default values of the Random Range node as **0** and **1** respectively (Figure 4-65).

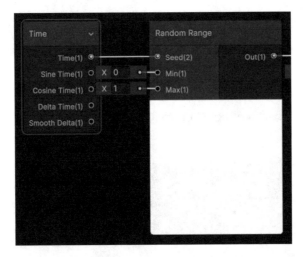

Figure 4-65. *Random Range nodes*

You may see in the **Random Range** node preview that it is blinking randomly at high speed. What is happening is that the **Random Range** node is going to output a value between **Min(1)** and **Max(1),** in our case, 0 and 1, respectively. The **Seed(2)** value will determine a defined random value between those inputs, so every time the **Seed(2)** value changes, a different random value between 0 and 1 is obtained.

We don't want the blink to happen constantly, but rather to happen with a random frequency, simulating a failure in the projection device. We want that blink to be controlled and also randomized in time. To achieve that do the following:

- Create a **Comparison node** and connect the previously created **Random Range node** output with its input **A(1)**.

- Set the **B(1)** input default value to **0.9.**

- Lastly, set the dropdown setting of the **Comparison node** to **Greater.** (Figure 4-66).

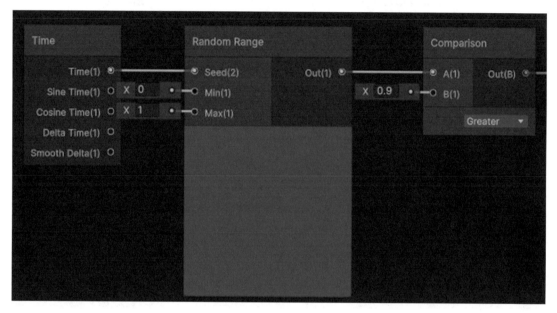

Figure 4-66. *Adding a Comparison node*

The Comparison node is used to compare two values and output a Boolean (true/false) result. It takes two inputs, usually two numeric values or vectors, and a comparison operator to determine how to compare them. The available comparison operators are: Equal, Not Equal, Greater Than, Greater Than or Equal To, Less Than, and Less Than or Equal To. For this use case select Greater, so, if A(1) is greater than B(1) it will output a true value; otherwise it will output a false value.

Knowing that the Random Range node is going to output a value between 0 and 1, it is obvious that we are only getting a true output when A(1) is greater than 0.9, which translates into a blink probability of 10 percent.

Now, let's use that Boolean output to generate a response when it is true using the Branch node. The **Branch** node will output the value of **True(1)** if the **Predicate(B)** value is true or the value **False(1)** if it is false. The whole result is a random blink effect that will happen once in ten ticks of time. Do the following:

- Add a **Branch node** whose input **Predicate(B)** will be fed with the **Comparison node** output, and the inputs **True(1) and False(1)** will be fed with 0.4 and 0 respectively. When the output value of the Comparison node is true, the output of the Branch node is 0.4; otherwise, the output of the Branch node will be 0 (Figure 4-67).

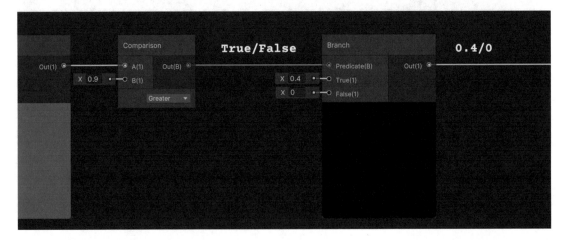

Figure 4-67. *Blink branch output*

To apply this effect in our current shader, do the following:

- Take the **output** of the **Branch node** and connect it to a new **Add node A(1) input**.

- The **input B(1)** of this **Add node** will be fed with the output of the previously created **Add node output** that was previously feeding the **Base Color input** of the **Fragment block**.

- Finally, connect the output of this **last created Add node** to the **Base Color input** of the **Fragment block** (Figure 4-68).

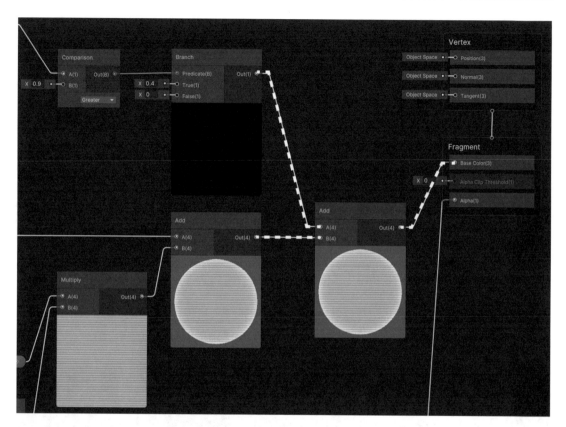

Figure 4-68.   *Adding a blinking effect*

After saving the asset, you will notice that the object is blinking randomly, causing a nice, random, noisy effect that really suits this hologram sci-fi effect.

Refactoring Shaders

That was a really beautiful but huge shader full of nodes and connections. Let's take this opportunity to look at how to group those nodes and how to organize the **Blackboard** in categories.

You can group by clicking and dragging your mouse over some nodes. After they are all selected, you can right-click and choose **Group Selection** or use CTRL + G as shortcut (Figure 4-69).

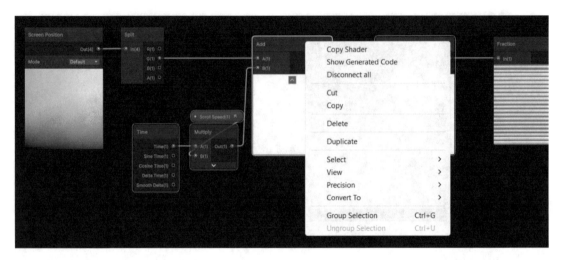

Figure 4-69. *Grouping nodes*

This will create a thin border around those nodes that you can drag, as it is one large node. Also, you can name it by double-clicking in the top label (Figure 4-70).

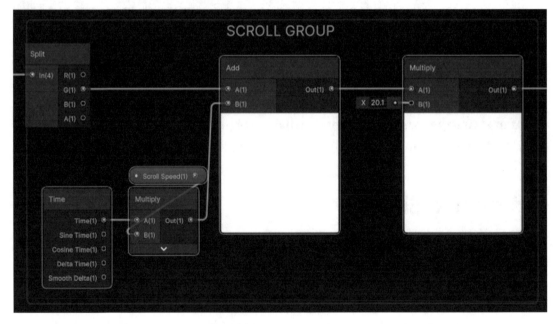

Figure 4-70. *Group created and renamed*

This is good practice as it divides your shader into readable and understandable sections.

You can also group exposed properties in your **Blackboard** by clicking the "+" button at the top-right corner of the tab and selecting **Category** (Figure 4-71).

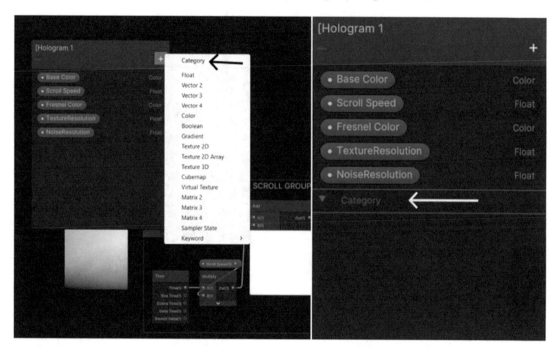

Figure 4-71. *Creating a category*

You can rename the category by double-clicking it, and you can also drag and drop properties into it (Figure 4-72).

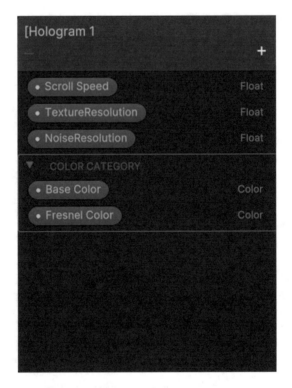

Figure 4-72. *Category name and properties*

This will keep things organized in the Material Inspector, as shown in Figure 4-73.

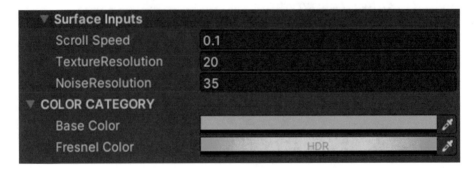

Figure 4-73. *Categories exposed in the Material Inspector*

Summary

I hope you had fun making these shaders and learned a lot about dynamic effects. We have also covered a lot of basic node implementation and graph refactoring, so take your time to review everything and play with the shaders you have created.

In the next chapter, we are going to focus on **Deformation** shaders, and we will study the **Vertex** block in the shader graph to deform and change the shape of our objects to create outstanding effects like **real-time snow generator, fish procedural animations, and more.**

CHAPTER 5

Vertex Shaders

In this chapter, we are going to access the **Vertex Position** node in the **Vertex** block of the master stack to change the position of the vertices of our mesh, which will also affect the disposition and orientation of the polygons formed by them. This will allow us to change the mesh surface of any shape in real-time. This technique is used when we want to create deforming effects, procedural animations, and more, as follows:

- **Procedural Fish Animation**: We are going to animate a fish mesh without doing the complex setup that is normally required to implement animations (skeletons, vertex weighting, setting up keyframes). We will deform the mesh of the fish using a sine wave pattern to make it feel like it is swimming under the ocean (Figure 5-1).

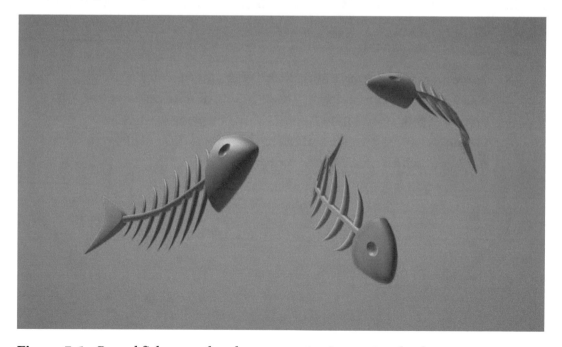

Figure 5-1. *Boned fish procedural movement using vertex shader*

Á. Alda, *Beginner's Guide to Unity Shader Graph*, https://doi.org/10.1007/978-1-4842-9672-1_5

- **Volumetric Snow**: If your game has a Christmas theme, having the objects in a scene with a deep and cozy layer of snow is a must. We will learn how to deform the vertices of a mesh to achieve what you see in Figure 5-2.

Figure 5-2. *Snow shader*

- **Spawning Objects from a Singularity Point**: Are you making a space- themed game and want a black hole to dramatically swallow objects in your scene like in Figure 5-3? We are going to study how to manipulate the position and reference of the vertices of different meshes to achieve that effect in your game.

Figure 5-3. *Singularity position absorbing elements in the scene*

Procedural Fish Animation

In video games development, to animate a mesh you need to make a previous setup (create a skeleton, weigh the mesh, set up the keyframes and animation curves, and more), which sometimes, depending on the 3D model, can be quite tricky. Obviously, we are not going to cover that way of animating here. We will make a shader to modify the vertices of our mesh to create an animation without a required setup. I will teach you how to use a vertex shader to create a runtime, natural and looping animation for a fish mesh by following these steps:

- Import and set up the fish mesh.

- Access the pointing direction coordinate of the fish.

- Create a wave pattern using **Sine** node.

- Make the wave movement dynamic.

- Deform the mesh on a selected axis.

- Adjust the wave pattern intensity.

Import and Set Up the Fish Mesh

To animate a fish, we need . . . you guessed it—a fish mesh. This book is not about 3D modeling, so I will use a FBX free model from a CC0 website called The Base Mesh[1]. This web page gives you access to more than 900 free license meshes that you can use in your personal or professional projects.

If you open the link provided, you will go to the home page of the website. On the home page you can click the middle button, **GoToLibrary**, highlighted in Figure 5-4.

Figure 5-4. *TheBaseMesh home page*

---

[1] https://thebasemesh.com

After clicking the GoToLibrary button, you will be redirected to a page where you can search for and download any of their meshes. Inside the Search tab write *Fish*, and you will find the mesh we are going to use in our project (Figure 5-5).

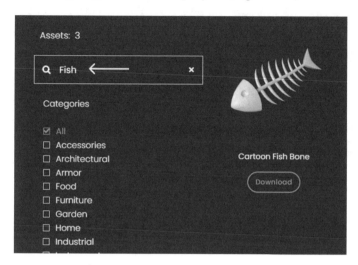

Figure 5-5. *Cartoon fish bone*

Click on the Download button under the preview of the mesh and a ZIP file will be downloaded to your computer. Inside the ZIP file, you will find several files (FBX, obj, and an image of the preview of the mesh). We are interested in importing the FBX file,[2] which stores information about the model, such as mesh, animations, materials, and more.

To import the FBX file into your Unity project, you have to drag the FBX file from the File Explorer (Finder in Mac) with the mouse and drop it anywhere inside the Project tab of Unity Editor (Figure 5-6).

---

[2] FBX (Filmbox) is a file format used in the video-game industry to store 3D models, associated animations, materials, and more information about the model.

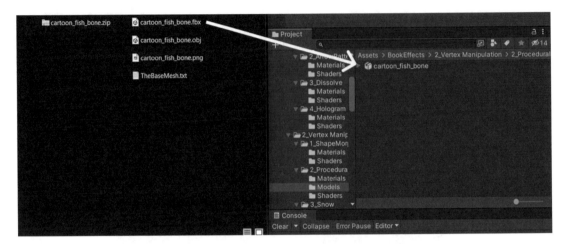

Figure 5-6. *Importing the .FBX file to the Unity project*

This FBX file can also be found inside the github project of this book inside **Assets ➤ BookEffects ➤ 2_VertexManipulation ➤ 1_Procedural Animation ➤ Models.**

Now, we are ready to start animating this fish inside Unity using a brand-new URP lit shader graph, as follows:

- Create a new URP lit shader graph by right-clicking anywhere inside the Project tab, and then select **Create ➤ Shader Graph ➤ URP ➤ Lit Shader Graph.** I called it **ProceduralAnimation.**

- Create a material by right-clicking the newly created shader graph and selecting **Create ➤ Material.**

- Now, drag and drop the fish FBX file from the Project tab to the Scene view, or go inside the Hierarchy tab to instantiate it inside the scene.

- Then, drag and drop the recently created material asset to the fish object to assign that material to its mesh renderer.

Now, you are ready to start making the shader graph to make your fish swim.

Access the Pointing Direction Coordinate of the Fish

The first thing we need to know is how a fish moves. If you've seen a documentary about the ocean or gone to an aquarium, you may have noticed that a fish performs a sinuous movement along its body to displace the water around it, pushing itself through the ocean.

Our task is to move the vertices of the fish, following a sine function so the fish object looks like it is swimming. To achieve that, let's first analyze Figure 5-7, in which I placed a photo of a fish over a plot of a sine function. You can clearly see that the fish shape is following that formula when moving in order to move itself through water.

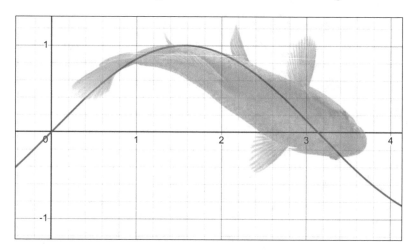

Figure 5-7. *Fish movement compared with a sine function*

We first need to identify the following two directions:

- The direction the fish is traveling; in other words, the local vector that the fish is pointing toward. This direction is going to be the input of the sine function.

- The direction to deform the vertices. The vertices of the fish mesh need to displace along the sides of the fish to create this movement, but which local vector defines that direction?

To know that information, we must go to Unity Editor and do the following:

- Set **local coordinates gizmos** to know the local orientation of the fish.

- Set the **movement tool** to display the vector arrows of the local coordinates of the fish.

- **Click on the fish object** in the scene or hierarchy to display the gizmo in the Scene view (Figure 5-8).

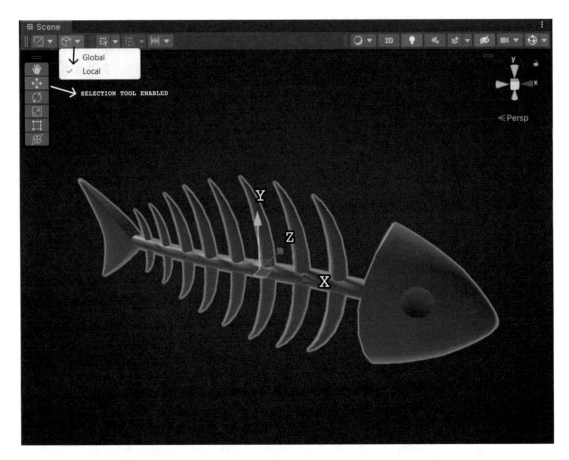

Figure 5-8. *Fish local coordinates displayed*

We can see, by color inspection, that the **orientation** of the fish is the **X/R** coordinate and the **displacing orientation** of the vertices is the **Z/B** coordinate.

Knowing that, we can start modifying the shader graph. Double-click the shader graph asset we previously created and follow these steps:

- Create a **Position node** and set its **dropdown** setting to **Object**, so as to access the local coordinates of the position of each vertex.

- Create a **Split node** whose input will be connected with the output of the **Position node** we just created, as in Figure 5-9.

- Connect the **Split node R(1)** output to the input of a new **Sine node**.

- Then connect the output of the **Sine node** to the **Base Color input** of the **Fragment block**. This will serve as a way to see if we are approaching the solution correctly (Figure 5-9).

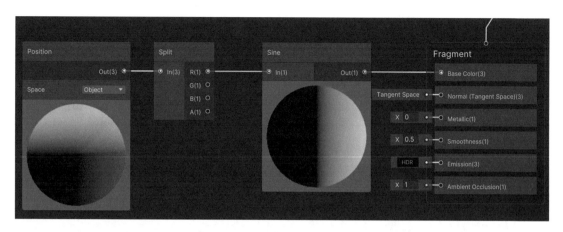

Figure 5-9. *Connecting the X/R component of the vertices to the input of a Sine node*

If you save the asset and take a look at the fish object (Figure 5-10), you will find that you are accessing the correct X/R coordinate, since the gradient is displayed in that direction. But as you can see, nothing is really "waving," because the value of R(1) goes from 0 to 1. To see some wave motion pattern, we need to multiply that output by a **WaveAmount** value.

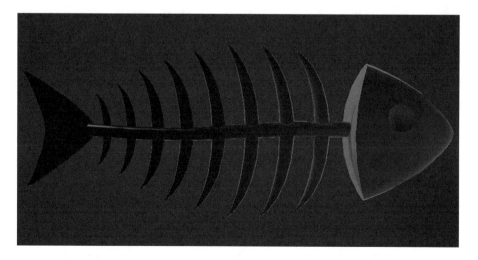

Figure 5-10. *Connecting the X/R component of the vertices to the input of a Sine node*

Create a Wave Pattern Using Sine Node

We need to increase the frequency of the sine function to achieve the desired wave pattern. If you take a look at Figure 5-11, you can clearly see that multiplying the input of the Sine node will increase the frequency of the wave pattern that is outputting this mathematical operation.

You can compare the function **Sin(2In(1))** and the function **Sin(In(1))**. Sin(2In(1)) has a frequency two times higher than that of Sin(In(1)).

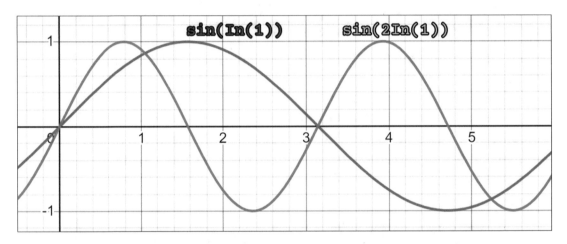

Figure 5-11. *Sin(2x) in blue vs. Sin(x) in red*

Let's now modify the frequency of the Sine node output by multiplying the output of the Split node before entering the Sine node, as follows:

- Create a new **Multiply node** and feed its A(1) input a new **Float Input node** with a default value of **5**. I exposed it for future tweaks inside the Inspector and named the property **WaveAmount**.

- Connect the **B(1)** input of the **Multiply node** with the input **R(1)** of the previous **Split node**.

- Finally, connect the output of the **Multiply node** to the input of the **Sine node** (Figure 5-12).

For now, we are going to connect the nodes to the Base Color input of the Fragment block to have a visual representation of the movement that the vertices of the shape are going to follow.

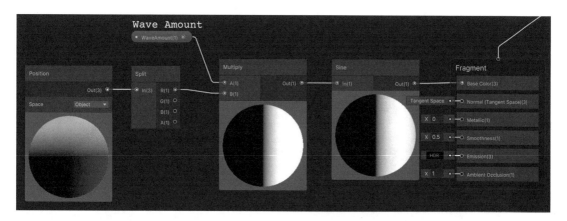

Figure 5-12. *Increasing the sine frequency using the wave amount*

If you increase the **WaveAmount** value to 60, you can see in the scene how the sine waves are displayed along the X/R coordinate of the fish (Figure 5-13).

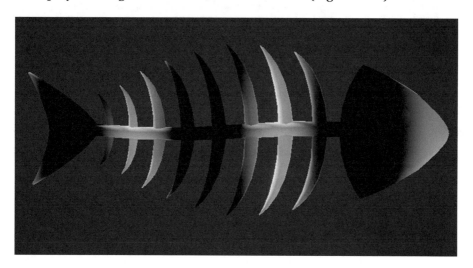

Figure 5-13. *Waves displayed along the X/R axis of the fish*

As you may have noticed, these waves are not moving along the *x*-axis, and the input value of the sine node is static, so the fish will not move at all. To fix that, let's offset the sine using the Time node.

Make the Wave Movement Dynamic

This method consists of adding a constant offset value to the input of the Sine node. If you take a look at Figure 5-14, you can see the comparison between the functions $\sin(In(1))$ and $\sin(2 + (In(1)))$. The second mentioned function will be offset in the x-axis two units.

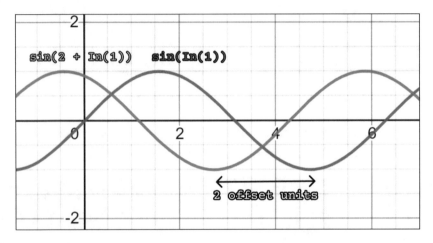

Figure 5-14. *Sin(2+In(1)) vs. Sin(In(1))*

The idea is to constantly increase that offset value to create a moving sine along the X/R coordinate. To achieve that we will use the Time node as follows:

- Create a **Time node** and connect the input **Time(1)** to a brand-new **Multiply node's input A(1)**. Then connect the **B(1) input of the Multiply node** with a **float input** that you can expose as **WaveSpeed** with a default value of **0.5** (Figure 5-15).

    We are using the **Sine node** in a similar way to how we used the **Fraction node** in previous effects. This node is useful to create repeating patterns but with a smoother finishing, unlike the Fraction node, which has hard-edged transitions between patterns, although the key concepts are the same:

    - Multiplying the input of the Sine node will generate more repetition patterns.

    - Adding values to the input of the Sine node will generate the displacement of the pattern.

Figure 5-15. *Time and Multiply nodes*

- Now, create an **Add node** that will be placed between the first created
  Multiply node and the **Sine node**. That Add node will be fed by both
  Multiply nodes' output, and its output will be connected to the **Sine
  node's input**, as in Figure 5-16.

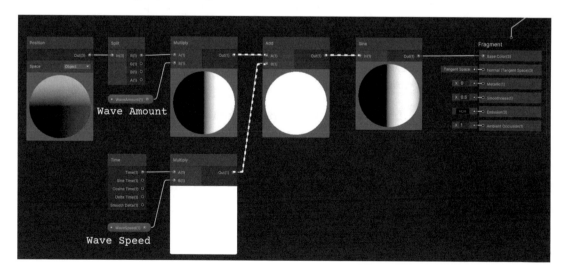

Figure 5-16. *Sine node movement*

This method will add a constantly increasing offset, moving the wave pattern along the **X/R** coordinate of the fish. You can check it out in the scene after saving the asset (Figure 5-17).

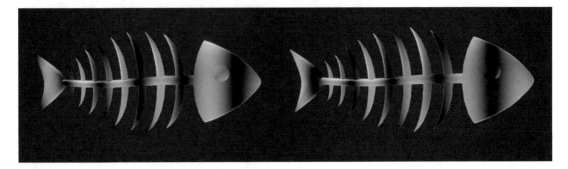

***Figure 5-17.** Fish displaying the moving wave pattern*

Deforming the Mesh along a Selected Axis

Now that we have displayed the sine function in the color of the mesh, it is time to actually deform the mesh using that pattern. Let's translate the result of this sine function into vertex movement along the Z/B axis of the vertices of the fish, moving the vertices along the sides of our fish. To achieve that, do the following:

- Create a **Vector3 input node** and set a default value of **(0,0,1)**.

- Create a **Multiply node** and feed its **A(3) input** with the output of the **Sine node** we created earlier.

- Then connect the **Vector3 input node** we created to the **B(3) input of the Multiply node** we just created.

The Position node of the Vertex blocks needs to be fed with a Vector3, indicating the new position of the vertex in the world. The output of the Sine node, however, outputs a float value, so the technique we are applying consists of storing the information calculated by the Sine node in a Vector3. In this case, as we want to move the vertices in the Z/B direction, we need to store the Sine node output in the Z component of a Vector3 (Figure 5-18).

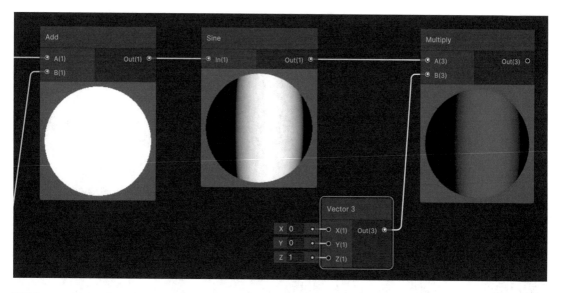

Figure 5-18. *Creating a Vector3 with the Sine node output stored in its Z/B component*

The first clue that we are doing things right is that the Multiply preview is now showing the sine pattern in a blue color, indicating that the Sine node output is stored in the Z/B component of a Vector3. Now we need to add that calculated deformation, stored in the Z component of a Vector3, to the current position of the vertices. Do the following:

- Access the local position of the vertices by creating a new **Position node** in the **Object space.**

- Create an **Add node** and connect the **Position node** output to the **Add node input A(3)** and the output of the **Multiply node to the input B(3)** of the new **Add node**.

- Finally, connect the output of the recently created **Add node** to the **Position input** of the **Vertex block** (Figure 5-19).

Now that we are going to modify the vertex position input in the Vertex block, we can delete the connection to the Base Color input of the Fragment block, since it is no longer needed for debugging.

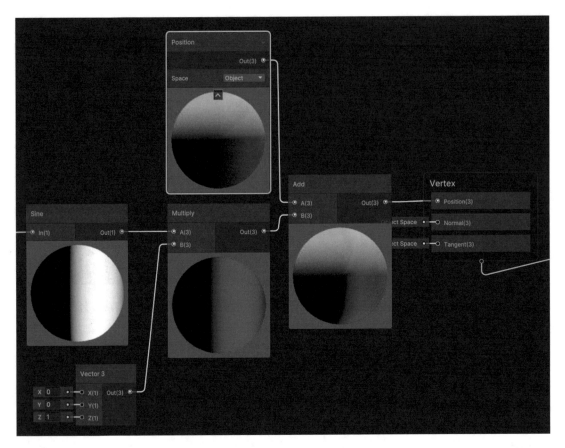

Figure 5-19. *Adding the sine operation to the Z/B component of the vertex positions*

If you now save the shader graph and go back to Unity Editor, you will find something weird happening (Figure 5-20).

The deformation pattern is following the sine pattern we created, but we are not controlling the strength of the deformation, so they are overstretching. We need to make the deformation of the mesh more subtle so as to avoid this ugly stretching.

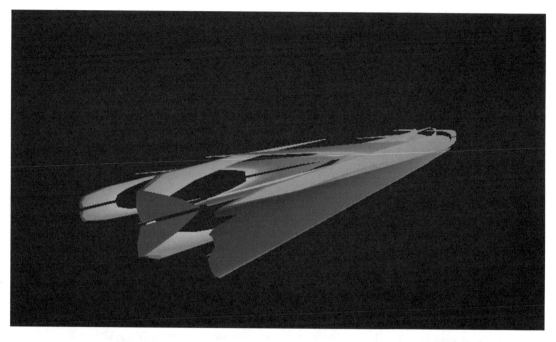

Figure 5-20. *Vertices of the fish mesh are too deformed along the Z/B axis*

Adjust the Wave Pattern Intensity

As you saw previously, the fish was being deformed far too much by the shader. We need to subtly decrease the output of the Sine node in order to achieve a more realistic and controlled effect. In other words, we need to reduce the amplitude of the sine function. We need to multiply the output of the sine function by a value between 0 and 1.

We can now modify the output of the Sine node and multiply it by a value between 0 and 1 to reduce its maximum and minimum values. For instance, in Figure 5-21 you can check a sample where a sine function was reduced in amplitude by half by multiplying the result by 0.5.

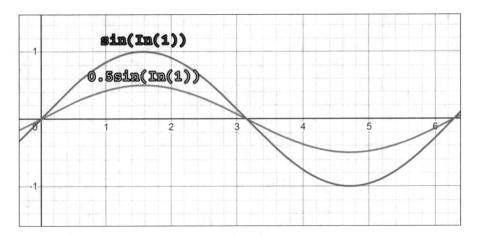

Figure 5-21. *Reducing the amplitude of the sine function by half*

- Let's translate this behavior in Shader Graph by creating a **new Multiply node** between the **Sine node** and the previously created **Multiply node** that was storing the Sine node output inside a Vector3 Z/B component.

- Then, create a **Float Input node**, which I exposed with the name **WaveAmplitude**, with a default value of 0.01, and connect it to the remaining input of the last created **Multiply node** (Figure 5-22). This will reduce the amplitude of the Sine node output by 100.

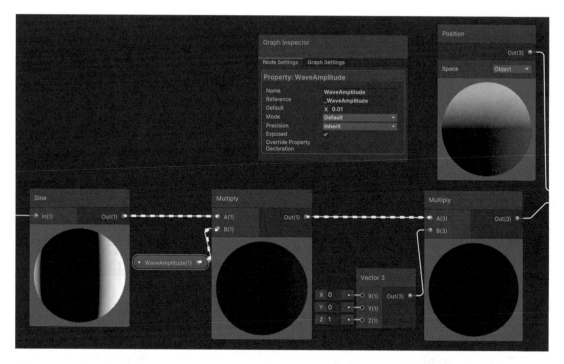

Figure 5-22. *Reducing the amplitude of the sine function a hundred times*

Finally, to end up with a really nice result, let's use the following property values:

- WaveAmount = 11

- WaveSpeed = 3

- WaveAmplitude = 0.01

Using these values will produce a smooth and subtle swimming animation effect (Figure 5-23).

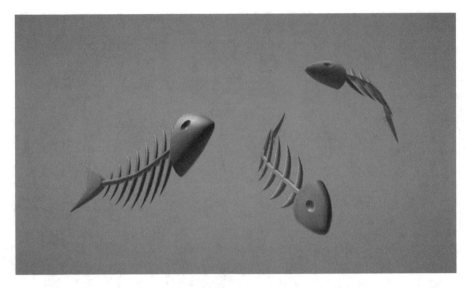

Figure 5-23. *Different fish animations in the scene*

This effect uses the Sine node to achieve a repetition pattern like the Fraction node but with a more subtle and wavy finish. You can use this technique when you want to create water waves or flags.

Volumetric Snow

Imagine making a Christmas-themed game. All elements in the scene need snow on top of them to be integrated inside the Scene, like some snow has fallen from the sky and set on top of them. To achieve a really nice snow effect we have to follow these steps:

- Import 3D models to scene.

- Define a snow direction mask.

- Use a gradient to mask the extrusion.

- Extrude geometry along normals.

- Fix broken extruded mesh.

- Add masked color.

- Add glowy fresnel effect.

Import 3D Models to Scene

As in the previous effect, we are going to use an imported 3D model—in this case, a bench. You can also find this asset inside the github project under the path **Assets ➤ BookEffects ➤ 2_VertexManipulation ➤ 2_Snow ➤ Models.**

I downloaded the bench mesh from the web page *The Base Mesh*. To do that, go to the Mesh Library section and write in the Search field: *park bench* (Figure 5-24).

Figure 5-24. *Bench mesh from The Base Mesh*

After clicking on download, you will have a ZIP file. Inside of the ZIP file you will find an FBX file among other files we don't really need. You can import the FBX file into your Unity project by dragging and dropping that file anywhere inside the Assets folder under the Project tab (Figure 5-25).

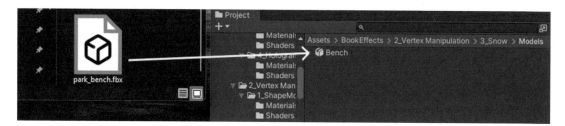

Figure 5-25. *Importing an FBX file inside a Unity project*

You can then drag and drop that FBX asset from the Project tab to your Scene view or Hierarchy tab to instantiate it inside of the mentioned view (Figure 5-26).

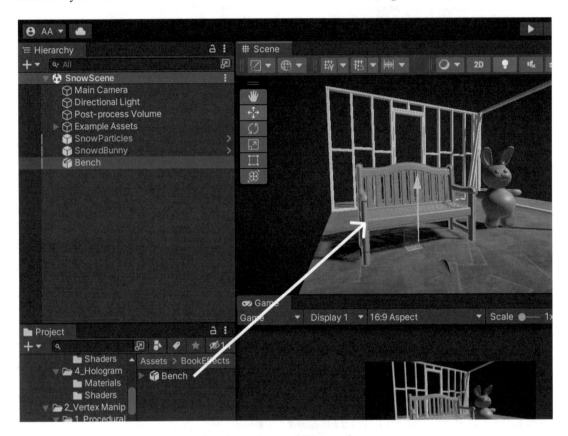

Figure 5-26. *Instantiating FBX bench model into the scene*

Define a Snow Direction Mask

Let's first take a look at a real-life snowy bench, completely covered by the snow (Figure 5-27).

Figure 5-27. Real-life snowy bench

We can see that the snow has been falling from the sky, depositing snow on top of the bench, "extruding" its shape. It feels that the surface of the bench has been extended, following the direction of the falling snow.

If we want a nice snow effect, we have to take into account the direction from which the snow falls. That falling direction will be useful to create a gradient, masking which vertices need to be extruded.

But first, let's create and set up a URP lit shader graph, as follows:

- Create a URP lit shader graph by right-clicking anywhere inside the Project tab and selecting **Create ➤ Shader Graph ➤ URP ➤ Lit Shader Graph**, which I called Snow.

- Then, create a material by right-clicking inside the recently created shader graph asset and selecting **Create ➤ Material.**

- Finally, drag and drop the material asset to the bench object we imported before.

Now, open the Shader Graph Editor by double-clicking on the shader graph asset just created, and then do the following:

- Create a new **Normal Vector node** and set it to **World Space** in its dropdown setting.

- We need to compare the **World** orientation between the falling snow vector and each vertex normal in the mesh.

- Create a **Vector3 node** with **default value (0, 1, 0)** and expose it as a property called **SnowDirection**. This will be the vector indicating the snow falling direction.

- Create a new Dot Product node and connect the **Normal Vector node** and **SnowDirection input** to the **Dot Product Node inputs B(3) and A(3)** respectively (Figure 5-28).

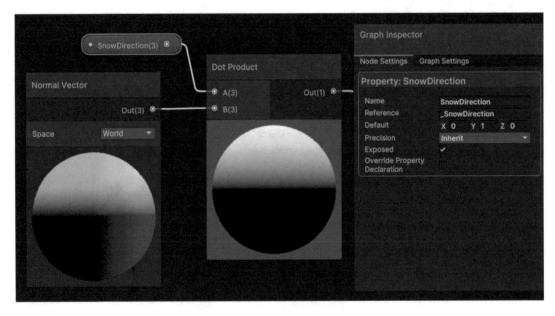

Figure 5-28. *Creating a gradient in a certain direction*

- We can test this by connecting the output of the **Dot Product node** to the **Base Color input** of the **Fragment block**.

You will see in the scene that both meshes have a black-and-white gradient pointing toward the SnowDirection vector (Figure 5-29).

Figure 5-29. *Gradient shown in the scene meshes*

Depending on the SnowDirection value, the Dot Product node can output values lower than 0 (creating weird stripes) and values greater than 1 (with uncontrolled glow). To avoid those unpredictable results, we will do the following:

- Connect a new **Saturate node** to the output of the **Dot Product node** to keep the output result of the **Dot Product node** between 0 and 1 (Figure 5-30).

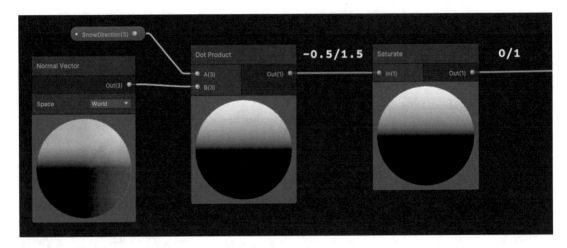

Figure 5-30. *Adding a Saturate node to the Dot Product output*

Now that we can access the vertices whose normals are pointing in the direction defined by the property SnowDirection, it is time to extrude them along their normal direction to create extra volume in the defined direction.

Extrude Geometry Along Normals

To create a nice snow effect, we have to extrude the vertices of the mesh in a given direction, which was already defined by the gradient we created. The extrusion has to be along the normals to achieve a nice effect and avoid snapping vertices and polygons one over another (Figure 5-31).

Figure 5-31. *Snow extrusion direction (along each vertex normal)*

Let's access the normal direction of each vertex inside the shader graph and mask them so only the vertices whose normals are in the direction determined by the property SnowDirection are extruded, as follows:

- Create a new **Normal Vector node**, but this time set it to **Object/Local space** since we are moving the vertices of the mesh along each local normal direction.

- Connect the output of the recently created **Normal Vector node** and the previously created **Saturate node** to a **Multiply node** (Figure 5-32).

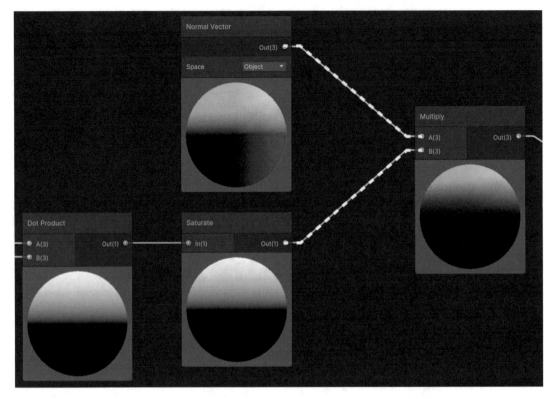

Figure 5-32. *Masking the Normal vector using the previously calculated gradient*

With this method, we have access to only the vertices whose normal directions are parallel to the direction indicated in the property SnowDirection.

Now, we can multiply those vertex normals by any value to determine how much the vertices are going to extrude in the direction of their normals, as follows:

- Connect the **Multiply node** output to another **Multiply node**, which will be fed by a **float exposed property** that I called **Snow Amount**, set to a default value of 0.2 (Figure 5-33).

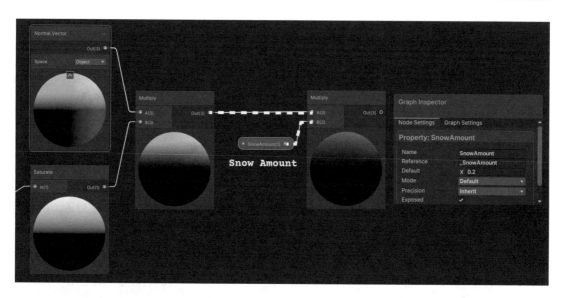

Figure 5-33. *Snow amount control*

Now, **SnowAmount** will let us control how much deformation the mesh is going to have; in order words, the amount of snow on top of the object.

Now that we have the direction and amount each vertex has to move to achieve the desired effect, it is time to add that extrusion to each vertex position, as follows:

- Access the vertex's position by creating a **Position node** in **Object space**.

- Connect the **Position node** output and the last created **Multiply node** output to the brand-new **Add node inputs A(3)** and **B(3)** respectively.

- Finally, connect the output of the Add node to the **Position input** of the **Vertex block** (Figure 5-34).

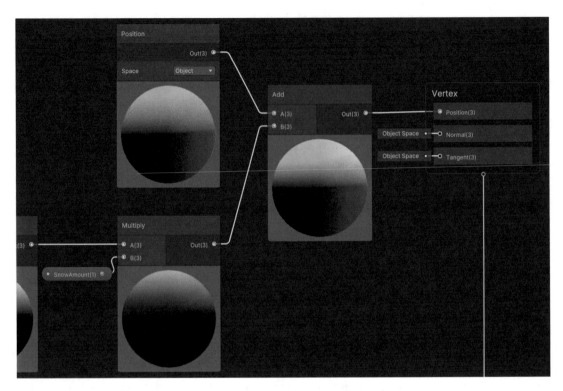

Figure 5-34. *Displacing the vertices using the Add node*

Only the vertices whose normals are parallel to the SnowDirection are being extruded toward their local normals direction in the amount we defined in SnowAmount. See Figure 5-35.

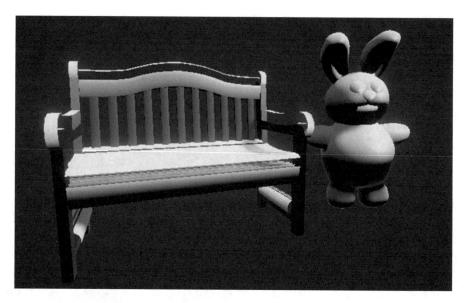

Figure 5-35. *Snow effect*

Notice that the bench seems quite off since its vertices have been separated out of the mesh, splitting the polygons and causing a weird glitchy effect. Let's examine why this is happening and how to fix it.

Fixing Broken Extruded Mesh

This issue happens when using any hard-edged mesh like our previously imported bench mesh. For contextualization, let's focus on a simpler use case. Take a look at the cube mesh in Figure 5-36, which is the simplest hard-edge mesh we can think of. You may notice that Unity is displaying in the mesh information that it has 24 vertices instead of 8.

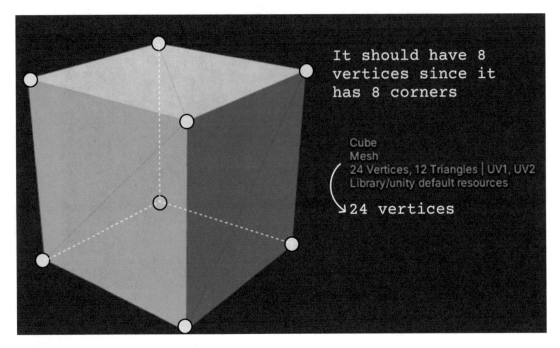

Figure 5-36. *Cube mesh information*

To obtain hard surface faces like in this cube, one must create duplicates of a vertex for each polygon surrounding each corner, so each new vertex normal will point toward the normal of each adjacent polygon. This way, the light will interact differently with each vertex normal in the same corner, generating solid-looking faces. Let's get a close-up of one corner of a cube in Figure 5-37.

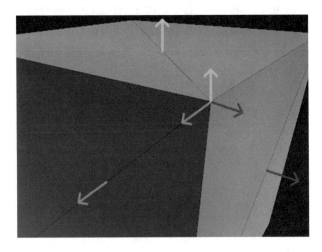

Figure 5-37. *Corner close-up*

In the case of this cube, there are three quads surrounding each corner; therefore, there are thee vertices coexisting at the same point, each one pointing toward the normal of each surrounding quad. That is why the Unity cube mesh has 24 vertices instead of 8 (**8 x 3 = 24**).

As you may conclude, when extruding the vertices along the normals, each individual vertex, coexisting at the same corner, will displace toward different directions, splitting the mesh (Figure 5-38).

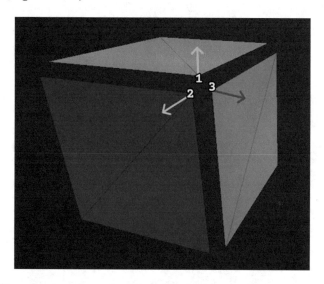

Figure 5-38. *Split cube mesh in the direction of the arrows*

These extra vertices are added by the 3D model software in which the artist created the mesh, so the light shader can create that hard lighting behavior properly. When the mesh is imported into Unity, we have the option of using those calculated normals or **letting Unity calculate the normals with a threshold angle value we set**. That threshold value will filter if an edge is considered hard or soft, depending on the angle between the quads that form that edge.

To customize the normals of our mesh, select the Bench.fbx file we imported before, under the Project tab. While selected, the Inspector tab will display all the internal FBX model settings we can tweak (Figure 5-39).

Take a look at the highlighted setting called **Normals**, which is set as **Import** by default. That option will import and set the normals calculated by the 3D modeling software, which would cause our mesh to break. You can change it to **Calculate** and set the **Smoothing Angle** to 90. Then click apply (Figure 5-40).

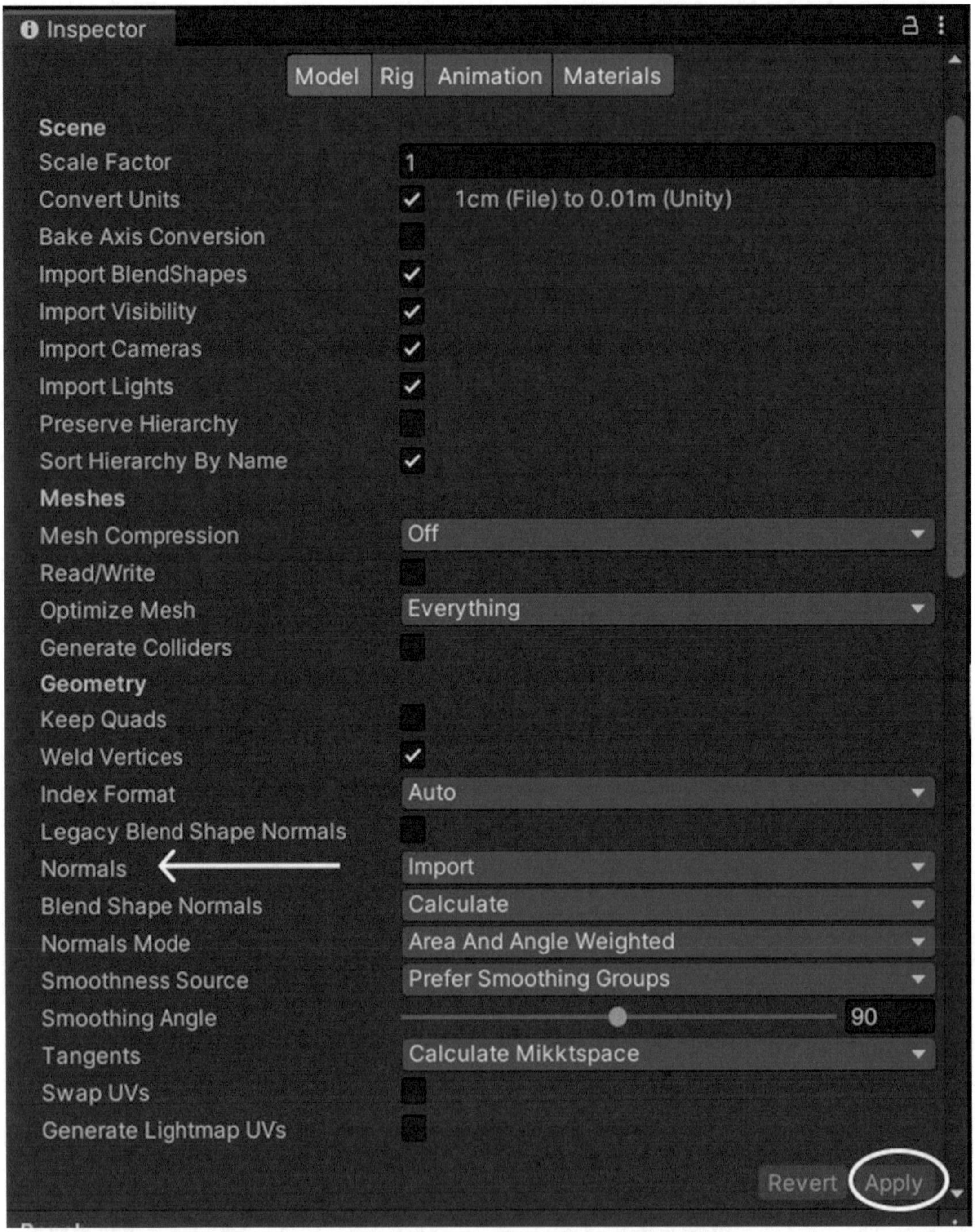

Figure 5-39. *Bench FBX settings*

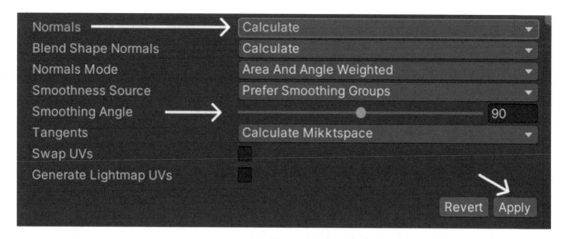

Figure 5-40. *Setting normals to Calculate and smoothing angle to 90*

After clicking the Apply button, you will see that extruding the vertices is no longer causing the bench faces to split (Figure 5-41).

Figure 5-41. *Smoothing bench normals to avoid mesh quads' splitting*

Now that our bench is extruding properly, let's finish this effect by adding some light and color to enliven the snow a little bit.

Adding Masked Color

We are going to reuse the masked direction gradient we created earlier to make a Lerp operation between the default color of the mesh and the white glowy color of the snow, as follows:

- Take the **previously** created **Saturate node** and duplicate it. We are doing this because the shader graph will not let you connect any output of a node that leads into the **Vertex block** to another branch that ends in the **Fragment block**. Creating a duplicate of the last node we want to use in both shader blocks will do the trick and lets us continue with the effect (Figure 5-42).

Note   To duplicate a node you can right-click on top of the node and then select Duplicate, or you can use the shortcut Ctrl +D with the node selected. This also works for copying/cutting and pasting nodes. Notice that the inputs of the duplicated nodes will also be connected to the same nodes as the original.

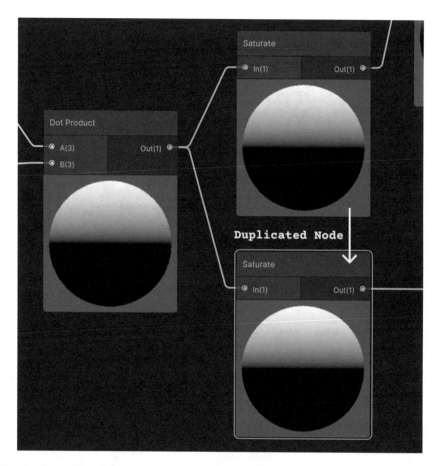

Figure 5-42. *Duplicating Saturate node to use the same gradient in the Fragment shader*

- Now, create a **Power node** whose input **A(1)** will be connected to the last created **Saturate node**, and the **input B(1)** of the **Power node** will be fed with a floating value of **0.42**. This will tighten the gradient so the snow is denser and more obvious, instead of a softer gradient (Figure 5-43).

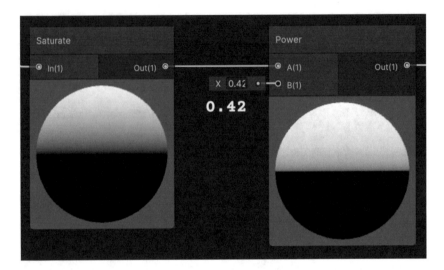

Figure 5-43. *Tightening gradient using the Power node*

- Add some color by multiplying the output of the **Power node** with a **Color input node** that you can expose as **HDR** and that I called **SnowColor**. It is shown in Figure 5-44 with the default value of **R =93, G =231, B =210 , A = 255**, and intensity value of **0.4.**

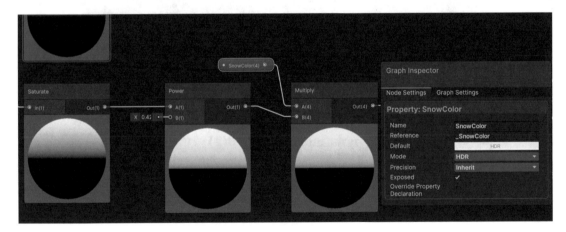

Figure 5-44. *Multiplying to change the snow color*

- You can check the result by connecting the output of the **Multiply node** to the **Base Color input** of the **Fragment block** (Figure 5-45).

Figure 5-45. *Snow color applied*

Snow in real life is really shiny because it is made of a bunch of little crystallized water shards. We are going to replicate that effect by adding a rim effect, also called a **fresnel** effect, on top of the color of our snow.

Adding Glowy Fresnel Effect

Let's create a glowy effect that characterizes stylish snow effects, as follows:

- Add a **Fresnel Effect node** and feed the **Power(1)** input with an **exposed float property**, which I called **RimPower**, with a default value of **2.37**.

- Then, take the output of the **Fresnel Effect node** and connect it to a **Multiply node**, which is also fed with a **Color input** that I **exposed** in **HDR** mode and called **RimColor** with a default value of (R = 255, G = 255, B = 255, A = 255) and intensity value of 1.2 (Figure 5-46).

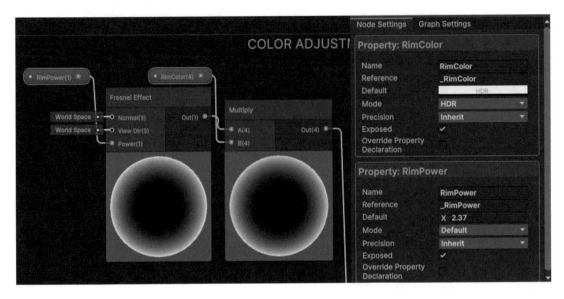

Figure 5-46. *Fresnel effect*

- Finally, multiply the output of the **Multiply node** and the output of the previously created **Power node** to mask the fresnel (Figure 5-47).

Using this technique, the gradient we achieved can be used to mask the fresnel effect, so it will only happen where the snow is appearing and not in the rest of the pixels of the surface of the object. Do the following:

- Drag the output of the last **Multiply node** to the input of the **Emission node** in the **Fragment block**.

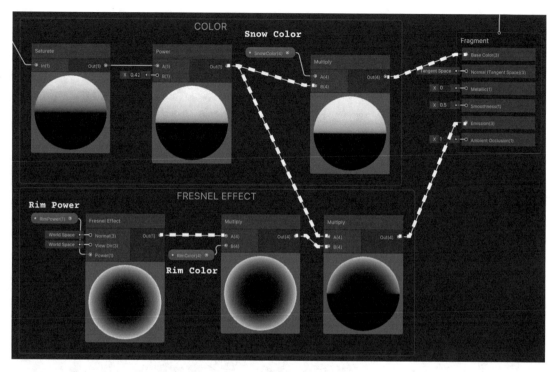

Figure 5-47. *Adding a fresnel effect to the snow shader emission*

After saving the shader graph asset in the top-left corner of the Shader Graph Editor, you can check out in Scene view the final result of this glowy and cozy snow effect on top of the meshes in the scene, as in Figure 5-48. Don't forget to review everything you have done and play with different exposed properties in different materials to achieve all kinds of snow.

Figure 5-48. *Snowed objects in the scene*

Spawning Objects from a Black Hole

This effect can be used either to spawn objects from a singularity or to make them disappear through a black hole. We will gradually modify the position of each vertex of the objects in the scene to collapse them into a single point, like a black hole would do. The steps are as follows:

- Do initial setup.
- Collapse the vertices to the center of the mesh.
- Set a collapsing destiny singularity.
- Collapse the vertices by distance.
- Add a traveling glowing color.

242

Initial Setup

To set up this sample I took advantage of the workbench object, whose children are prop objects with a variety of referenced meshes (jigsaw, hammer, safety hat, workbench, etc.), highlighted in Figure 5-49. You can find those objects in the sample scene inside the template URP project. Use these assets or create your own objects and import them into your project since every mesh is valid for this example.

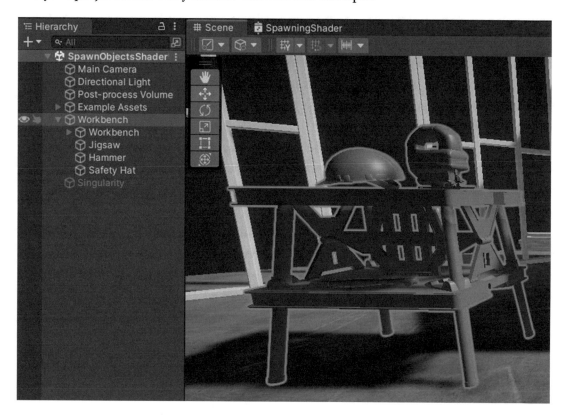

Figure 5-49. *Workbench assets*

Let's now set everything up as follows:

- Create a new URP lit shader graph by right-clicking inside anywhere in the Project tab and selecting **Create ➤ Shader Graph ➤ URP ➤ Lit Shader Graph**; I called it **SpawningShader.**

- Create a new material with the shader graph attached by right-clicking on top of the recent shader graph asset we created and selecting **Create ➤ Material.**

- Finally, drag and drop the material to any object that you want to be affected by the shader we are going to create. In my case, I dragged and dropped it to every individual object with a mesh renderer component inside the workbench parent object.

Collapse the Vertices to the Center of the Mesh

First, let's describe a black hole. A black hole is a region of spacetime where gravity is so strong that nothing, including light or other electromagnetic waves, has enough energy to escape it. In its center, there is an infinitesimal small spot, called the **singularity**, into which all the matter that the black hole absorbs is collapsing. This whole effect will replicate this behavior so we can collapse the objects in our scene into a single point with a dramatic glow effect.

We want to start by replicating the behavior of collapsing the mesh vertices into a single **local** point. This will be the first step in the process of making the whole absorbing effect, because we want, in fact, every vertex of the mesh to collapse into a single point in space.

We are going to take every vertex in the mesh and Lerp between its current position and its local origin, defined by the **local Vector3 (0,0,0)**. Using a Lerp node, we can make a transition between the original mesh and a collapsed or shrunken mesh (all the vertices of the mesh in the same spot).

Double-click the shader graph asset we have created, and inside the Shader Graph Editor do the following:

- Add a **Position Node** in **object** space to access the vertices connected to the mesh.

- Then, connect the **Position node** output to a **Lerp node input B(3)**.

- Feed the other **Lerp node input A(3)** with a **Vector3 input with value (0, 0, 0)**.

- Finally, connect the **interpolator input T(3)** with a Float Input node with a default value of 1; I exposed it as a property and called it **Transition**. Take the output of the **Lerp node** and connect it to the **Position(3) input** of the **Vertex block** (Figure 5-50).

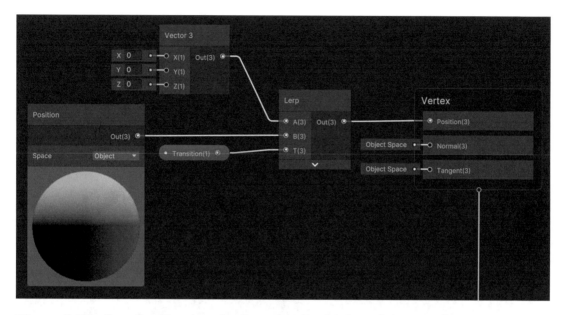

Figure 5-50. *Local collapsing shader using Position and Lerp nodes*

As you can see, the Transition value (between 0 and 1) is going to determine the position of the vertices of the mesh (all the vertices in the origin of the mesh, or all the vertices in their original position).

This effect will create a collapsing effect of the vertices of the meshes into their local center position, from totally collapsed with a **Transition** value of 0 to a default state with a **Transition** value of 1 (Figure 5-51). The property Transition is going to represent the state between the idle mesh and the collapsed mesh.

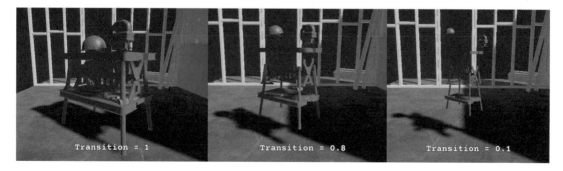

Figure 5-51. *Local collapsing in scene depending on Transition value*

Set a Collapsing Destiny Singularity

But this is not how a black hole works. We need the meshes' vertices to collapse to a single point in space, common for all of the objects, which will be the position of the center of the black hole.

To achieve that, we need to change the Vector3 input value we created from object reference to world reference, as follows:

- **Expose the recently created Vector3 input node**. I called it **SingularityPosition** (Figure 5-52). This will allow you to change the collapsing destiny point whenever you want, from Unity or from a custom script.

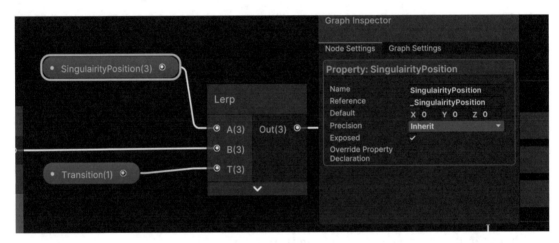

Figure 5-52. *SingularityPosition node*

Since we are working with the local (object) space of the vertices, this SingularityPosition node is read by the shader as a local position, instead of a **world position** (so every object will collapse to its local origin, instead of to the origin of the scene, common to all objects).

To trick the shader into reading the SingularityPosition node as a world position transformed to a local position, we are going to use the **Transform node (Figure 5-53)**.

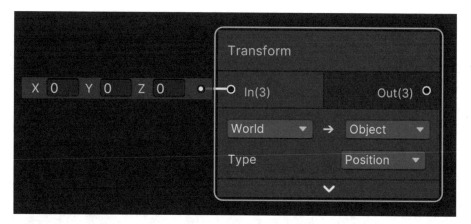

Figure 5-53. *Transform node*

This useful node is going to take a Vector3 as an input in any coordinate space and output the same vector but transformed to another coordinate space. It has the following dropdown settings we have to tweak:

- The **top-left** one is for choosing the origin coordinate space. In our case, we are going to select **World**, because we want to tell the shader that the position (0,0,0) is the origin in the world and not the local origin of the mesh.

- The **top-right** dropdown represents the destination coordinate space, which we are going to set as **Object,** to translate the origin (0,0,0) of the world to a local reference of the mesh, so the vertices will now have a destination point in local coordinates.

- The **bottom-right** one is for choosing if the vector to be transformed represents a position or a direction; in our case, a **Position**.

With the same value of SingularityPosition, each node will have it translated into its local reference to the center of the scene. Do the following:

- Connect the **SingularityPosition** property to the input of the **Transform node**.

- Connect the **output of the Transform node** to the **input of the Lerp node A(3)** (Figure 5-54).

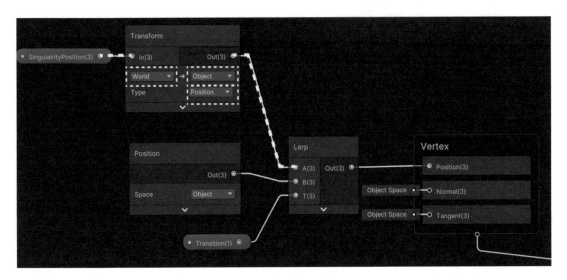

Figure 5-54. *Transform node connection to set the SingularityPosition node as a world reference*

If we save the shader graph and come back to the Scene view, we can see that changing the Transition property to 0 will make the mesh vertices collapse into the position determined by the SingularityPosition property (Figure 5-55). You can change the SingularityPosition property value to set another destiny point.

Note   The objects are created by default in the position (0,0,0) in the Scene view so make sure that you move them from that specific point when trying the effect.

Figure 5-55. *All meshes collapsing to the same world position (origin 0,0,0)*

The vertices are all moving at the same time. It seems more like a displacement and rescaling effect, which is not the intended effect. We want the vertices to be absorbed **gradually** by the singularity point, starting from the vertices closest to the black hole and ending up collapsing the furthest vertices of the meshes.

Collapse the Vertices by Distance

The vertices of the objects in the scene have to be attracted gradually to the interior of the black hole depending on the distance to the singularity position. We are going to implement that effect by taking into account each vertex's distance to the singularity position. The vertices closest to the singularity are the ones that are going to be attracted first, deforming the mesh and creating a swallowing effect.

To achieve that, let's make these nodes and connections inside the shader graph:

- Create a new **Position node** in **world space**, because now we want to access the distance in world space between the vertices' position and the singularity position.

- Create another instance of the **SingularityPosition** property by **dragging and dropping it from the Blackboard** or copying and pasting the instance we created before.

- Connect the recently created **Position node** output and the **SingularityPosition node** output to a **Distance node** (Figure 5-56). This node is going to calculate the distance between the two vectors we connected as inputs (A(3) and B(3)).

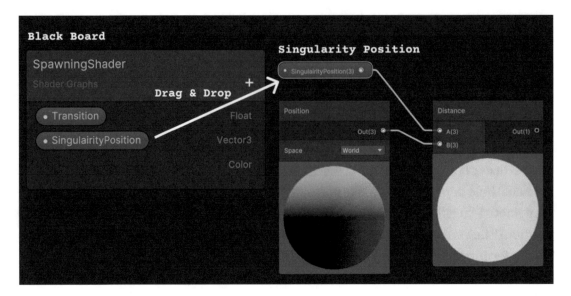

Figure 5-56. *Calculating distance between singularity and position*

Note   As the Position node is set in world space, we don't need to transform our SingularityPosition space of coordinates because it is already referenced in world space.

- Connect the **Distance node** output to a **Subtract node A(1) input.**

- Then, disconnect the Transition property node from the T(3) input of the Lerp node and reconnect it to the **B(2) inpu**t of the **Subtract node** (Figure 5-57).

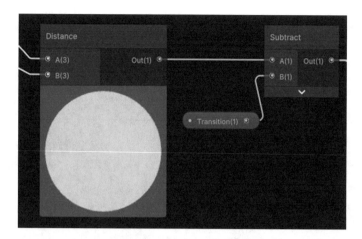

Figure 5-57. *Subtracting the distance with transition*

The **Subtract node** will create a **dependency relation** between the **distance** and the **Transition property.** The vertices will be dragged to the center of the singularity depending on how close they are to its center, achieving a really nice swallowing effect.

For instance, when the transition value is greater than 0 they will be absorbed by the singularity, depending on their distance to it. However, if the transition value is 0 they will be barely affected by the singularity, unless they are in almost the same position. The greater the transition value, the bigger the influence of the singularity will be on the objects. Do the following:

- Connect the **Subtract node** output to a new **Saturate node input** to avoid operating in nodes with values below 0 or beyond 1 that can create unexpected results.

- Connect the **Saturate node** output to the previously created **Lerp node T(3)** interpolator (Figure 5-58).

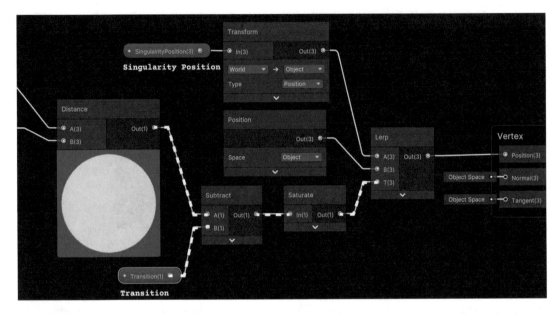

Figure 5-58. *Interpolating the position of the vertices depending on the distance to the singularity*

This will create a nicer effect, and the object's vertices are going to be gradually absorbed by the singularity, depending on the distance and the Transition property value, as you can see in Figure 5-59.

Figure 5-59. *Absorbing effect depending on the singularity distance*

Apart from deforming the mesh when absorbed, creating a nice swallow effect, we managed to influence the objects depending on their distance to the singularity.

Adding a Collapsing Glowing Color

Other than seeing it is deformed, we do not see when an object is being influenced by the black hole. To add that extra detail, we are going to add a traveling color to simulate that the black hole is dragging the objects so hard that they are heating up and dissolving into a single point in space, as follows:

- Connect the output of our previously created **Subtract node** to a new **Saturate node**.

    Remember, from the snow effect, that if we want to use previous node connections that end in both master stack blocks we have to copy the last common node ending in both blocks (Figure 5-60).

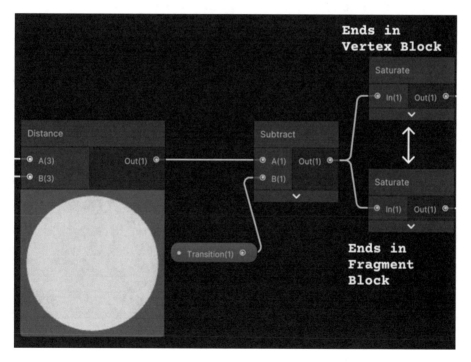

Figure 5-60. *Separated block branches that use the same previous calculations*

Now, we want the object to emit color when it is collapsing, so we need to invert the output value of the Saturate node created second, as follows:

- Create a **One Minus node** and feed it with the last created **Saturate node** output.

  The Distance node is outputting higher values the farther the fragments are from the SingularityPosition node. As we want the closer fragments to be affected by the color mask, we are using this node to invert the Distance node output.

- Then, **Multiply** the output of the **One Minus node** with a **Color input**, which I **exposed** with the name **EmissionColor**, and set up as **HDR** with **default value (R = 191, G = 62, B = 0, A = 255)** and **intensity value** of **2.5**.

- Finally, connect the output of the last created **Multiply node output** with the **Emission input** of the **Fragment block** (Figure 5-61).

Figure 5-61. *Adding color to the traveling fragments*

After saving these last changes, you can check the final result, as in in Figure 5-62. You can see how the objects are being collapsed to the position introduced in the **SingularityPosition** property.

Figure 5-62.   *Objects collapsing into the singularity*

Summary

In this chapter, we have created vertex displacement effects and learned how we can access the Vertex block to change the position of the vertices, deform the meshes, extrude the polygons, and even animate the meshes.

We have also accessed both master stack blocks in the same shader, learning about the limitations of Shader Graph regarding this topic and how to work around them.

In the next chapter, we will study the distortion shaders and how to use them to access and modify the scene color to create incredible effects like a black hole space-bending distortion or ice refraction.

CHAPTER 6

Distortion Shaders

Visual distortion refers to the modification, deformation, or manipulation of visual stimuli resulting in a deviation from their original or expected appearance. It involves a change or deformation in the characteristics, properties, or perception of an object, signal, or concept. In other words, the illusion of the deformation of what you are seeing.

A clear sample of a distortion is the refraction of the light that travels through different densities, like air and water, or through different crystal arrangements in materials, like stained glass or ice. In Figure 6-1 you can see a glass deforming the visual representation of some fruits behind it, following the same pattern defined by the glass texture.

Figure 6-1. *Refraction of the glass deforms the visual representation of the fruits behind*

Á. Alda, *Beginner's Guide to Unity Shader Graph*, https://doi.org/10.1007/978-1-4842-9672-1_6

In this chapter, we are going to talk about **screen space distortion**, which involves distorting the image on the screen based on the pixel's position and the distortion texture. It requires rendering the scene normally and then applying a post-processing shader that modifies the UV coordinates of the pixels on the screen using a distortion texture (downloaded or procedural). The effects that we are going to cover in this chapter are as follows:

- **Ice refraction**: We are going to replicate the effect seen in Figure 6-1. We are going to place an ice plane in front of the scene to generate a nice refraction effect (Figure 6-2).

Figure 6-2. *Ice refraction effect*

- **Black Hole Distortion**: The gravity of a black hole is so strong that it can deform the space around it, creating a spiral mirage around its surface. In this section, we are going to study how to create a spiral dynamic distortion effect around a black hole (Figure 6-3).

  - **BONUS**: This effect also includes a simple black hole center shader.

Figure 6-3. *Black hole distorting space around*

Ice Texture Refraction

This effect will consist of recreating the refraction of light that occurs when it travels through irregular crystal–made materials, like stained glass, ice, or moving water. We will follow the following steps to recreate the shader effect:

- Do initial setup.

- Modify the scene color to create distortion.

- Use an ice texture to modify the scene color.

- Customize the shader with the ice texture and color.

Initial Setup

For this effect, we don't require any special mesh or special setup, but, for a more understandable use case, we are going to use a plane mesh that is going to be positioned in front of other assets in the scene so we can see the effect of this shader properly. Do the following:

- Create a plane in the scene by right-clicking in an empty space inside the Hierarchy tab and selecting **3D object ➤ Plane.** I called it **IceWall.**

  A plane object will then be created in the middle of the scene. You can move it and rescale it until it is properly placed between the camera view and the objects you want to see distorted (Figure 6-4).

- Now, create a URP lit shader graph by right-clicking anywhere inside the Project tab and selecting **Create ➤ Shader Graph ➤ URP ➤ Lit Shader Graph.**

- Create a material out of that shader graph by right-clicking on the recently created shader graph asset and selecting **Create ➤ Material.** A material asset will be created with the shader graph referenced.

- Finally, drag and drop the material asset to the plane object in the Scene view or to the referenced plane object in the Hierarchy tab.

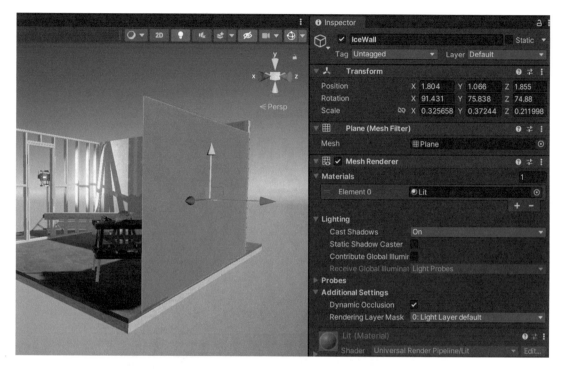

Figure 6-4. *Created plane object*

After the preceding step, the shader will be attached to the material that is referenced in the mesh renderer component of the plane object, ready to be modified.

Modify the Scene Color to Create Distortion

As we mentioned before, we are going to use **screen space distortion**, which involves distorting every frame the camera is rendering based on the pixel's position and the distortion texture.

As we are accessing and modifying the last rendered frame, we can be sure that it is a **post-processing effect**. These effects were described previously in **Chapter 2**, under the "Post-Processing Effects" subsection, and we have to take into account that they affect the performance of the game, especially when we want our game or app to be released for mobile platforms.

We can access the last rendered frame information using the **Scene Color** node. This node is going to output the color buffer of the camera, expecting as UV inputs the normalized screen coordinates **(Screen Position node output in Default mode)**.

Let's open our recently created shader graph by double-clicking on it in the Project tab; then do the following:

- First, set the Surface Type field to Transparent in the Graph Settings in the Graph Inspector tab (Figure 6-5). We want to see through the plane, so it must be set as transparent.

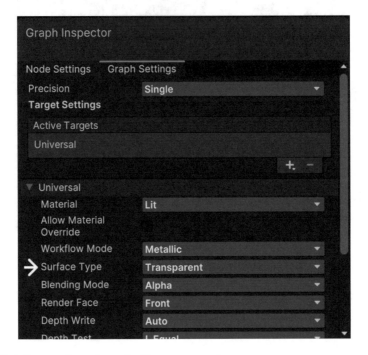

Figure 6-5. *Set the surface type to Transparent*

- Create the **Scene Color node** inside the Shader Graph Editor.

- As the Unity documentation says, the **Scene Color node needs to have as input the screen position**. Create a **Screen Position node in Default mode** and connect its output to the input of the Scene Color node.

- Finally, connect the output of the Scene Color node to the **Base Color input of the Fragment block (Figure 6-6)**.

- Save the asset in the top-left part of the Shader Graph Editor and go back to the Scene view.

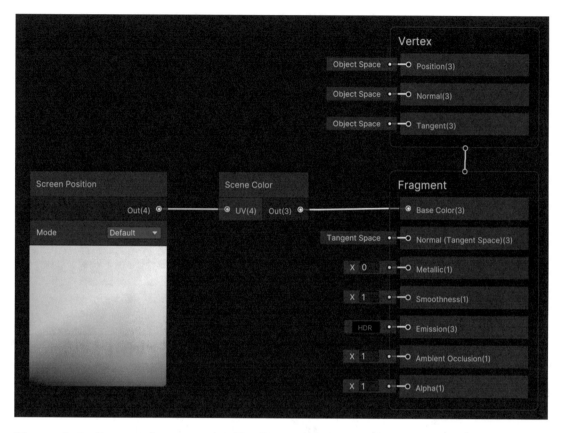

Figure 6-6. *Scene color access in Shader Graph Editor*

We expect to see the rendered frame placed on top of the plane, making it look transparent, since we are not modifying that frame yet, but, as you can see in Figure 6-7, nothing has changed at all—**the plane still looks to be in its default form.**

Figure 6-7. *Scene color not working in the Scene view*

This is happening because the ability to access the **scene color** (also called **Opaque Texture**) is not available by default. Every post-processing effect requires a lot of work from the GPU; therefore, in URP, Unity decided to disable this feature by default. We need to activate it.

As we know from **Chapter 2** in the "RenderPipelines" section, there is an asset that holds all the settings of the render pipeline. To find that asset in particular, you need to go to **Edit ➤ Project Settings**. If you select the **Graphics** dropdown at the left of the Project Settings window, you will find a scriptable object referenced in the section **Scriptable Render Pipeline Settings** (Figure 6-8).

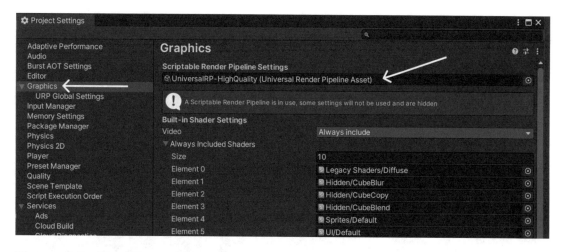

Figure 6-8. *Pipeline settings asset*

If you left-click on top of the referenced asset, the Project tab will highlight it so you can select it (Figure 6-9).

Figure 6-9. *Project tab, highlighting the pipeline settings asset*

Then, with the highlighted asset selected, the **Inspector tab** will show you all the render pipeline settings available. You can now **toggle on** the Boolean setting named **Opaque Texture** (Figure 6-10).

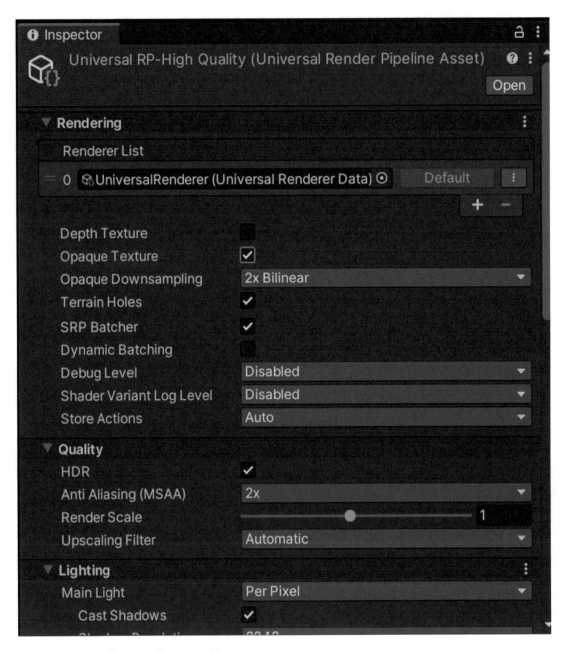

Figure 6-10. *Setting Opaque Texture on*

If you go back to the Scene view, you will see that the shader is working as intended (Figure 6-11). Now, we are letting our project access the last rendered frame of the Scene view, when requested.

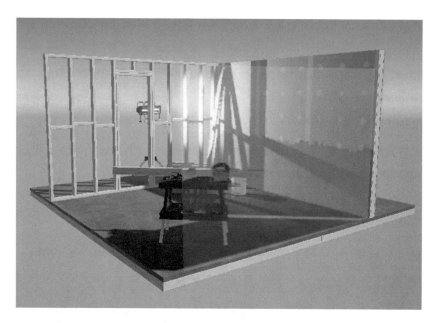

Figure 6-11. *Opaque texture*

If the game performance is dropping too much when using this type of effect, you can change the resolution of the frame captured by the camera in the setting **Opaque Downsampling** (Figure 6-12).

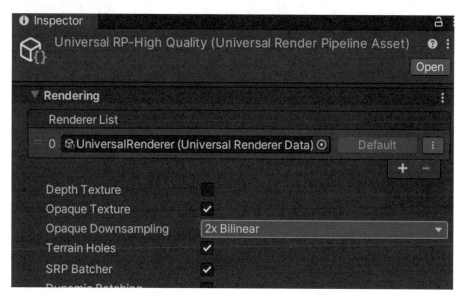

Figure 6-12. *Opaque Downsampling*

The **Opaque Downsampling** is a dropdown setting with the following options to be selected:

- **None**: Is going to use the frame without reducing the resolution. It is the least performant.

- **2x Bilinear**: Is going to reduce the resolution of the frame by half.

- **4x Box**: Produces a quarter-resolution image with box filtering. This produces a softly blurred copy.

- **4x Bilinear**: Produces a quarter-resolution image with bilinear filtering.

In Figure 6-13, you can see a visual comparison of the different options.

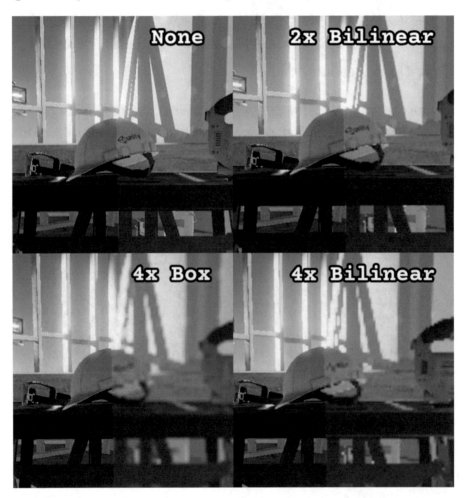

*Figure 6-13. Comparison of different **Opaque Downsampling** values*

I will keep it as 2x Bilinear because it has a nice quality–performance curve, but you can use whichever you want in your projects. Take into account that the better the quality, the worse the performance.

Now that we have access and control over the camera-captured frames, we need to distort it using an ice texture.

Use an Ice Texture to Modify the Scene Color

Let's now use an ice texture to modify the screen position coordinates that are being inputted into the Scene Color node. This will create a distortion effect.

First, get any black-and-white texture you want. In my case, I created one using artificial intelligence (Figure 6-14). You can find that asset in the Github project in **Assets ➤ Book Effects ➤ 3_Distortion ➤ 1_IceRefraction ➤ Textures.**

Figure 6-14. *Ice texture created by AI. Source: Stable Diffusion*

Now, let's use that texture inside Shader Graph, as follows:

- Create a **Texture 2D Asset** node.

- Connect the ice texture to the **Texture 2D Asset node** by dragging
  and dropping the image asset from the Project tab to the reference
  box inside the Texture 2D Asset node (Figure 6-15). You can also
  reference an asset by clicking the Reference button at the right of the
  reference box inside the Texture 2D Asset node, and then searching
  and selecting the ice texture asset.

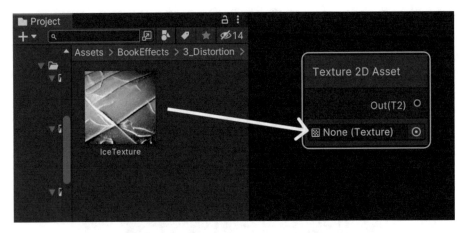

Figure 6-15. *Reference the ice texture by dragging and dropping it inside the
reference box*

- Now, create a **Sample 2D Texture node**.

  This node is going to take a texture asset and the UV coordinates
  to output the colors of the fragment to be painted. We can also
  access the individual color components (**R**ed, **G**reen, **B**lue,
  Alpha) with the corresponding output (R(1), G(1), B(1), A(1))
  (Figure 6-16).

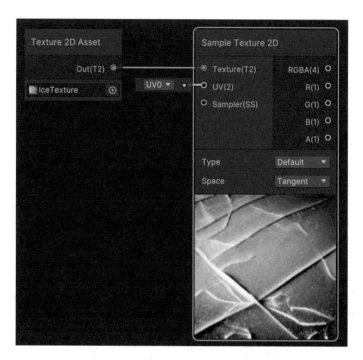

Figure 6-16. *Sample Texture 2D node*

- Create a new Lerp node and connect the output R(1) of the Sample Texture 2D node to the B(1) input of the Lerp node.

  We are using the R(1) output, which stores the black-and-white values of the texture, since we don't need more channels for this effect.

- Connect the previously created Screen Position node output to the A(4) input of the new Lerp node.

- Create a **Float Input node** with a **default value of 0.02** and expose it as a **property**. I called it **DistortionAmount**.

- As we already studied, the Lerp node is going to output a linear interpolation between the Screen Position value and the Sample Texture value inside the Scene Color node. When the value of DistortionAmount is between 0 and 1 it is going to mix the texture information with the Screen Position coordinates, modifying its value. This will be read by the Scene Color node, which will output a refraction effect, following the texture details. The closer the value of DistortionAmount is to 1 the more noticeable the refraction effect is.

- Finally, connect the Lerp Out slot to the original Scene Color node, replacing the original connection (Figure 6-17).

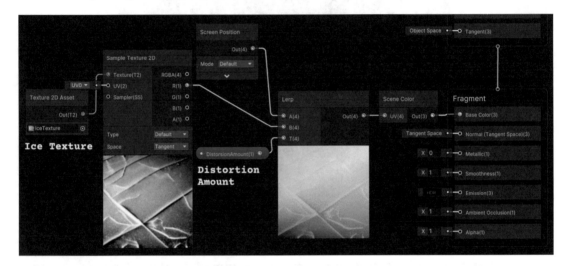

Figure 6-17. *Using the Lerp node to blend the texture and the screen coordinates*

After saving the asset and going back to the Scene view, you will see a really nice distortion effect (Figure 6-18).

Changing the value of the **DistortionAmount** property will change how much the ice texture is blending in the Screen Position value, deforming the view through the plane.

Figure 6-18. *Distorting the view through the plane object*

If you don't see any distortion effect like in the figure, remember to crank up the value of the DistortionAmount property we created.

Let's now use the texture to put in some color details, and then use the Color node to implement some icy color on the shader.

Customize the Shader with the Ice Texture and Color

Our distortion effect is behaving correctly, but to simulate some icy effect we want to emphasize the ice cracks of the texture. To achieve this, we will multiply the black-and-white ice texture with a floating value that will indicate how much of the ice texture we want to apply as details, and add it to the final base color. Do the following:

- Create a **Multiply node**, with its input A(1) fed with the output R(1) of the **Sample 2D Texture node**.

    Create a **Float Input node** with a **default value of 0.25** and connect it to the B(2) input of the recently created **Multiply node**. Expose that Float Input node as a **property**. I called it **TextureBlend** (Figure 6-19).

This property will control how much of the texture detail is shown in the final color.

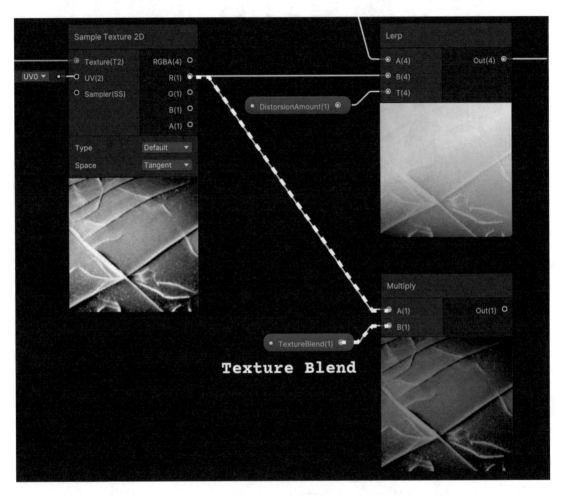

Figure 6-19. Multiply node with the TextureBlend property

- Then, create a new Add Node and connect the output of the **Scene Color node** to the input A(3) of the **Add node**, and the output of the previously created **Multiply node** to the input B(3) of the **Add node**.

  The Scene Color node is going to output the color of the plane so we can add the details of the texture on top of it to blend the texture color with the distortion effect.

- Take the output of the **Add node** and connect it to the **Base Color input** of the **Fragment block** in the master stack (Figure 6-20).

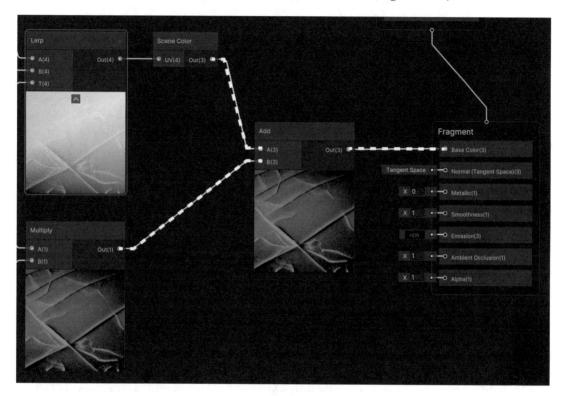

Figure 6-20. *Adding texture details to the final color*

Save the asset and go back to the Scene view, where you can check the details of the ice texture on the plane object (Figure 6-21). As you can see in the figure, we added the color of the texture on the plane surface to achieve a very subtle icy effect, with the ice cracks marked on top.

Figure 6-21. *Displayed texture details on the final color*

- To change the color of the texture, create a new **Multiply node** and connect to its A(3) input the **Color Input node** that I exposed as a property called **TextureColor.**

As before, we can now multiply the output of the Add node with a desired color to generate a colorful result with the Multiply node, as follows:

- Connect the output of the last created **Add node** to the input B(3) of the **Multiply node**.

- Finally, connect the output of the **Multiply node** to the **Base Color input** of the **Fragment block** (Figure 6-22).

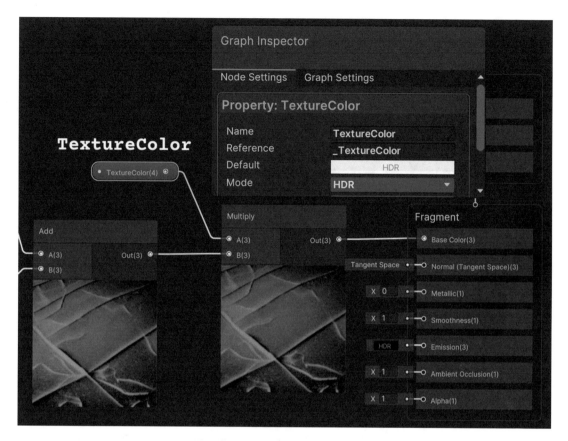

Figure 6-22. *Apply color to the texture details*

After saving the asset, go to the Scene view and check the final result. It will display an icy color over the texture details (Figure 6-23).

You can play with different property values and different textures to achieve completely different effects.

Figure 6-23. *Final ice distortion effect*

In the next section, we are going to recreate a new outstanding effect that will simulate the spatial blending distortion that a black hole makes around its singularity. We are going to learn how to create a custom procedural spiral texture for the distortion effect using the Twirl node.

Black Hole Distortion

We mentioned the power of black holes in the previous chapter when we created an absorption effect. A black hole is capable of absorbing even light itself, which is why you cannot see the center of it in space. But what you can see is the space around the black hole, completely distorted, dragged to the center of the singularity in a spiral pattern.

In Figure 6-24, you can check a NASA simulation of a supermassive black hole, located in the middle of a galaxy. Because no light can escape the black hole, you can see it as a plane silhouette in the middle of the image. The black hole's gravity is so strong that it is causing a spiral distortion around the edge of the black hole, which is the effect we are going to reproduce.

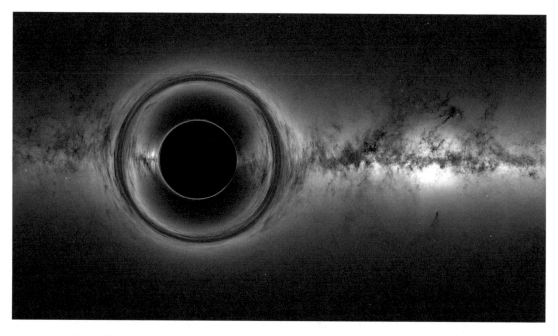

Figure 6-24. *Black hole in the middle of an ultra dense galaxy. Source: NASA's GSFC*

In this section, we are going to follow these steps to generate a more complex effect with two different objects, one of them representing the black spherical silhouette of the black hole and the other one representing the plane that is going to deform the visual of the space around the black hole center. We will do the following:

- Create the center of the black hole.

- Use particle systems for a billboard effect.

- Create a spiral texture using the Twirl node.

- Modify the scene color.

- Mask the spiral texture.

- Add dynamic rotation to the spiral texture.

Creation of the Center of the Black Hole

The complete black hole effect is complex, involving more than one object with different shaders. We will start by creating the dark center, whose shader is going to be the simplest one. Let's set up everything in our scene first:, as follows

- Create an unlit shader graph by right-clicking anywhere inside the Project tab and selecting **Create ➤ Shader Graph ➤ URP ➤ Unlit Shader Graph**; I called it **BlackHoleCenter.** We are using an unlit shader because, as the light is absorbed by the black hole, there is no actual interaction with the light around the surface of the object, which is why it seems like a 2D silhouette in the referenced NASA images.

- Create a material out of the shader graph asset we just created by right-clicking on the shader graph asset and selecting **Create ➤ Material.**

- Finally, create a sphere in the scene by right-clicking in an empty space inside the Hierarchy tab and selecting **3D Object ➤ Sphere.** Drag and drop the material asset to the recently created object in the Scene view or in the Hierarchy tab to connect the material to its mesh renderer component.

Change the scale of the sphere down to (**0.2, 0.2, 0.2**) for a better look inside the template scene (Figure 6-25).

Figure 6-25. *Unlit sphere inside the Scene view*

Now, to create the dark effect with a shiny border we are going to use the fresnel effect and apply some shiny color to it, as follows:

- Open the shader graph asset BlackHoleCenter by double-clicking it.

- Inside of the Shader Graph Editor, create a **Fresnel Effect node** with a default Power(1) input value of 8.

- Then, create a **Color Input node** in HDR mode with default values **(R = 191, G = 37, B= 0, A= 255) and intensity value of 3**.

- Create a **Multiply node** and feed it with the **Fresnel Effect node** output and the **Color Input node** we just created.

- Finally, connect the output of the **Multiply node** to the **Base Color input** of the **Fragment block** (Figure 6-26).

The fresnel effect node is going to create a white rim around the black sphere, simulating the same rim that we can see in the referenced Figure 6-24.

The Multiply node with a Color Input node will assign that color to the gradient defined by the Fresnel Effect node. You can set any color you want for this.

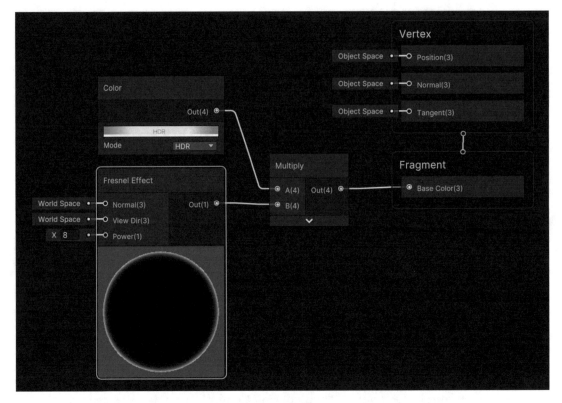

Figure 6-26. *Black hole center shader graph*

Save the asset and go back to the **Scene view** to see the result (Figure 6-27).

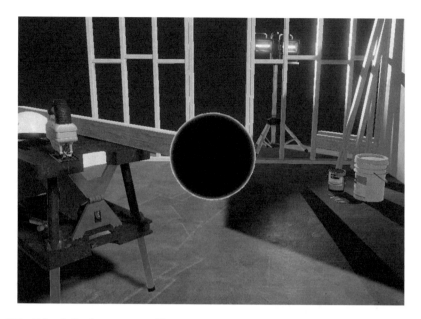

Figure 6-27. *Black hole center effect*

Now that the black hole is done, let's create a distortion effect around it, using the **Scene Color** modification technique we used in the previous section.

Using Particle Systems for a Billboard Effect

For this part of the effect we can also create a plane object as a child of the black hole center and apply the distortion shader to it, as we did with the ice wall effect. The problem is that when you turn the camera around the black hole you will notice the 2D plane edges, losing the spherical feeling that this effect should have (Figure 6-28).

Figure 6-28. *Distortion effect applied in a plane object*

To simulate the three-dimensional distortion produced by a spherical black hole, we are going to use a technique called billboarding.

Billboarding is a visual technique often used in video games that consists of the constant rotation of an object toward the camera to make a three-dimensional illusion. It is commonly used to represent objects that would otherwise be computationally expensive to be rendered in full 3D, such as trees, vegetation, or distant objects.

In Unity, there is a component called **particle system** that applies this rendering technique by default. We will take advantage of this component to create our distortion effect, as follows:

- Create a particle system as a child of the black hole center object by right-clicking on the black hole center object and selecting **Effects ➤ Particle System.**

You will see that some default particles will start traveling from the black hole toward the camera when this object is selected in the hierarchy (Figure 6-29).

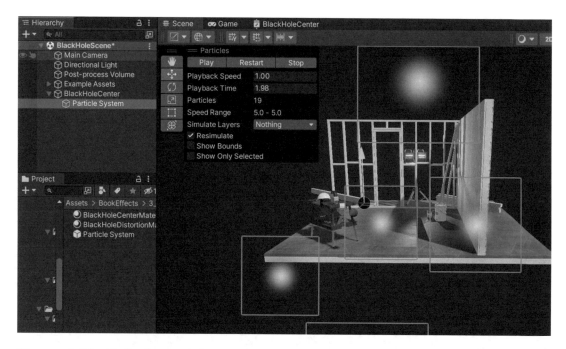

Figure 6-29. *Default particle system*

If you select the **particle system object**, you can see the particle system component in the **Inspector tab**, where you can change every setting regarding the emitted particles (movement speed, lifetime, size, rotation, traveling direction, etc.). We are going to change some parameters inside the particle system component to simulate a **static quad** that is always looking at the camera. Do the following:

- Change the **Duration** to **1**. This value in seconds indicates the duration of the particle system.

- Set **Prewarm** to **true**. This will pre-calculate the particles to start the scene with them activated; if not you will see a flick of the quad when the game starts.

- Set **Start Lifetime** to **1**. So the particles are going to live the same length of time as the whole duration. This will simulate that they are not being recycled, and it will look like there is just one static quad.

- Set **Start Speed** to **0**. This will keep the particles from moving, setting them static inside the emission shape (Figure 6-30).

Figure 6-30. *Main module changes in particle system component*

- Now, open the **Emission** module by left-clicking on it, making sure the checkbox at the left is marked.

- Change its **Rate over Time value** from **10** to **1** (Figure 6-31). This will ensure that 1 particle is emitted per second. So, when one particle dies, another will instantly appear in the same position.

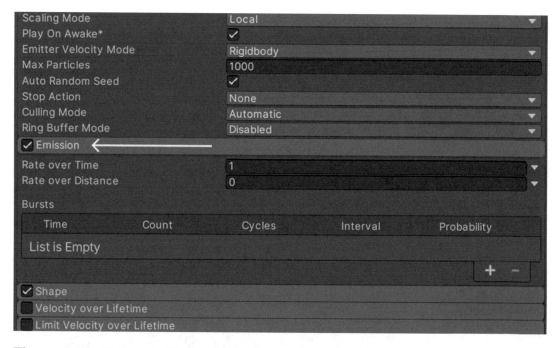

Figure 6-31. *Rate over Time changed from 10 to 1*

- You will see that the particles are spawning one by one along a cone shape. To change that into a single spot, open the **Shape module** just below the **Emission module**.

- Change the **Shape** dropdown value to **Edge.**

- Finally, change the **Radius** value to **0**. It will be rounded to 0.0001, but it is virtually identical (Figure 6-32). This will ensure that all particles are appearing in the same exact position every time.

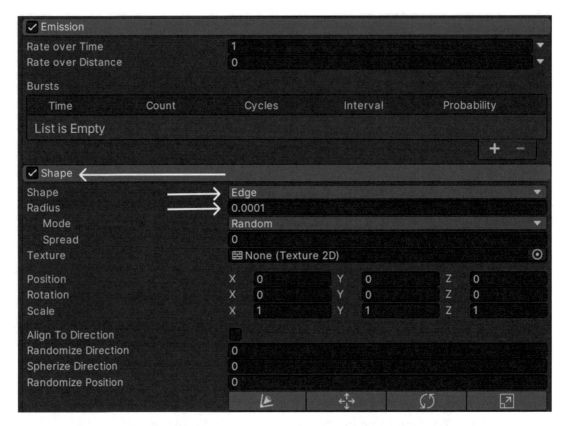

Figure 6-32. *Emission shape set to Edge with Radius value 0.0001*

Now, you will see in the Scene view something like in Figure 6-33, where we created a plane that is always looking at the camera.

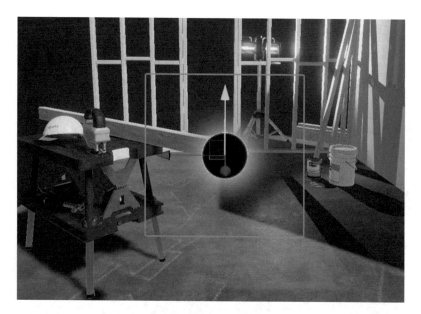

Figure 6-33. *Billboard panel particle system*

Note   Particles in the particle system are not always displayed in the editor. To trigger the particles, keep the particle system object in the Hierarchy tab selected or click on the Play button, starting the game to see them animated, keeping the setting ***Play On Awake*** enabled inside the particle system component.

The particle system has a default particle material attached under the **Renderer** module, at the very bottom of the particle system component (Figure 6-34).

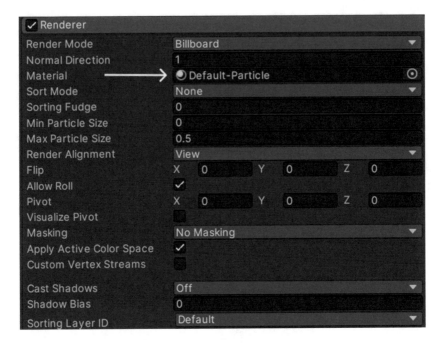

Figure 6-34. *Default particle material inside the Renderer module*

We will swap it with a brand-new material, which is going to apply the distortion effect, as follows:

- Create a unlit shader graph by right-clicking in the Project tab and then selecting **Create ➤ Shader Graph ➤ URP ➤ Unlit Shader Graph.** I called it **BlackHoleDistortion.** We don't need the light to interact with the distortion panel itself, since it is a pure distortion effect; no shadows or reflections are going to be represented.

- Create a material out of this shader graph asset by right-clicking on it in the Project tab and selecting **Create ➤ Material.**

- Drag and drop the material asset from the Project tab to the particle system object inside the hierarchy or inside the Scene view to attach the material to the **Renderer module** of the particle system component.

You will end up with this initial setup in the Scene view (Figure 6-35). Now, everything is ready to start creating the spiral texture that is going to distort the scene color.

Figure 6-35. *Custom unlit material loaded in the particle system*

Creating a Spiral Texture Using the Twirl Node

The Twirl node (Figure 6-36) is a UV modification node type that is going to output the input UVs, or texture coordinates, deformed, following a spiral pattern that is determined by the other inputs in the node. These are as follows:

- **Center**: Center of the spiral. By default it is at 0,0.

- **Strength**: A float number that will determine how many turns the spiral performs. By default it is 10.

- **Offset**: Offsets the influence of the x and y coordinates. By default its value is 0,0.

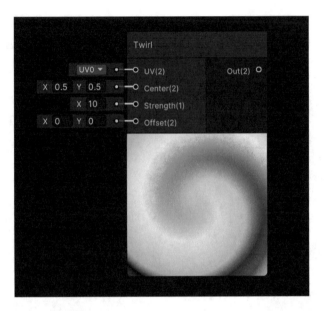

Figure 6-36. *Default Twirl node*

Let's start to make a spiral texture in our new shader graph. Double-click the last shader graph, BlackHoleDistortion, we created, which is the one that is going to create the distortion effect. Inside of the Shader Graph Editor, do the following:

- Create a **Twirl node** and then create a new **Float Input node connected to the Strength(1) input of the Twirl node**.

- Set the **default value of the Float Input node** as **25** and expose it as a property named **TwirlScale** (Figure 6-37).

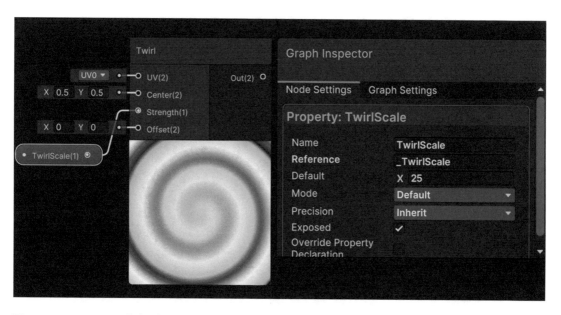

Figure 6-37. *Modified strength of the Twirl node*

- Now, to create a noisy twirl texture suitable for the black hole, create a **Simple Noise node** and connect the **output of the Twirl node** to the **input UV(2)** of the **Simple Noise node**.

- Create a **Float Input node** with a **default value of 10** and connect it to the input Scale(1) of the Simple Noise node. I also **expose** this Float node as a property called **NoiseScale**.

- Then, connect the output of the **Simple Noise node** to the **Base Color input** of the **Fragment block** so we can check the texture we are going to use to distort the scene behind the particle we created.

If you save the asset and go back to the scene you will find the successfully made texture on the particle system object (Figure 6-38).

Figure 6-38. *Spiral texture shown in the particle surface*

We are going to use the displayed texture in the next section to distort the scene color, as we did in the previous effect with the ice texture.

Modifying the Scene Color Using the Spiral Texture

First, make sure that the Boolean setting **Opaque Texture** in your pipeline settings asset is enabled (Figure 6-39). If not, the effect will not perform correctly, and you won't see any distortion applied. As we did in the "Initial Setup" section of the previous effect in this chapter, we need to enable the **Opaque Texture boolean**.

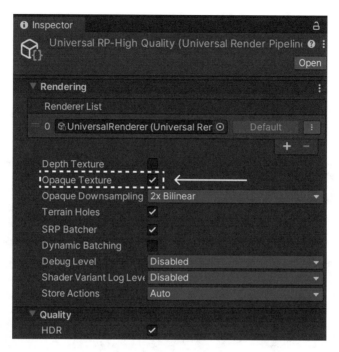

Figure 6-39. *Opaque Texture enabled in pipeline settings asset*

- Back in the Shader Graph Editor of the BlackHoleDistortion shader graph, set the Surface Type to Transparent in the Graph Settings under the Graph Inspector tab, as we did in the previous shader effect.

- Create a **Screen Position node** and an **Add node**.

- Connect the output of the previously created **Simple Noise node** to the **B(1) input** of the **Add node** and connect the **Screen Position node output** to the **A(1) input** of the **Add node**.

When you add the output of the ScreenPosition node to a black-and-white texture using an Add node in Shader Graph, you are essentially combining the positional information of each pixel on the screen with the grayscale values of the texture. This is translated into a deformation of the Screen Position components following the texture details; in this case, following a noisy spiral pattern. The preview of the Add node in the Figure 6-40 explains this interaction visually.

You can experiment using the Subtract, Multiply, or Divide nodes to obtain different interactions and dependencies between the Screen Position coordinates and textures.

- Then, create a **Scene Color node** and connect the output of the **Add node** to the input of the **Scene Color node**, whose output will be connected to the Base Color input of the Fragment block (Figure 6-40).

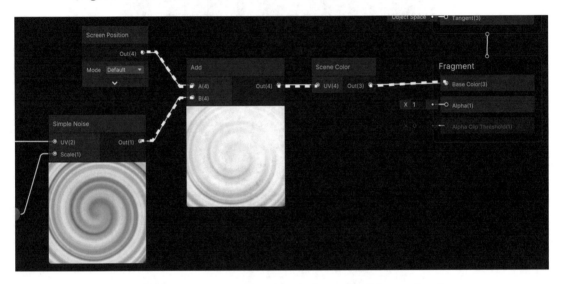

Figure 6-40. *Modifying the scene color using the Spiral Texture*

After saving the asset, go back to the Scene view and check how the texture is now distorting what is behind the particle quad, following a spiral distortion effect (Figure 6-41).

Figure 6-41. *Spiral texture deforming the view behind the particle quad*

If you take a close look at the edge of the quad of the particle (Figure 6-42), you will notice that there is a hard cut between the view altered by the distortion and the view that is not altered, ending up in an artificial and not good-looking effect.

Figure 6-42. *Hard edge of the distortion effect*

To avoid this hard transition, we will create a circular gradient mask to make a subtle change between distorted and non-distorted views.

Masking the Spiral Texture

There are many ways to create a circular gradient texture. The one we are going to cover here uses the Distance node, as follows:

- Inside the Shader Graph Editor of the BlackHoleDistortion shader, create a **UV node** to access the texture coordinates.

- Create a **Vector2 input node** with default value of **(0.5, 0.5)**.

- Then, create a **Distance node** and connect the output of the UV node to the input A(2) of the Distance node and connect the Vector2 input node to the input B(2) of the Distance node (Figure 6-43).

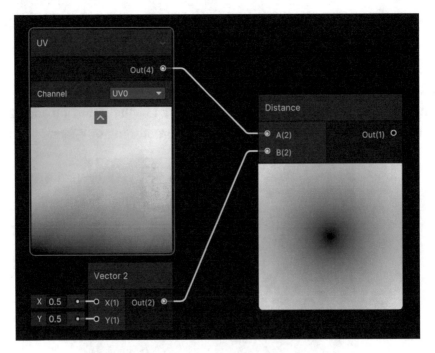

Figure 6-43. *Obtaining a dark gradient spot using Distance node*

The Distance node will display values between 0 and 1 depending on how far the corresponding UV coordinate value is from the center of the texture (0.5, 0.5), displaying a dark-to-white gradient from closest points from the center to farthest points from the center.

- Now, connect the output of the **Distance node** to a new **One Minus node**.

The One Minus node is useful when we want to invert the texture values. In this case, as we want to hide the outer fragments of the plane, we need to invert the texture of the Distance node to have a white circle fading to black in the corners.

- Then, connect the output of the **One Minus node** to a **new SmoothStep node** with **Edge(1)** default value of **0.5** and **Edge(2)** default value of **1.2** (Figure 6-44).

The SmoothStep node will adjust the radius of the mask and the intensity of it, meaning that we will control how big the distortion will be along the quad and how strong. You can adjust these values as you please, but **make sure** that the hard limits of the texture are completely black so the visible edges of the particle quad are not noticed anymore.

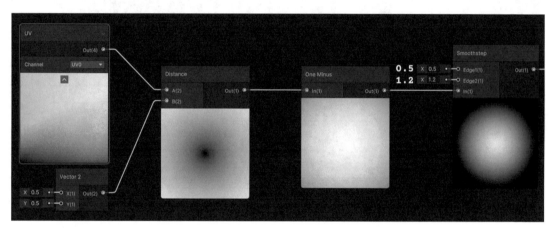

Figure 6-44. *Gradient circular mask using the Distance node*

- Finally, to **apply the mask in our spiral texture**, create a **Multiply node** whose input B(1) is fed with the output of the SmoothStep node we created and the input A(1) is connected with the output of the **Simple Noise node** we created before.

The Multiply node multiplies the corresponding pixel values of the mask texture (B input) and the spiral texture (A input). The result is that the areas where the mask texture is white (value of 1) will retain the original base texture, while the areas where the mask texture is black (value of 0) will become transparent or masked out. Also, as the visible parts of the mask are below 1, adjusting how much of the base spiral texture is passing through the mask will smooth the effect down.

- Now, the output of the **Multiply node** we have just created is the one that will connect with the input of the **Add node** that was fed with the **Screen Position node output**. (Figure 6-45).

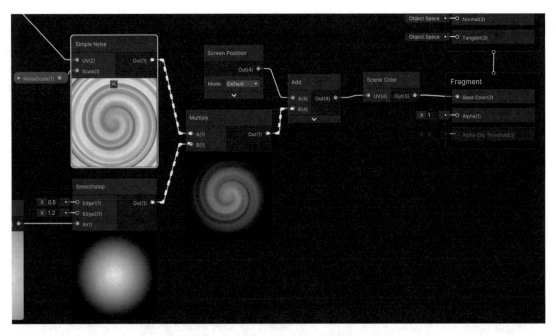

Figure 6-45. *Applied the circular mask to the Spiral texture*

The mask is successfully applied to the Spiral texture. Check the result in the Scene view after saving the shader graph asset (Figure 6-46).

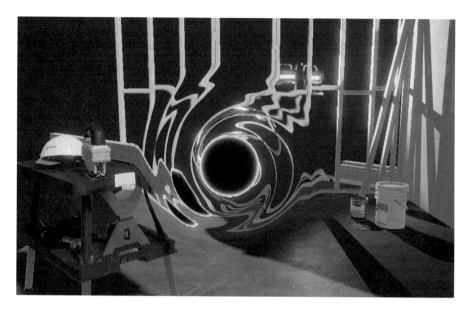

Figure 6-46. *Masked distortion effect around the black hole*

With these changes, we do not see hard-edge distortion transitions, and, what is more, the distortion is stronger in the closer points to the black hole's center, which is very realistic, thanks to the Distance calculation and the One Minus node. But there is one thing left: In real life, black holes create dynamic orbits so the spiral effect should be constantly rotating, creating a nice effect.

Adding Dynamic Rotation to the Spiral Texture

To add some constant rotation to the spiral texture, let's make some nodes at the left of the **Twirl node**, to modify its UVs in time, as follows.

- Create a **Time node** and a new **Multiply node**.

- Connect the **Time(1) output** of the **Time node to** the **input** A(1) of the newest Multiply node.

- Create a **Float Input node** with default value of **1.75** and connect it to the **Multiply node input B(1)**. Expose that input as a **property** and call it **RotationSpeed**.

- Create a **Rotate node** and connect the output of the recently created **Multiply node** to the input Rotation(1) of the Rotate node (Figure 6-47).

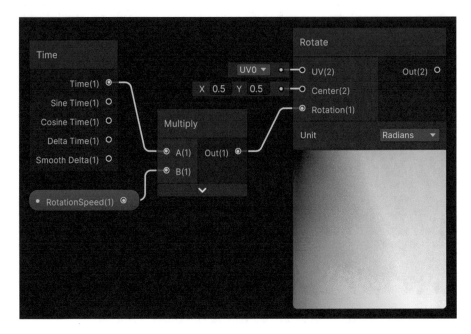

Figure 6-47. *Create a constant rotation with the Rotate node*

The **Rotate node** will rotate the UV coordinates a desired amount (defined by the **Rotation input**) around the axis determined by the center input, which we will keep as **(0.5, 0.5)**, representing the center of the texture.

- Finally, connect the output of the **Rotate node** to the input UV(2) of the **Twirl node** (Figure 6-48).

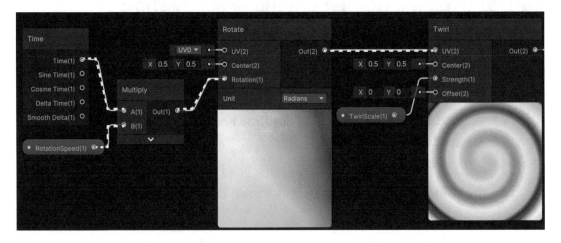

Figure 6-48. *Rotating the Twirl UVs*

As we did previously, we access the Time node to generate a continuously incrementing variable that will feed the Rotation input of the Rotate node, generating a constant rotation in the Twirl node. This will be translated into a constantly (and hypnotical) spinning spiral texture.

If you save the shader graph asset and click Play, you will see in the Scene view that the distortion effect is doing a really nice and subtle rotation, ending up wth the final black hole distortion effect (Figure 6-49).

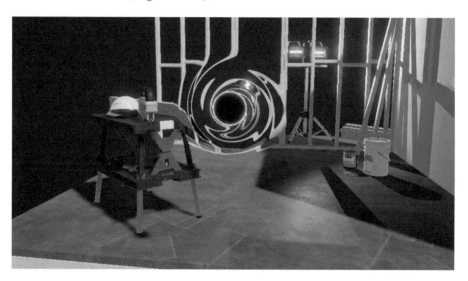

Figure 6-49. *Final black hole effect*

Play with the exposed property values to get different types of black hole distortion effects.

Summary

In this chapter, we dove deep into the power of the **Scene Color node**, accessing the color buffer of the frames renderer in the screen to modify it, creating amazing distortion effects that are going to give your games an extra kick of realism and quality. But be aware that this post-processing resource has a cost in the performance of the device that is running the game.

We have been creating amazing effects throughout this book, learning about the fragments and vertex shader principles using the Shader Graph Editor. We have learned all the tools available, including advanced post-processing techniques like bloom or opaque texture access. **In the next chapter,** we are going to use new and already learned knowledge to create outstanding, high-quality, and professional-level shaders that you can use in your AAA or mobile platform games.

CHAPTER 7

Advanced Shaders

Throughout this book, we have delved into the fascinating world of shader programming, exploring various techniques to enhance the visual quality and realism of Unity projects. In this chapter, we will push the boundaries of our knowledge further by focusing on two exciting shader effects: a cartoon water shader and a realistic bubbles shader. The following is a brief summary of their features:

- **Cartoon Water**: We begin this chapter by diving into the enchanting realm of cartoon water. You will learn how to create a visually captivating water surface that perfectly captures the essence of animated worlds by leveraging the principles of stylized rendering and using new advanced techniques like **scene depth.** I will also teach you how to reuse node calculations of your shader in different graphs using **SubGraphs**, a specific shader graph technique to reuse shader parts.

- **Bubble Particles**: Next, we will explore realistic bubble particles. Bubbles have an inherent allure and can add a touch of magic to any scene. You will discover how to simulate their behavior realistically by leveraging various properties, such as metallic reflection, rim color to simulate surface color, and iridescence noisy dynamic texture. By combining shader graph functionalities such as noise functions, color gradients, texture mapping, and the default Unity default particle system, you will create shaders that breathe life into bubbles, making them appear dynamic, transparent, and mesmerizing.

© Álvaro Alda 2023
Á. Alda, *Beginner's Guide to Unity Shader Graph*, https://doi.org/10.1007/978-1-4842-9672-1_7

Cartoon Water Shader

Water is a commonly used element in games and animations, and achieving a stylized, cartoon-like appearance can add visual interest and appeal to your projects (Figure 7-1).

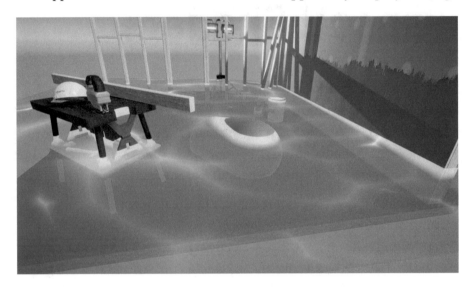

Figure 7-1. *Cartoon water shader*

We will use the **Voronoi Noise node** to create stylized water caustics and the **Scene Depth node** to access depth-buffer information to detect when another object in the scene is next to the surface of the water, causing a foamy water, beach shore effect. We will do the following:

- Perform initial setup.

- Access the depth buffer to create foam with the Scene Depth node.

- Create water caustics.

- Use SubGraph to reuse groups of nodes.

- Add radial deformation using radial shear.

- Add movement to the Voronoi cells.

- Add extra caustic layers.

- Add color to the water caustics texture.

- Deform the vertices of the water surface.

Initial Setup

As usual in this book, start a new scene using the template project **3D Sample Scene (URP)** shown in Chapter 3. Then, create a 3D plane and accommodate it in the scene as you like. This plane is going to be our future water, and is made as follows:

- To create a plane object, right-click in any empty space inside the Hierarchy tab and select **3D Object ➤ Plane.** A 3D plane object will be instantiated in the scene. I called it **WaterObject**.

- I changed its **position** in the Transform component to **(1.82, 0.4, 0)** and its **scale** to **(0.5, 0.5, 0.5)**, as you can see in Figure 7-2.

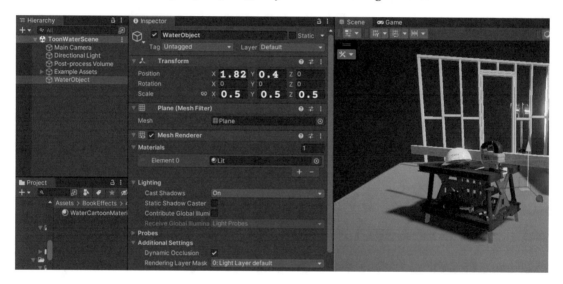

Figure 7-2. *Water plane object in the scene*

With the plane object created in the scene, it is time to create the shader graph that is going to perform the effect, as follows:

- Right-click anywhere inside the Project tab and select **Create ➤ Shader Graph ➤ URP ➤ Unlit Shader Graph**, and the shader graph asset will appear. I called it **WaterCartoon**.

I am using an unlit shader because for stylized or cartoon finishes there is no need to create light interaction. We are going to simulate our light reflections using caustic procedural textures, as follows:

- Create a material out of the shader graph asset **water cartoon** by right-clicking on top of the asset and selecting **Create ➤ Material.** Then, a material asset with the water cartoon referenced will be created in the Project tab.

- Drag and drop the material asset to the **WaterObject** in the **Hierarchy** tab or in the **scene** to reference the material to its **MeshRenderer** component.

I also created a capsule object by right-clicking inside the Hierarchy tab and selecting **3D Object ➤ Capsule.** This capsule will be an addition to demonstrate the next subsection issue clearly. I also set its transform component with the following values:

- **Position:** (1.5, 0.1, 0.5)

- **Rotation:** (80, −35, 0)

- **Scale:** (0.65, 0.65, 0.65)

Accessing the Depth Buffer to Create Foam with the Scene Depth Node

If you take a closer look at Figure 7-1, you can clearly see that the water is, in fact, interacting with other objects in the scene, creating a white foamy gradient in the intersection with those elements (Figure 7-3).

Figure 7-3. *Water shore gradient*

But how can a shader access the position of the rest of the objects in the scene? How can I have the information of the objects below the plane? Which node gives me information about the depth in the scene?

Scene Depth Node

To detect this interaction with parts of the scene, we are going to use the Scene Depth node (Figure 7-4). This special node provides access to the depth information of the scene at a particular pixel. It allows you to retrieve the distance between the camera and the current pixel being shaded. The depth buffer is an intermediate buffer that stores the depth or distance information of objects in the scene from the camera's viewpoint. The depth buffer, also known as the Z-buffer, is used for depth-based calculations and effects during rendering.

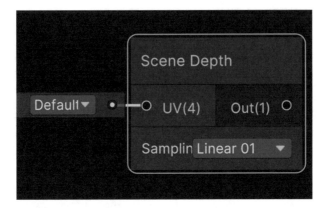

Figure 7-4. *Scene Depth node*

This node has the following main modes that you can choose from in the dropdown inside the Scene Depth node:

- **Linear 0-1**: In this mode, the Scene Depth node provides the depth value normalized between 0 and 1, where 0 represents the nearest object to the camera and 1 represents the farthest object.

- **Raw**: Raw mode outputs the raw depth value without any modification or transformation. It represents the depth as an absolute distance in the camera's coordinate system.

- **Eye**: Eye mode provides the depth value relative to the camera's eye space. The resulting depth value takes into account the camera's position, orientation, and field of view. It is useful when you need to perform calculations based on the eye-space depth.

In this case, we are going to use Eye mode because it is the one that performs a realistic finish in terms of representing the water depth relative to the camera position and orientation.

Be aware that accessing the depth buffer of the camera is pretty expensive in terms of performance, and it can cause GPU drops because of the rendering workload, so try not to overuse this feature, especially in mobile games. Due to that, in URP this tool is disabled by default. To enable it, go to the URP settings asset where we activated the Opaque Textures for the effects in Chapter 6's "Initial Setup" section, under **Edit ➤ Project Settings ➤ Graphics ➤ Scriptable Render Pipeline Settings.** Click in the referenced asset to highlight it under the Project tab. Select it in the Project tab, and in the Inspector tab set the option **Depth Texture** as true (Figure 7-5).

Figure 7-5. *Enabling the depth texture access in the URP settings asset*

In Figure 7-6 you can see what the camera is outputting as depth buffer or Z-buffer. It is mapping the object's pixel information from 0 (closer) to 1 (farther). This image is a replica of what the camera is calculating when you are accessing the depth buffer.

Figure 7-6. *Scene depth*

Implementing the Depth Information in the Shader

Open the WaterCartoon shader by double-clicking on top of the asset in the Project tab. Then, inside the Shader Graph Editor, do the following:

- First and most important, as we want to see the objects below the water and we need to access the information of the objects through the WaterObject, the material has to be **transparent**. Open the **Graph Inspector** and in the **Graph Settings** tab set the **Surface Type** to **Transparent**.

- Create a **Screen Position node** and set its mode as **Raw**.

- Drag out from the Screen Position node to create a Split node.

- Then, create a **Subtract node** and feed **its A(1) input** with the **output** of the **Scene Depth node** and its **B(2) input** with the **output** A(1) of the **Split node** (Figure 7-7).

- Finally, create a **Saturate node** and connect its input with the **Subtract node output** and its output with the **Base Color input** of the **Fragment block**.

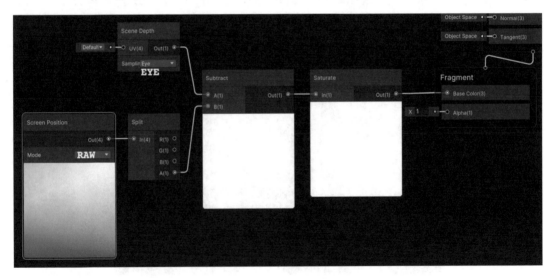

Figure 7-7. *Scene Depth node*

If you save the shader graph asset and go back to the Scene view you will find that a black gradient has been represented around the part of the objects that are intersecting with the plane, fading out the deeper parts (Figure 7-8).

Figure 7-8. *Black gradient, representing the objects under the plane object*

With these calculations, we are creating a relationship between the depth information of the **Scene Depth node** and the **clip space position of the screen coordinates** held in the last component of that vector that we accessed using the Split node A(1) output.

The scene depth texture has the information of the pixels that are closer to the camera. Using the clip space of the **Screen Position node**, we are mapping that texture in the plane, using and setting that object as the reference for that depth texture to be created. This relationship is created with the Subtract node. The pixels of objects that are closer to the plane (less deep) are going to be represented in black, and the pixels of the objects far enough from the plane (deeper from the plane) are going to be represented in white.

These types of calculations use the Subtract node and normally output values lower than 0 and/or greater than 1, creating visual glitches when accessing color information to be displayed. To avoid that, we created the Saturate node so the output will always be clamped between 0 and 1.

Controlling the Depth Gradient with Divide Node

We now want to control the depth gradient intensity; in other words, the **depth** threshold value, which will control how much of the objects below the plane are going to be represented. To do that, perform the following steps:

- Create a new **Divide node** between the already created **Subtract** and **Saturate nodes**.

- Create a new **Float Input node** with a **default value** of **0.3** and expose it as a property under the name **Depth.**

- Connect the **output of the Subtract node** to the **input A(1) of the Divide node** and connect the **Float Input node Depth** to the **input B(1)** of the **Divide node**.

  The value of the property **Depth** will control how deep we are detecting the objects below the panel object.

- Finally, connect the output of the **Divide node** to the input of the **Saturate node**, whose output is still connected to the Base Color input of the Fragment block (Figure 7-9).

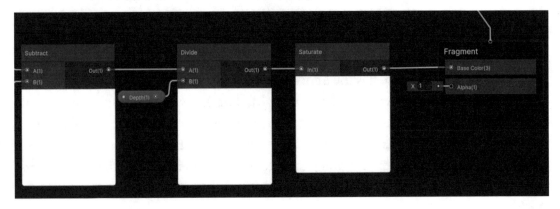

Figure 7-9. *Divide node to control Depth property*

The Divide node will increase the value of the gradient, detecting deeper below the WaterObject panel, if the **Depth** property value is greater than 1; however, if the **Depth** value is less than 1, only the pixels nearest to the plane will be detected. Figure 7-10 shows these two possibilities. Feel free to adjust the height in your water plane object to achieve different effects, as well as to change the Depth value.

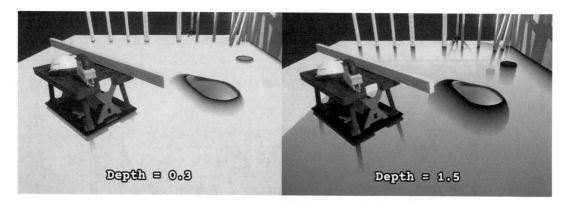

Figure 7-10. Different Depth property values

The final part consists in inverting the black and white values because we want that gradient to be a white foam around the edges of the objects under the water, like in Figure 7-1.

As before, use the One Minus node to invert the output of the Saturate node, as follows:

- Create a **One Minus node** and connect its input to the output of the previously created **Saturate node**.

- Connect the output of the **One Minus node** to the **Base Color input** of the **Fragment block (Figure 7-11)**.

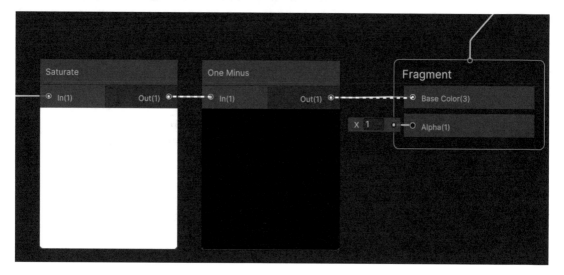

Figure 7-11. Inverting the gradient using the One Minus node

The One Minus node will invert the values output by the Saturate node, so the black gradient will be transformed into a white gradient. This seems more like the foamy shore we saw in Figure 7-1.

Save the shader graph WaterCartoon asset and go back to the Scene view to see the result (Figure 7-12).

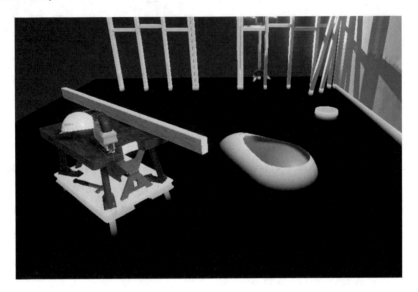

Figure 7-12. *Shore foamy gradient*

In the next section, we are going to study water caustics and how to replicate that phenomena using the Voronoi Noise node. That texture is going to be finally added to the foam gradient we have created to achieve a nice cartoon water effect.

Create Water Caustics

Water caustics refers to the patterns of light and shadow that are created by the refraction and reflection of light as it interacts with the surface of water. When light passes through or reflects off the surface of water, it undergoes a change in direction due to the varying refractive index of water. This bending of light rays creates intricate and dynamic patterns of light and shadow on surrounding surfaces, as shown in Figure 7-13.

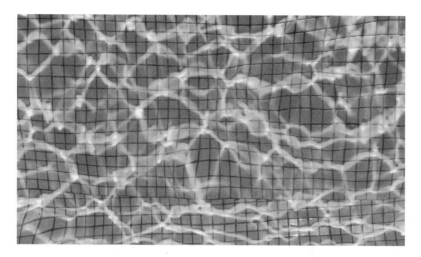

Figure 7-13. *Water caustics in real life*

These patterns arise due to the complex interplay between the geometry of the water surface, the angle of incidence of light, and the refractive properties of water. A mathematically perfect caustics effect requires a very complex setup, whose impact on performance makes it not worth implementing in a video game, especially if it is intended for mobile platforms. We will make a simpler yet beautiful workaround using the Voronoi Noise node.

Using the Voronoi Noise Node

We talked about the Voronoi Noise node in Chapter 3 in the "Procedural Noise Nodes" section. Voronoi or Worley noise is a type of procedural noise that generates patterns based on the division of space into cells or regions. Each cell represents a unique point called a seed or a feature point, and the noise value at any given position is determined by the distance to the nearest seed.

This pattern is frequently used in graphic computation to obtain natural textures like cells, muscle tissue, insects, and, of course, water.

Let's start using this node in our shader graph, as follows:

- Open the shader graph **WaterCartoon** and create a **Voronoi noise node**.

- Create a **Float Input node** with a **default value of 8.5** and expose it as a property with the name **RipplesDensity.**

- Connect the output of the **RipplesDensity property** to the input **CellDensity(1)** of the **Voronoi Noise node**.

Take into account that all the calculations regarding the caustics are going to be added to the already made calculations for the foamy shore we already implemented in the same shader.

- Create a new **Add node** and connect the output **Out(1) of the Voronoi Node** to its input **A(1)**.

- Connect the output of the **One Minus node**—which was already connected to the **Base Color input of the Fragment block**—to the **B(1) input of the Add node** we just created (Figure 7-14).

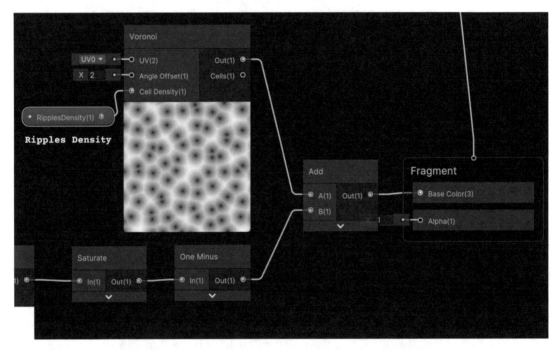

Figure 7-14. *Using the Voronoi node to create caustic ripples*

If you save the asset and come back to the Scene view you will see that we are getting some ripples, but the white gradient is too wide (Figure 7-15). We need to define thinner borders, so let's use the Power node to tighten the white gradient a bit, as follows:

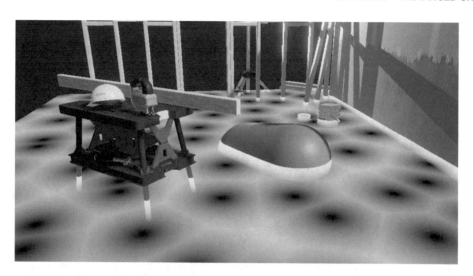

Figure 7-15. *Wide caustic ripples*

- Add a **Power node** after the **Voronoi node** and connect its **input A(1)** to the **Voronoi node Out(1) output**.

- Create a new **Input Float node** with a default value of **4.5**. I exposed that parameter as a **property named RippleStretch**. Connect it to the B(1) input of the Power node.

- Finally, connect the output of the **Power node** to the **input A(1)** of the previous **Add node (Figure 7-16).**

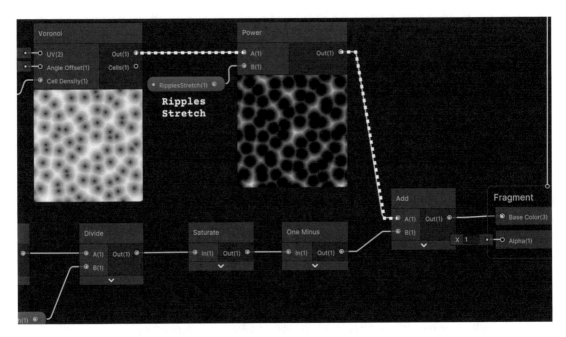

Figure 7-16. *Using the Power node to stretch the caustic ripples*

Remember how elevating values between 0 to 1 to values bigger than 1 (4.5 in this case) will reduce drastically the output values, except those closest to 1. Visually, it will stretch the gradient into the whitest parts.

Take a look at the result in Figure 7-17. We can see now that we are getting something similar to real caustic ripples along the plane. Furthermore, the foamy shore around the objects now makes more visual sense.

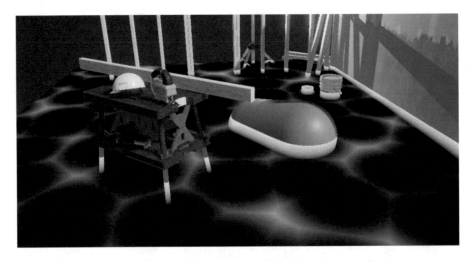

Figure 7-17. *Using the Power node to stretch the caustic ripples*

As we saw in our water reference image in Figure 7-13, we are looking to achieve the same style with a lot of blurry layers of caustic ripples instead of one. Since this is a cartoon approximation of that effect, we can keep it simple and make just one caustic layer, but I think we should add at least one more layer to create a nicer effect. We can copy and paste all the nodes that we made to create the caustic effect, or we can take advantage of a powerful shader graph tool used to reuse nodes, called SubShader.

Using SubGraph to Reuse Groups of Nodes

A SubGraph is a reusable collection of nodes and connections that can be encapsulated and treated as a single node within a larger shader graph. SubGraphs allow you to create modular and organized shader networks by grouping related functionality into separate units.

This is very flexible because you can reuse those groups of nodes in different graphs, and every change you make to them will be reflected in all shader graphs currently using it.

Let's create one SubGraph out of the caustics calculations we have performed already, as follows:

- Select the **RippleDensity** and **RippleStretch** properties instances as well as **both Voronoi and Power nodes** we created (you can drag and drop with the arrow to select a bunch of elements in the shader graph or by clicking on top of each one with the Ctrl key pushed).

- Right-click on one of the selected elements and select **Convert to ➤ SubGraph.**

- A file explorer (or finder in Mac) pop-up will appear asking you where you want to save your **SubGraph asset**. Save it anywhere inside the root Assets folder of the project. I called it **CausticSubGraph**.

After saving the SubGraph asset and going back to the **WaterCartoon** shader graph you will find that all the selected nodes and connections have collapsed into a single node called **CausticSubGraph** (Figure 7-18). This can now be instantiated in any other shader graph as you would do with another node.

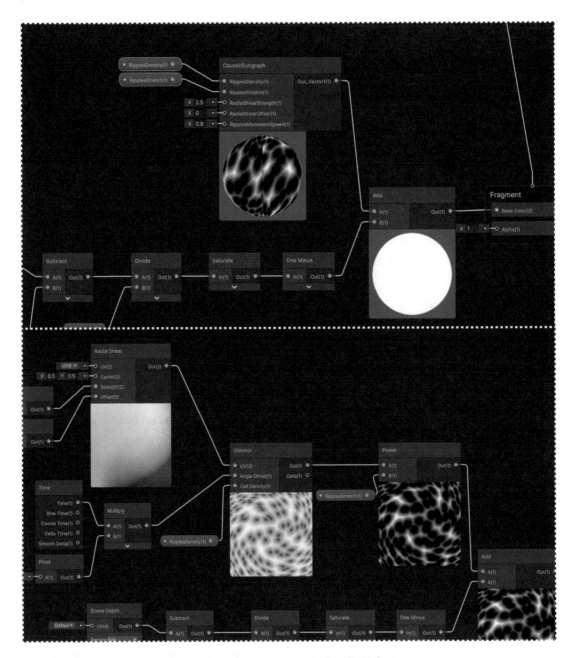

Figure 7-18. *SubGraph (top); bunch of nodes (bottom)*

If you double-click the **CausticSubGraph** node or double-click the SubGraph asset that was created in the Project tab (Figure 7-19), you will open a new Shader Graph Editor instance where all the connections, nodes, and properties are stored (Figure 7-20). Notice that now the properties are treated as node inputs from outside the SubGraph.

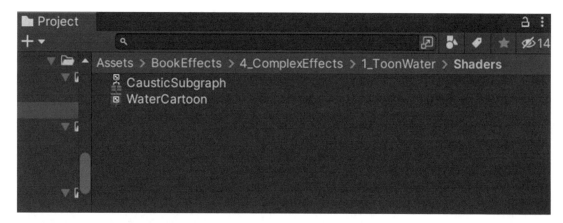

Figure 7-19. *SubGraph asset*

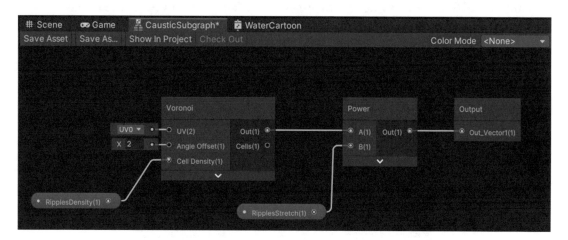

Figure 7-20. *Caustic SubGraph*

The properties found inside the SubGraph are no longer the same that we set up in the **WaterCartoon** shader graph, so make sure to set proper default values for those properties (8.5 for Ripples densities and 4.5 for RipplesStretch).

Now, we can access the SubGraph to modify the caustics effect in a reusable and flexible way.

Add Radial Deformation Using Radial Shear

Water is not a perfect arrangement of ripples; it is a fluid and is constantly moving. Flow maps are usually used to deform the UVs to create more vivid and natural flow effects. In this case, we are going to use the Radial Shear node.

Radial shear, also known as circular shear, is a geometric transformation that distorts an object or image by displacing its points along radial lines from a central point. This transformation produces an effect where the points in the object or image are shifted outward or inward, creating a shearing or stretching effect in a circular pattern. The Radial Shear node performs that type of deformation to the texture coordinates (UV). It can be used to perform flow deformation on any kind of image with a UV as input, like the Voronoi Noise node.

The **Radial Shear node** has several inputs that define the center of the radial deformations, the strength of the deformation around the center, and the offset of the deformation in the U and V components of the texture coordinates (Figure 7-21).

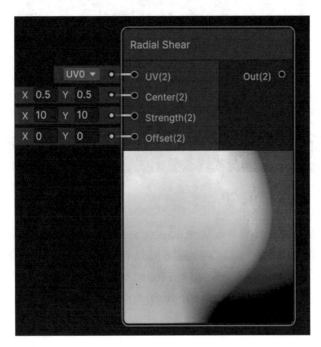

Figure 7-21. *Radial Shear node*

To use it, open the **CausticSubGraph** asset and do the following:

- Create a **Radial Shear node**.

- Create a **Float Input node** with a default value of **2.5** and expose it as a property called **RadialShearStrength**. Connect it to the **Strength**(2) input of the **Radial Shear node**.

- Create another **Input Float node** with a default value of **0** and expose it as a property called **RadialShearOffset**. Connect it to the **Offset(2)** input of the **Radial Shear node**.

- Finally, connect the output of the Radial Shear node to the input UV(2) of the Voronoi node (Figure 7-22).

You can see right away in the Voronoi Noise node preview that the pattern is now following a circular flow. The UV values have been deformed using the Radial Shear formula. Then those UVs are used to input the Voronoi function to perform a more natural flowy texture.

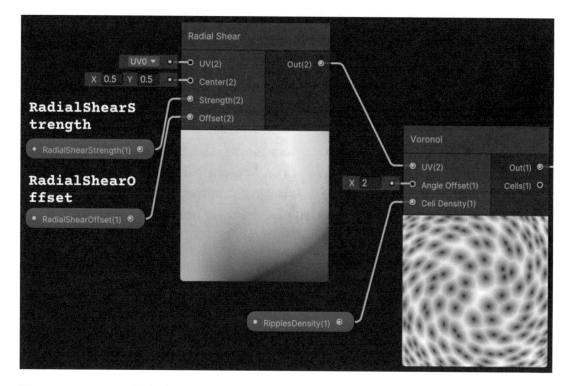

Figure 7-22. *Radial Shear UVs*

If you save the SubGraph asset and go back to the **WaterCartoon** shader graph, you will find out that the **CausticSubGraph** node now displays two more entries to tweak (**Figure 7-23**), which are the recently created properties inside the SubGraph (Radial Shear Strength and Radial Shear Offset), both initialized with the default values we set in those properties inside the SubGraph.

This is fantastic, as now we can have different layers of caustic textures by using more **CausticSubGraph** nodes with different entry values.

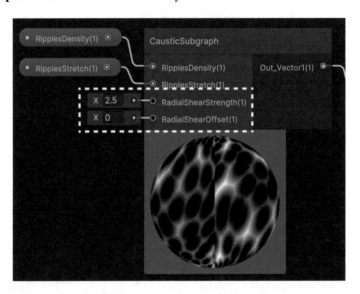

Figure 7-23. *New inputs in the CausticSubGraph node*

If you go back to the Scene view you will see that the shear deformation is applied right away, creating a radial flow distortion to the Voronoi texture, giving a feeling of moving water (Figure 7-24). Although it is not really moving at all, let's add some movement to the texture by constantly changing the **angle offset** of the **Voronoi Noise node**.

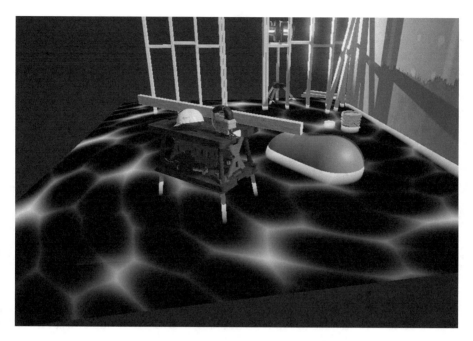

Figure 7-24. *Voronoi radial distortion*

Adding Movement to the Voronoi Cells

When the Voronoi Noise node is calculated, some random seeds (the center of the cells) are displayed in the texture, taking into account the UV coordinates as limits. Then, for each cell, the distances to the proximity neighbors are calculated, displaying a gradient between the cells and their neighbours.

The Voronoi Noise node has another input called **Angle Offset**, which will generate a rotational offset when calculating the distance between seeds. This will generate a change in the arrangement of the Voronoi cells in the texture. For instance, take a look at these two pure Voronoi Noise nodes with different Angle Offset values (Figure 7-25).

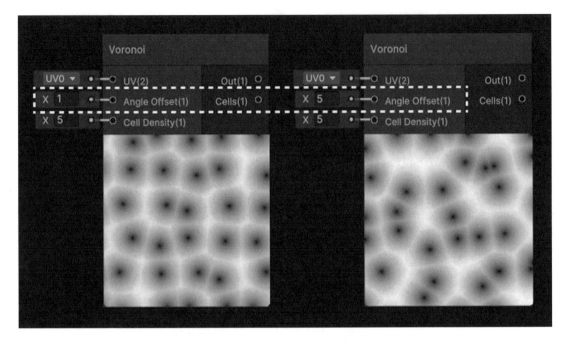

Figure 7-25. *Voronoi Angle Offset values comparison*

If you keep increasing the Angle Offset value you will notice a beautiful movement of the different cells along the texture. To keep increasing that value **in the Voronoi Noise node** of the **CausticSubGraph** shader we will use a Time node as usual.

Open the **CausticSubGraph** asset by double-clicking it and doing the following inside:

- Create a **Time node** and a **Multiply node**.

- Create a **Float Input node** with a default value of **0.8**. Expose it as a property with the name **RipplesMovementSpeed**. This property will represent the speed of movement of the ripples in the water texture.

- Drag from the output Time(1) of the Time node to create a Multiply node connected to its A(1) input.

- Feed the input B(1) of the Multiply node with the property we just created.

- Finally, connect the output of the **Multiply node** to the input of the **Voronoi Noise node AngleOffset(1) (Figure 7-26).**

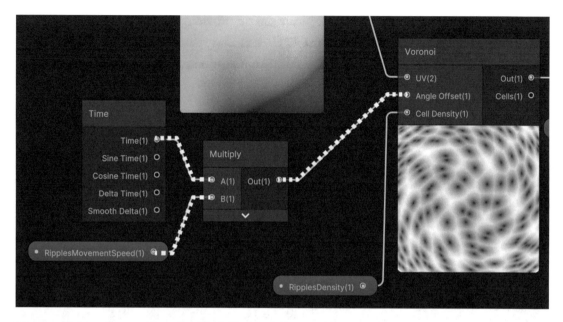

Figure 7-26. *Increasing Angle Offset in time*

As we did in so many effects so far, the **Time node** will output a constantly increasing value from the initialization of the shader. This constantly increasing value ratio is controlled with the property we created using the Multiply node. The Voronoi node will receive that constantly increasing value to the Angle Offset input, creating a moving Voronoi pattern.

Save the SubGraph asset and go back to the Scene view to check the result by clicking on Play or interacting with the editor.

The moving ripples will create a deep-water feeling, and the ripples will naturally move around, creating the visual effect that some light is going through the water causing those reflections. The radial shear creates an amazing flow sensation, making the ripples move through the center of the texture. Now it's time to add more ripple layers.

Adding Extra Caustic Layers

If we open the WaterCartoon shader graph we will find that the CausticSubGraph node has a new input called RipplesMovementSpeed, which is in fact the property we created inside the SubGraph. Now that we have a lot of inputs in our node it is time to create different layers of water caustics.

You can duplicate the Caustic node as we did on previous occasions by selecting it and then pressing **Ctrl+D (or Ctrl+C and Ctrl+V to copy and paste).**

As you can see in Figure 7-27, both of them share the same RipplesDensity and RipplesStretch properties.

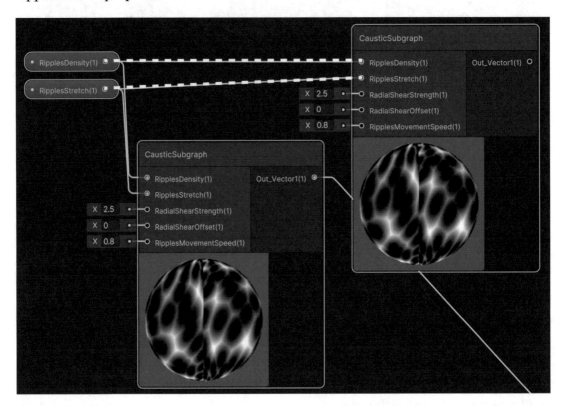

Figure 7-27. *Sharing properties*

As we want to be able to have a different effect with the new Caustic layer, remove the connecting nodes to the original properties, allowing you to customize the second layer a bit more, delete the property input connections in the duplicated node so we can add different values for those parameters by selecting them, and then click in **Delete** or **right-click** and select **Delete.**

Now, put these default values in the duplicated node to generate a totally different caustic pattern (Figure 7-28):

- RipplesDensity = 5

- RipplesStretch = 12

- RadialShearStrength = 5

- RadialShearOffset = 2

- RipplesMovementSpeed = 0.6

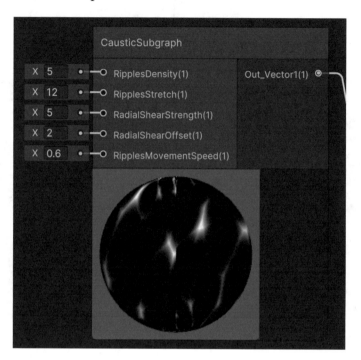

Figure 7-28. *Duplicated Caustic node values*

Now we can add both nodes' resulting patterns using the Add node, as follows:

- Create a new **Add node** and connect the original **Caustic node** and the duplicated **Caustic node** outputs to the **B(1) and A(1)** inputs of the **Add node** respectively.

- Then, connect the **output** of this **recently created Add node** to the **A(1) input** of the **first Add node** that was adding the depth calculations to the water texture (Figure 7-29).

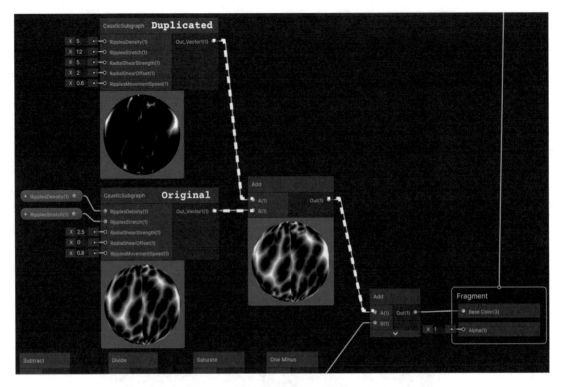

Figure 7-29. *Duplicated Caustic node values*

Adding both patterns, one on top of the other, will perform great, realistic, but still cartoonish water-moving caustic reflections in the scene (Figure 7-30). Adding another caustic layer will create a more complex flow movement across the surface of the plane, as there are different caustic layers moving asynchronously, creating a more natural and realistic effect.

Figure 7-30. *Complex caustic pattern*

Adding Color to the Water Caustics Texture

With the desired black-and-white texture achieved, we can add some blue- and green-toned colors to it to get a desired cartoonish water texture.

We will keep it simple and just color the original Caustic node output using the Lerp node inside the WaterCartoon shader graph, as follows:

- Create a **Lerp node** after the **first Caustic node**.

- Connect the **Lerp output to the B(1)** input of the **Add node** to which both Caustic textures were added.

- Connect the output of the first **Caustic node** to the input **T(1) of the Lerp node** (Figure 7-31).

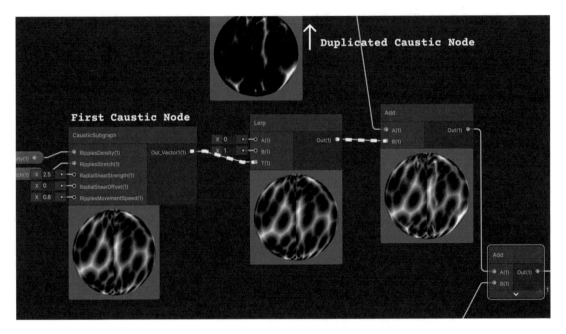

Figure 7-31. *Lerp node between the first Caustic node and the Add node*

Remember that the purpose of using a black-and-white texture as the T(1) input is to control the interpolation, or blending effect. Darker areas (values closer to 0) in the texture will result in colors closer to the A value, while lighter areas (values closer to 1) will produce colors closer to the B value. The grayscale texture acts as a mask, determining the distribution and intensity of the interpolation between A and B.

Taking the previous reasoning into account, we will input in A the base color of the water and in B the color of the ripples, as follows:

- Create a Color Input node and expose it as a property called **BaseWaterColor** with default values of (R = 73, G = 173, B = 192, A = 255).

- Create another Color Input node and expose it as a property called **RipplesColor** with default values of (R = 125, G = 238, B = 237, A = 255).

- Connect the **BaseWaterColor node** to the input **A(4)** of the **Lerp node** and connect the **RipplesColor** property node to the **input B(4)** of the **Lerp node** (Figure 7-32).

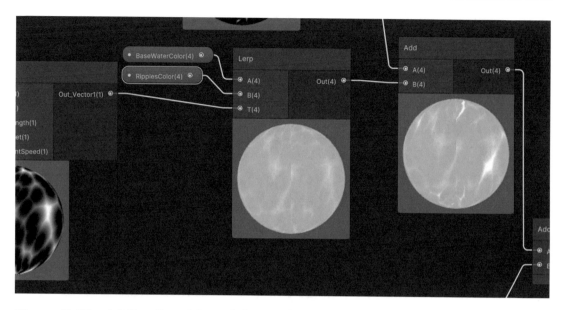

Figure 7-32. *Adding BaseWaterColor and RipplesColor*

As a final tweaking, reduce the default value of the **Alpha input** of the **Fragment block to 0.7**. This will give the water a nice translucent feeling (Figure 7-33).

Save the asset and go back to the Scene view and click Play. You can see how complex our shader effect got, having layers of cartoon caustic reflections moving in a plane object, causing a really nice and living water effect (Figure 7-34).

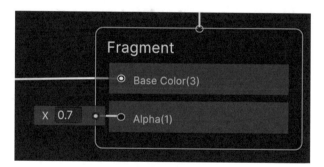

Figure 7-33. *Reducing the Alpha value to 0.7*

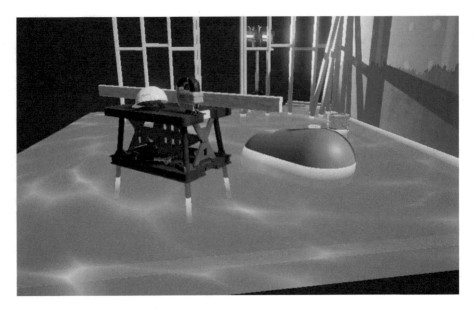

Figure 7-34. *Colored dynamic, multilayer, caustic texture*

Here we are having a really nice and "deep" water effect, but I think water in real life is a moving and living thing, affected by tidal forces, creating a constant displacement of the water up and down. Our water effect definitely needs that. In the next subsection, we are going to add vertex movement to our shader, deforming the vertices.

Deforming the Vertices of the Water Surface

Our shader graph is really complex at this moment, with tons of calculations and even with SubGraphs inside of it. We need to target every detail possible when making shaders. In this case, we will add a random deformation of the vertices along the *y*-axis of the plane to create a tidal fluctuation in the water.

Open the **WaterCartoon** shader graph asset and do the following in the Shader Graph Editor:

- Create a **Simple Noise node**. This node will create the random amount of deformation at each vertex on the plane to be displaced along the *y*-axis.

- Now, we need to make it more subtle so as to create a smooth noisy pattern. To achieve that, change the **Scale (1) input** of the **Noise node** from **500 to 4** (Figure 7-35).

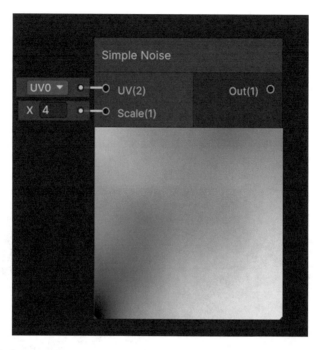

Figure 7-35. *Subtle Noise node*

To add some displacement, we need to add a few nodes before the Simple Noise node. As we have done previously, we will add a Time node, among others, to introduce this displacement.

To create a constantly increasing value at a defined rate we will do the following:

- Create a **Time node** and drag from its output **Time(1)** to create a new Multiply node connected to its input A(1).

- Create an **Input Float node** with **default value 0.2** and expose it as a property called **DisplacementSpeed.**

- Connect the **DisplacementSpeed property node** to the **B(1) input** of the recently created **Multiply node.**

- Create a **Tiling and Offset node** with its input **Offset(2)** fed with the output of the **Multiply node** and connect its output to the **Noise node UV(2)** input (Figure 7-36).

The Tiling and Offset node will perform a deformation to the UVs depending on the inputs Tiling(2) and Offset (2), as follows:

- **Tiling(2):** This vector2 will multiply the U and V coordinates of the UVs, generating a tiling or repetition of the pattern on the *x*- or *y*-axes.

- **Offset(2):** This vector2 will be added to the U and V components of the texture coordinates to create a displacement along either the *x*- or *y*-axis (or both).

We use the **Offset** input to constantly create a displacement in **Time** of the **Noise node** texture along both *x*- and *y*-axes.

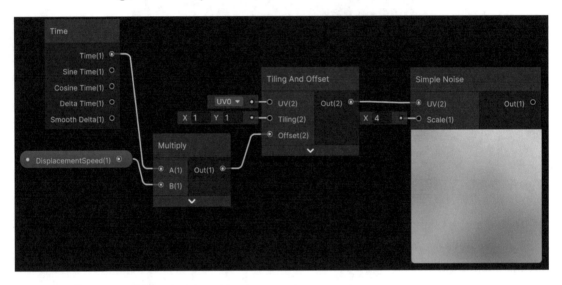

Figure 7-36. *Scrolling the Noise texture*

Now, let's control the intensity of the displacement, manipulating how much the vertices are going to move up on the *y*-axis. Do the following:

- Create a **Multiply node** and connect the output of the **Simple Noise node** to the input **B(1)** of this **Multiply node**.

- Create a **Float Input node** with a default value of **0.8** and expose it as a property called **DisplacementAmount.**

- Connect this property node to the **A(1) input** of the recently created **Multiply node** (Figure 7-37).

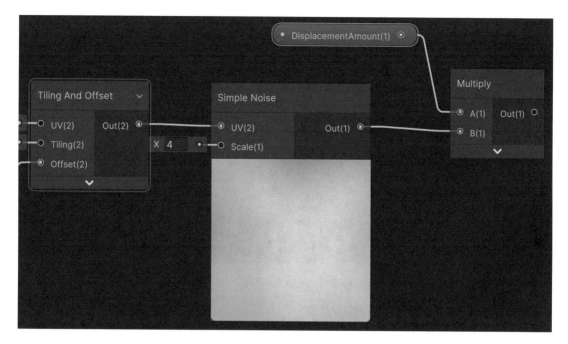

Figure 7-37. *Controlling the displacement intensity of the Noise node*

The output of this set of nodes will increase the amount of noise, using the DisplacementAmount to multiply the amount of noise generated. Increasing that value will increase the amount of vertical displacement of the vertices of the plane, and reducing it will reduce the vertex displacement of the water plane object.

Now it is time to move the vertices on the *y*-axis using the output of the last node we created.

Drag the output of the Multiply node we just created and create a Vector3 node connected by its Y(1) input. This node will output a Vector3 whose *y* component has been fed with the noise pattern we calculated earlier. So now we are telling the shader that we want the displacement to happen in the *y* coordinate of the vertices. Let's now add this information to the current vertex positions, as follows:

- Create a **Position node in Object space**. This position node will have the information of the default position of the vertices of the plane.

- Now, create a new **Add node** and **feed its inputs A(1) and B(2)** with the **Position node** output and the **Vector3 node** output respectively.

- Finally, connect the output of this **Add node** to the **Position(3) input** of the **Vertex block** in the **master stack**. (Figure 7-38).

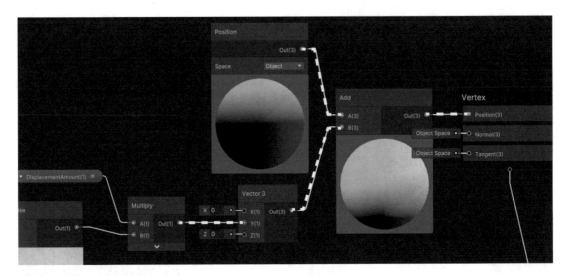

Figure 7-38. *Vertex displacement*

Save the shader graph asset and go back to the Scene view to check the final result. As the Time node is involved in this calculation, you can get a better sense of the dynamic vertex deformation if you click the Play button to see the game running.

You can check Figure 7-39 to see how the plane is performing a wave displacement pattern. The water will now feel totally alive, covering the different elements in the scene but still showing its contour when the elements are near the surface with a foamy but still cartoon silhouette.

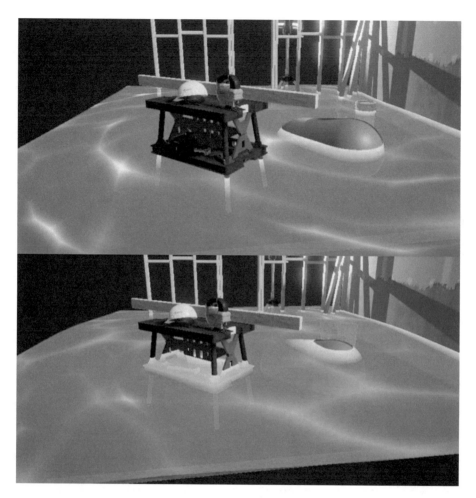

Figure 7-39. *Water waves*

This is the most complex effect we have developed so far, full of properties, SubGraphs, caustic effects, and both fragment and vertex shader calculations. Check the final shader in Figure 7-40.

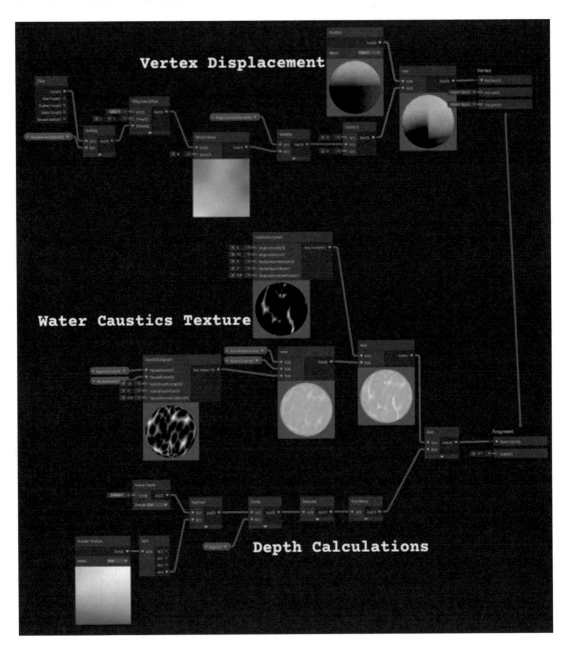

Figure 7-40. *Full WaterCartoon shader graph*

I recommend you review everything, including the **caustic SubGraph**, and play with the property values to achieve fully different water effects before continuing with the next complex effect: **the bubble shader**.

Iridescent Bubble Shader

In this section, we are going to recreate iridescent bubbles. As usual, when making complex shaders I recommend that you search for a reference of the final result you want to achieve (Figure 7-41).

Figure 7-41. *Iridescent bubble*

Iridescent bubbles exhibit a shimmering, rainbow-like appearance caused by the interference and diffraction of light waves as they interact with the thin film of the bubble's surface. We can get a close up of the bubble surface to see the layers of soap running through the watery surface of the bubble to create this amazing effect (Figure 7-42).

Figure 7-42. *Iridescent soap bubble close-up*

In the reference images, we can see the following behaviors of the surface of the bubble that we are going to target in our shader:

- It has a reflective surface, so you can see the elements around reflected in the surface of the bubble (**metallic**).

- The soap causes random iridescent random patterns around the bubble (**noise**).

- The pattern performs a defined gradient of beautiful colors around the bubble (**color gradient**).

- Its center, from the point of view, is transparent, and you start noticing colors and reflections in the **outer rim** of the surface (**fresnel**).

- The surface of the bubble is constantly deformed by the air and the actual movement of the bubble (**vertex displacement**).

This step-by-step analysis we did is called an abstraction exercise, in which we extract the main visual features of the effect we want to achieve and make a relationship with the tools we have available in Shader Graph to replicate them, breaking down the steps to reproduce this effect, as follows:

- Perform initial setup.

- Create and set up metallic reflections.

- Create an iridescent dynamic pattern.

- Add thin film interference gradient.

- Add rim transparency and color.

- Add random vertex displacement.

Initial Setup

As usual, I recommend using the 3D Sample Scene (URP) described in Chapter 3 because it has already set up some features that we will describe later. Now, let's start by creating a shader graph and setting up the main properties of the shader in the Graph Inspector, as follows:

- Create the **bubble** URP lit shader graph by right-clicking anywhere inside the Project tab and selecting **Create ➤ Shader Graph ➤ URP ➤ Lit Shader Graph.**

- Create a material out of the shader by right-clicking the recently created **bubble shader graph asset** in the Project tab and selecting **Create ➤ Material.**

- Now create a sphere in the scene by right-clicking in the Hierarchy tab and selecting **3D Object ➤ Sphere.** I placed the sphere at position **(2, 1, 0)** and called it **Bubble**.

- Then drag and drop the recently created material from the Project tab to the **bubble** object in the scene or in the Hierarchy tab to reference the material to its Mesh Renderer component.

Now, open the bubble shader graph by double-clicking the shader graph asset and opening the Graph Inspector. In the Graph Settings tab, change the **Surface Type** to **Transparent** and be sure that the **Workflow mode** is set up as **Metallic** (Figure 7-43).

Figure 7-43. *Metallic and Transparent*

We have everything ready to start developing our bubble shader. Let's start by creating some surface reflections.

Create and Set Up Reflections

In Chapter 2, when we were reviewing the different inputs of the Fragment block in the master stack, we found the **metallic input**.

The metallic property is represented as a value ranging from 0 to 1. A value of 0 typically represents a non-metallic or dielectric material, such as plastic or wood, while a value of 1 represents a fully metallic surface.

A metallic surface has a high density of free electrons that are not bound to individual atoms and move freely within the metal surface. When light strikes the metallic surface, these free electrons are excited and oscillate, generating their own electromagnetic waves, which are in the same frequency and direction as the incoming light, creating a total reflection.

In our case, the bubble is not made out of metal, but the surface of it is totally reflective, so our first step is to create that metallic appearance, as follows:

- Open the bubble shader graph and change the default value of the **Metallic input in the Fragment block** to **1**.

Metallic surfaces have to be totally **polished** to reflect the incident light. The Smoothness setting represents that value, as we reviewed in Chapter 2, along with the metallic property.

- Change the Smoothness input default value in the Fragment block to 1 (Figure 7-44).

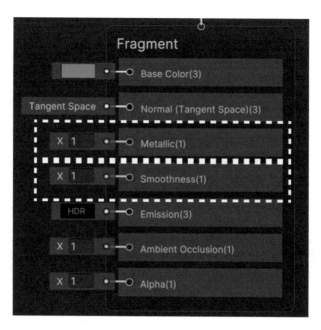

Figure 7-44. *Metallic default value set to 1*

If you save the shader graph asset and come back to the Scene view, you can see two different things:

- A sphere with environment reflections, reflecting the image of every object in the scene around it (Figure 7-45)

Figure 7-45. *Full scene reflection*

- A black sphere with no reflections (Figure 7-46)

Figure 7-46. *No reflections*

Having the surface of the sphere reflect every object in the scene depends on having a reflection cubemap calculated by a **reflection probe** set up in the scene. But what is a **reflection probe**? What is a **reflection cubemap**?

Reflection Probes and Reflection Cubemaps

Your reflections will work as expected, reflecting the environment props around the bubble object we created. This is because the **example assets** object in the scene has a child called **Reflection Probes**, which, in turn, has three single objects as children, which have the **Reflection Probe component** (Figure 7-47).

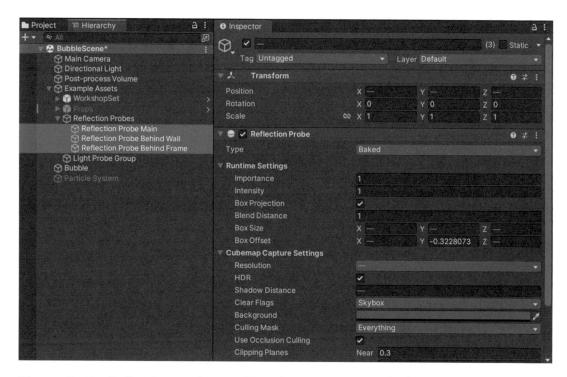

Figure 7-47. *Reflection probes in the **3D Sample Scene (URP)** project default scene*

While selected, they will be displayed in the scene as metallic balls that reflect everything around them (Figure 7-48).

Figure 7-48. *Reflections probes in the Scene view*

The reflection probe captures the surrounding environment from a specific position in the scene and stores the information in a cubemap texture. The cubemap texture contains six 2D images that represent the reflections from different directions (up, down, left, right, front, back). You can see an example of the cubemap generated by a reflection probe in Figure 7-49.

Figure 7-49. *Reflection cubemap*

These cubemaps are then used by shaders to calculate accurate reflections for objects within the probe's influence, represented by the Box Size property.

The **Reflection Probe component** has several important properties; let's define the most relevant ones here:

- **Type**: It determines the type of reflection probe, which can be either Baked or Realtime. Baked probes capture static reflections that are precomputed and stored in lightmaps or reflection probes. Realtime probes update in real-time, allowing for dynamic reflections but with a **higher performance cost**.

- **Box Size**: It sets the distance from the probe at which its reflections affect objects. Objects within this box's boundaries will receive accurate reflections from the probe, while those outside might receive less accurate or no reflections.

- **Box Projection**: If enabled, it allows the reflection probe to use a box shape for capturing reflections instead of the default sphere shape. This can be useful for specific environments or situations where a box shape is more appropriate.

- **Resolution**: It specifies the resolution of the cubemap texture used to store the reflections. Higher resolutions provide more detailed and accurate reflections but come at the expense of performance.

In conclusion, to create realistic reflections on any metallic surface we have to set up at least one reflection probe that contains the metallic object inside its influence boundaries and bake a reflection cubemap.

If you need to create a new reflection probe to add reflections to another scene different than this template one, do the following:

- Right-click anywhere in the Hierarchy tab and select **Create Empty.** This will create an empty object with just the Transform component (Figure 7-50).

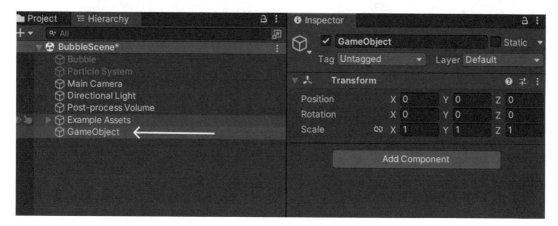

Figure 7-50. *Empty game object*

- Change the name of the object to Reflection Probe for legibility.

- Then, inside the Inspector tab, with this new object selected, click on the **Add Component** button and search for **Reflection Probe (Figure 7-51).** Select that component to be added to the object.

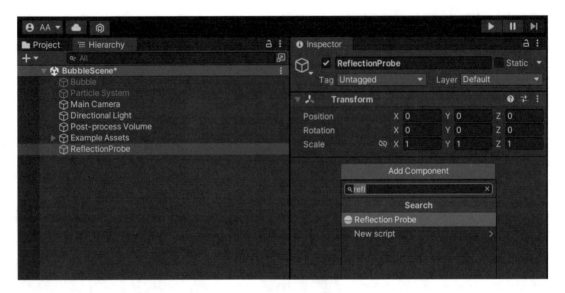

Figure 7-51. *Adding reflection probe component*

- I also changed the position of the reflection probe object to be at (2, 1, 0) which is the center of the Template Scene.

If you select the recently created reflection probe you will notice that it seems like a sphere with an unlit material (Figure 7-52). This is because the reflection cubemap associated with this reflection probe is not baked (calculated).

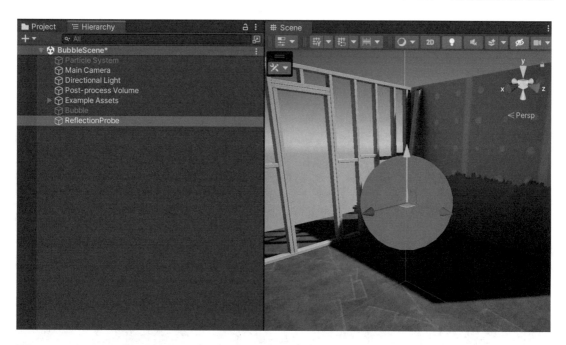

Figure 7-52. *Reflection probe with no cubemap baked*

If you enable the bubble object, you will see that it is completely black because the **bubble shader** doesn't have a reflection cubemap to read and represent on the surface of the object (Figure 7-53).

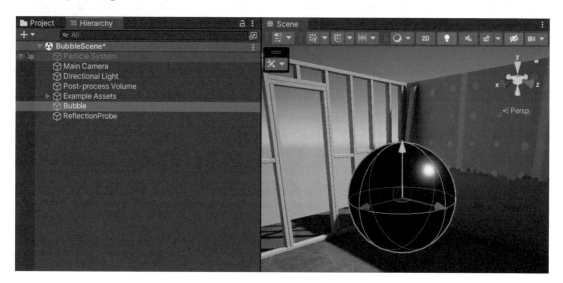

Figure 7-53. *No cubemap loaded*

To bake a reflection cubemap you just have to go to the reflection probe object we created and, at the lowest part of the reflection probe component, click the button **Bake** (**Figure 7-54**).

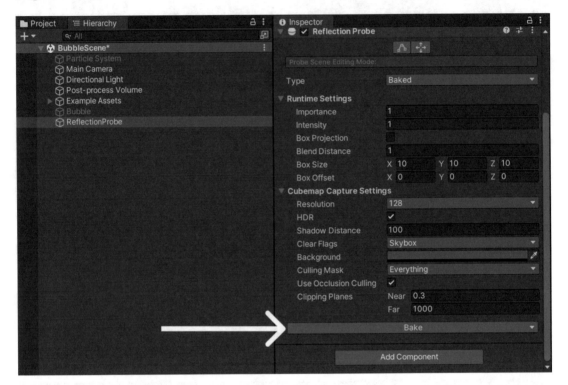

Figure 7-54. Click **Bake** button in reflection probe component

After a loading time that will depend on the **Resolution** property (the bigger the resolution, the longer it is going to take to create the cubemap), our reflection probe object will turn totally reflective, as you can see in Figure 7-55, taking into account every object inside its boundaries (10, 10, 10) set in **Box Size.**

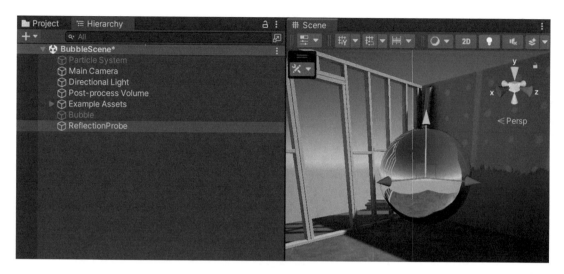

Figure 7-55. *Reflection cubemap calculated*

Note   To avoid baking all the cubemaps every time you change the position of
influence of the reflection probe, you can go to Window ➤ Rendering ➤ Lighting,
and at the very bottom of that window toggle on the Auto Generate setting. This
will constantly generate all the settings regarding light and reflections so you don't
have to do it manually, and it will do it every time you change any setting of any
component regarding lighting. When automatic lighting generation is active, the
Bake button of the reflection probe component will be hidden because you won't
need it anymore. But be aware that if your scene is really huge and full of detail
and light sources you may experience a lot of waiting time.

Inside the same folder where the scene asset is stored, a new folder will be created to
hold the cubemap file of the reflection probe (Figure 7-56). This folder normally stores
every setting related to lighting and reflection configuration of the scene.

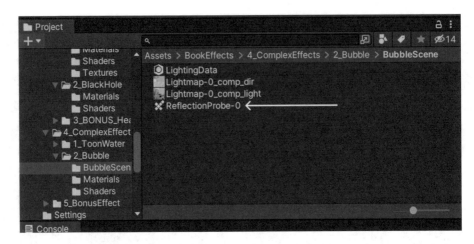

Figure 7-56. *Cubemaps*

If you now enable the bubble object, you will see how the reflections are properly set up, as in Figure 7-57.

Figure 7-57. *Bubble object successfully reflecting the objects around it*

Now that our bubble is reflecting properly, we need to give it an iridescent look instead of a polished metal appearance.

Creating an Iridescent Dynamic Pattern

As we said in the introduction to this effect, bubbles show an iridescent pattern on their surface, a beautiful random pattern created by the light traveling through the soap and water flowing across the surface of the bubble. We have to recreate that random pattern texture and make it flow in a desired direction through the surface of the sphere.

To achieve this effect, open the bubble shader graph asset. Inside the Shader Graph Editor, do the following:

- Create a **Time node** and a **Float Input node** with a default value of **0.1**. Expose that **Float node** as a **property** called **PatternScrollingSpeed**.

- Drag from the Time(1) output of the Time node to create a Multiply node connected to its A(1) input.

- **Connect the PatternScrollingSpeed** property to the input **B(1)** of this **Multiply node**.

- Create a new **Position node** with the **Space** setting set as **Object**.

- Drag from the Position node output to create a new Add node connected to its A(1) input.

- Create a Simple Noise node with a Scale(1) default value of 15.

- Take the output of this **Add node** and connect it to the input **UV(2)** of the **Simple Noise node**.

- Connect the output of this Simple Noise node to the Base Color input of the Fragment block, as shown in Figure 7-58.

We need that noise texture to flow along the surface of the sphere. One simple way to achieve that is to take the position values of the fragments referenced and add or subtract a constantly increasing value.

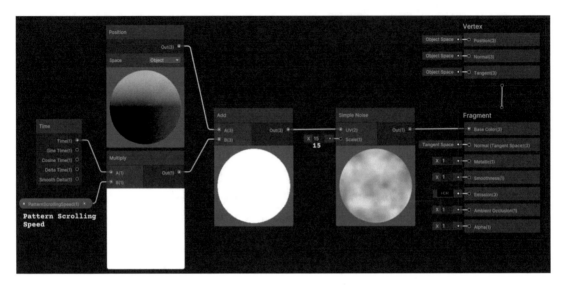

Figure 7-58. *Noise scrolling pattern*

We are reading the position of the fragments of the surface of the sphere relative to the screen with the Position node; this way, the noise pattern is not going to be deformed by the UVs of the sphere, because it is going to take into account the relative fragment position.

We are scrolling the screen position value of the fragments, creating a moving pattern with the Time node and controlling the speed with the Float Input and Multiply nodes.

Finally, those moving fragment positions are truncated to a Vector2 and used as UVs by the Noise node to be mapped on the surface of the sphere (Figure 7-59). **Remember to click Play to see the scrolling movement better**, and if you cannot see the pattern clearly enough, reduce the Metallic value.

Figure 7-59. *Noise scrolling pattern*

The pattern is scrolling correctly across the surface. But it is not changing at all—it seems really static and lacks movement and randomness. To add flow and variation to the scrolling texture, we are going to use a technique in which we add a black-to-white gradient. This gradient will be added to the scrolling texture to generate a constant variation in its noise pattern, along the gradient direction. This is a simple approximation for texture flow variation:

- In the **bubble shader,** add a new **Dot Product node**. Connect its input **A(3)** with the output of the **Position node** we created earlier (remember that one output can be connected to different inputs).

- Set the input **B(3)** of the **Dot Product node** with a **default value of (1, 1, 0).**

- Create a new **Add node** and connect to its **A(1) input the output** of the **Dot Product node** and to its **B(1) the output** of the **Simple Noise node**.

- Then, connect the output of this **Add node** to the **Base Color input of the Fragment block** (Figure 7-60).

359

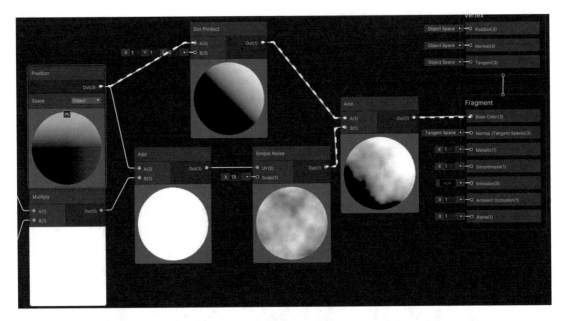

Figure 7-60. *Using the Dot Product node to create a gradient*

The noise texture will constantly change along the gradient direction as it scrolls because its value from 0 to 1 will be altered by the gradient, causing a more dynamic feeling.

Now, let's analyze why bubbles display that beautiful color gradient across their surface.

Adding Thin-Film Interference Gradient

Thin-film interference is a colorful phenomenon that happens when light waves reflect off a very thin layer of material, like **soap bubbles** or oily surfaces. When light hits the surface of the thin layer, some of it bounces back and some goes through.

The interesting part is that the light waves can bounce back and forth between the top and bottom surfaces of the thin layer. When this happens, the waves can either line up and reinforce each other (constructive interference), or they can cancel each other out (destructive interference).

The colors we see in thin-film interference happen because certain colors of light get reinforced while others get canceled out. The specific colors we see depend on the thickness of the thin layer.

These color gradients usually represent the color spectrum, and by inspecting references, like Figure 7-61, we can identify colors like blue, green, pink, yellow, etc.

Figure 7-61. *Oil stain, creating a thin-film interference color gradient*

Let's now use a **Gradient node** and **Sample Gradient node** to replicate this gradient as follows:

- Create a **Gradient node** (don't mistake it with the **Gradient Noise node**). This node generates a smooth transition between two or more colors or values, interpolated between 0 and 1.

- You can open the Gradient Editor by clicking in the black-to-white gradient rectangle inside the Gradient node (Figure 7-62).

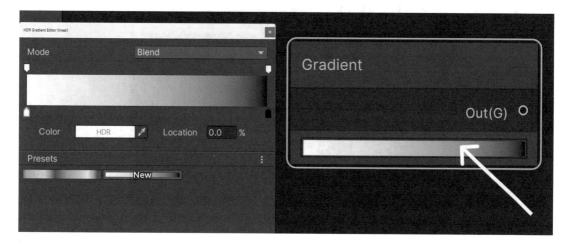

Figure 7-62. *Gradient node and Gradient Editor*

- At the top part of the Gradient Editor you can see the final Gradient sample and two key sections: one at the top of the gradient and another at the bottom of the gradient.

- The top part defines the alpha key values. You can set different keys with different alpha values, which will be interpolated along the gradient.

- In the bottom part you can define color keys.

You can create any key by clicking in any empty space at the top or bottom part of the gradient, and then you can select any created key to change its location in the gradient as well as its value.

To create our desired effect, I came up with these eight key values (the maximum supported by this tool), seen in Figure 7-63:

- **Key 1**: Color = (0, 41, 195), Location = 0.0

- **Key 2**: Color = (16, 191, 0), Location =12.4

- **Key 3**: Color = (191, 146, 0), Location = 27.1

- **Key 4**: Color = (115, 0, 191), Location = 40.9

- **Key 5**: Color = (5, 92, 130), Location = 57.1

- **Key 6**: Color = (44, 184, 0), Location = 70.3

- **Key 7**: Color = (255, 195, 0), Location = 83.2

- **Key 8**: Color = (115, 41, 191), Location = 100.0

Figure 7-63. *Resulting gradient*

These values are a sample reference on how to display a thin-film interference color pattern, but you can try different variations to create a similar effect. This gradient can be saved for later uses by clicking the **New** button in the lowest part of the Gradient Editor window. These **presets** can later be loaded by just clicking on them in the Gradient Editor window.

Now that we have created and set a **Gradient node** we need to sample it. The **Gradient node** output needs a value between 0 and 1 to know which color from the gradient has to be output. That where the **Sample Gradient** node comes in, as follows:

- Create a **Sample Gradient node** and connect the **Gradient node** output to its **Gradient(G)** input.

- Connect the output of the **last created Add node** to the **Time(1) input of the Sample Gradient node.**

- Finally, connect the output of the Sample Gradient node to the Base Color input of the Fragment block **(Figure 7-64)**.

The **Sample Gradient node** is going to take the black-and-white texture output by the Add node and convert the 0 to 1 value to a sampled color value defined in the gradient.

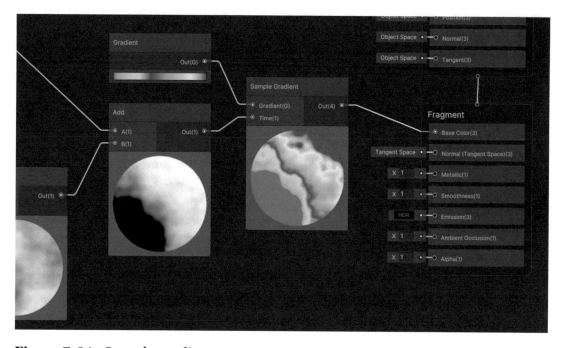

Figure 7-64. *Sample gradient*

If you save the asset and go back to the Scene view, you will find a really beautiful metallic ball with a colorful marble pattern flowing in its surface (Figure 7-65).

Figure 7-65. *Colorful noisy pattern through the bubble*

We have added the thin-film interference dynamically, creating a beautiful and dynamic pattern across the surface of the sphere. But it still looks like a solid metal ball, so we have to give it a transparent touch to make it feel light and bubbly.

Adding Rim Transparency and Color

As you saw in the reference image (Figure 7-42), the bubble is almost fully transparent in the middle and gradually gets translucent at its outer rim.

Mentioning a **rim** or border is a hint telling us to use the **Fresnel Effect node.** This node, used in a few of the effects in this book, creates a gradient at the outer rim of the faces of the mesh, taking into account the view vector and a fresnel power that adjusts the thickness of the gradient.

We are going to use this node to create a transparency mask around the outer rim of the sphere, as follows:

- First, be sure that the **Surface Type** is still set as **Transparent** in the **Graph Settings tab**.

- Inside the bubble shader graph, create a **Fresnel node** and set the **Power(1) input** default value to **1**.

- Connect the output of the Fresnel Effect node to the Alpha(1) input of the Fragment block (Figure 7-66).

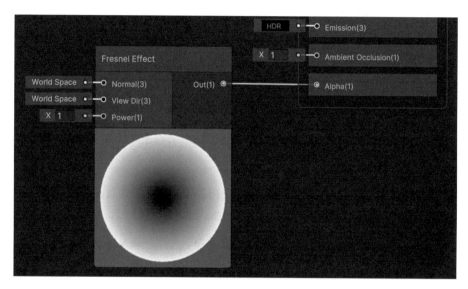

Figure 7-66. *Fresnel effect alpha mask*

The darker the values of the texture, the more transparent the surface of the sphere; and the whiter the values of the texture, the more opaque that part of the surface of the bubble will be (Figure 7-67).

Figure 7-67. *Bubble transparency*

We are getting closer to the desired effect. Let's add another rim, but this time to the emission input to achieve a glowing, bright-blue border, simulating the water reflection of the surface. Do the following:

- Create another **Fresnel Effect node**, this time with a **Power(1)**
  default value of **20**.

  We want this fresnel effect to be really stretched, to be really thin,
  which is why the default Power value is so high.

- Create a **new Multiply node** and feed its input **A(1)** with the **Fresnel Effect node output.**

- Create a **Color Input node** in **HDR** mode with a default color value of
  (R = 0, G = 190, B = 190) and with intensity of **1.5**.

- Connect the **Color Input node** to the **B(4)** of the recently created
  Multiply node.

- Connect the output of the **Multiply node** to the **Emission input of
  the Fragment block** (Figure 7-68).

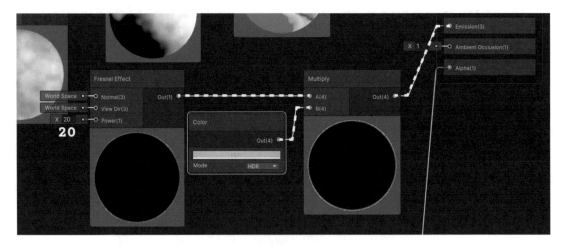

Figure 7-68. *Bubble transparency*

The Fresnel Effect node will create a black-to-white gradient at the outer border of the sphere from the perspective of the player. Its high-value power will stretch that gradient a lot, creating a really thin fresnel gradient. Then we color that gradient by multiplying the Fresnel Effect node output with a blue tone, causing the effect shown in Figure 7-69.

We have added two fresnel effects in the same shader, and you may be thinking that this implementation would be really expensive, but, in fact, the fresnel calculation is so optimized that it is implemented by default as an addition to the default lit shader in Unity URP and HDRP. This creates an extra layer of light interaction detail in the objects in the scene. Fear not using it in your shaders.

Figure 7-69. *Bubble blue outer rim*

We have a really nice bubble effect, **but I am not done yet!** Bubbles' surface morphology is not a perfect sphere, as their surface is constantly and randomly fluctuating because of external phenomena like the air.

Adding Random Vertex Displacement

When deforming a sphere using a noise, it is essential to do it in the direction of the normals of the vertices, because, as shown in Figure 7-70, the vertex normals point outward from the center of the sphere.

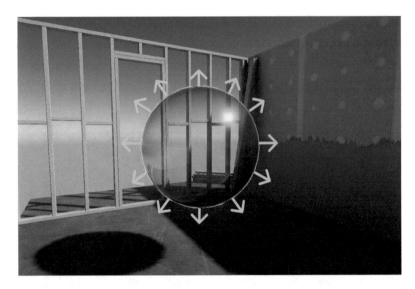

Figure 7-70. *Sphere vertex normals directions*

With that information, we can displace the vertices in the negative and positive directions of the normals to generate different surface morphology (Figure 7-71).

Figure 7-71. *Displacing the vertices along the normal directions a random amount*

To tell each vertex to be displaced a random amount, we can use a noise texture and scroll it continuously over time to make the vertex move along its normal direction.

Open the **bubble shader graph**. Let's use the vertex position information and offset it constantly in time to make the noise texture scroll so each vertex moves along its normal direction, as follows:

- Create a **Position node** with **Space** set as **Object.**

- Create a **Time node** and a **Multiply node**.

- Connect the **Time(1) output** of the **Time node** to the **A(1) input** of the **Multiply node** and set its **B(1) input** as **0.1**. This value will determine the deformation speed.

- Create a **Subtract node** and feed its **A(3)** input with the **Position node output** and its **B(3)** input with the recently created **Multiply node output.**

- Create a Simple Noise node with default Scale(1) value of 7.5.

This noise will determine the amount of displacement each vertex is going to perform.

- Now, just connect the **Subtract node output** to the **Simple Noise input** (Figure 7-72).

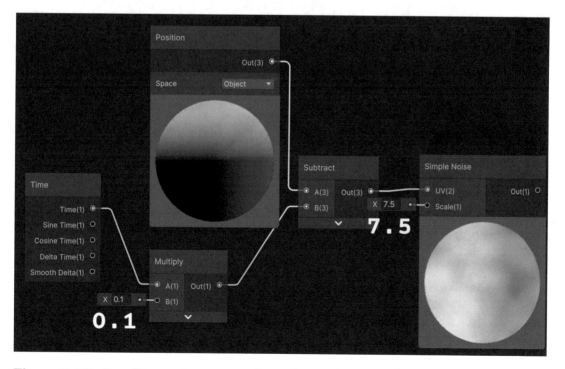

***Figure 7-72.** Scrolling noise pattern for a dynamic vertex displacement*

Now, let's customize this vertex displacement pattern. For example, we can add negative values using the Subtract node, as follows:

- Create a new **Subtract node** and feed its **input A(1)** with the **Simple Noise output** and set a **default** value for the **B(1)** as **0.3**.

The Subtract node will reduce some noise values below 0, causing a negative displacement of the vertices along its normal, which will make a more natural morphology.

- Now, let's control the amplitude of the displacement using a new **Multiply node**, setting its **A(1)** connection with a **default** value of **0.1** and connecting the **B(3) input** to the output of the **Subtract node** (Figure 7-73).

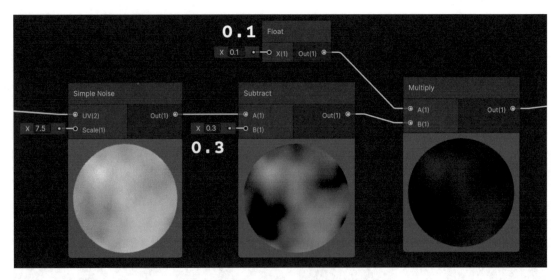

Figure 7-73. *Customizing the vertex displacement texture*

Now that we have the displacement amount as a black-and-white texture, we need to create a Vector3 in the direction of the vertex normal to be applied to the vertex position, as follows:

- Create a **Normal Vector node** with **Space** set as **Object**.

This node will output the normal direction of the vertex that we are going to modify using the displacement texture.

- Create a new **Multiply node** and connect its **input B(3)** with the previous **Multiply node** output and its **input A(3)** with the **Normal Vector node output**.

This operation will output a Vector3 in the direction of the normal of the vertex but with its amplitude changed according to the noise texture. It is time to add this new normal vector to the current position of the vertex to move it.

- Create another **Position node in Object space** and a new **Add node**, whose **input A(3)** will be connected to this **Position node output** and whose input **B(3)** will be connected to the last created **Multiply node output.**

- Finally, connect the output of this **Add node** to the **Position(3)** input of the **Vertex block** to set the new vertex position (Figure 7-74).

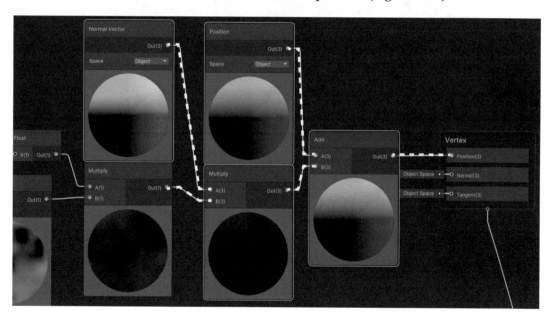

Figure 7-74. *Apply the vertex displacement to each vertex along its normal direction*

You can tweak the noise scale default value to change the resolution of the deformation, or the default values in the Multiply nodes to set different displacement speed or displacement scales. Check the subtle result after saving the asset (Figure 7-75).

Figure 7-75. *Subtle vertex displacement*

Summary

This was the most complex chapter so far, and you've made it to the finish! You have learned a lot of new complex tools and techniques like the SubGraph and the depth texture to create an immersive water, using the Voronoi node to create cartoon water ripples.

You studied everything related to reflections, like the Metallic workflow, the reflection probes, and the reflection cubemaps, and how to set up your project to create amazing reflective effects. You have also created amazing and complex shaders using all the techniques we have learned throughout this book, like dynamic patterns and vertex displacement effects.

In the next and final chapter, you will learn how to make interactive snow, a complex environmental element with which your characters will interact by creating footprints!

CHAPTER 8

Interactive Snow Effect

We have been producing nice visual effects throughout this book, using different techniques and post-processing calculations. But there is one thing we didn't tackle yet—user interaction with the shaders, or how to interact with the values inside the shader graph.

In this final chapter, we are going to make an interactive snow terrain in which our character will create real-time footprints while walking (Figure 8-1).

To achieve this effect, we will introduce the concept of **render texture.** We will also use a script to control our character with the keyboard so we can move it around the scene, stepping on the snow. This complex effect requires a lot of techniques and tools so is worthy of having a chapter dedicated to it.

Figure 8-1. *Interactive snow*

© Álvaro Alda 2023
Á. Alda, *Beginner's Guide to Unity Shader Graph*, https://doi.org/10.1007/978-1-4842-9672-1_8

Let's break down the steps we are going to follow to create this amazing and fun-to-play-with effect:

- Set up scene.

- Give movement to the character.

- Make snow plane 3D object.

- Create interactive snow shader graph.

- Interact with the snow.

Scene Setup

We are going to start by opening the template project we have been using with this book: **3D Sample Scene (URP).** Then, we are going to rearrange some props to have a better playground in which to test our interactive snow effect, as follows:

- The **Props** object inside **Example Assets** object is not really needed, so you can disable it.

- Change the WorkShopSet object position t: (2.5, 0, −1.5).

Inside the **WorkShopSet** object there are a bunch of panels and walls that we will move and rotate around:

- **DrywallPanel**: *Position* = (0.5, 0, −2.25) ; *Rotation* = (0, −30, 0)

- **Ground**: *Position* = (−3.70, 0, −0.8) ; *Rotation* = (0, 0, 0) ; *Scale* = **(3, 3, 3)**

- **OSB Panel:** *Position* = (0.75, 0, 5.5) ; *Rotation* = (0, −130, 0)

- **Stud Frame:** *Position* = (0, 1.2, 1.8) ; *Rotation* = (0, 0, 0)

- **Stud Pile:** *Position* = (0, 0, 0) ; *Rotation* = (0, 0, 0)

Adjust the **MainCamera object** position and rotation as well, as follows:

- *Position* = (2.7, 2.5, 3.5)

- *Rotation* = (19, 200, 0)

Finally, you can instantiate a 3D object that will act like a character (preferably a **capsule**) in the middle of the scene at **position (1.5, 0.5, 0.2)** (if you are using a **capsule**, change its **scale** to **(0.5, 0.5, 0.5)**); call it **Character.** In my case, I used the bunny object you can find in the GitHub project.

If you follow the previous steps, you should finally have in front of you the scene playground shown in Figure 8-2.

Figure 8-2. *Scene playground*

We modified the template scene in this way to have a nice playground with marked limits in which we can display the interactive snow and have a free space in which to move our character around.

The only issue here is that, if you are using a capsule as your character, you may get confused about where it is pointing. You can create some extra 3D objects as children of the character object to represent the direction. As we set up in the script, the object is moving toward the local *z* coordinate. So, we need to add the pointing indicators in the part of the surface that is pointing toward the *z*-axis, as follows:

- Make sure you have selected the local representation of the gizmos to identify its local *z*-axis when selecting the object (Figure 8-3).

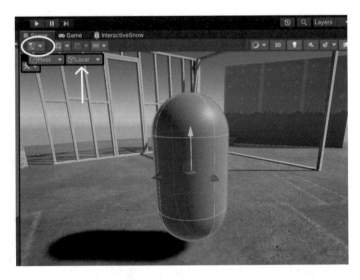

Figure 8-3. *Identifying the local z-axis of the character object*

- Now, add any 3D objects as children of the character controller; for
  example, a pointy cylinder with transform values:

    - Position: (0, 0.4, 0.5)

    - Rotation: (90, 0, 0)

    - Scale: (0.3, 0.3, 0.3)

Now your character has a big nose pointing toward the z-axis so you can follow its
movement and orientation better when playing (Figure 8-4).

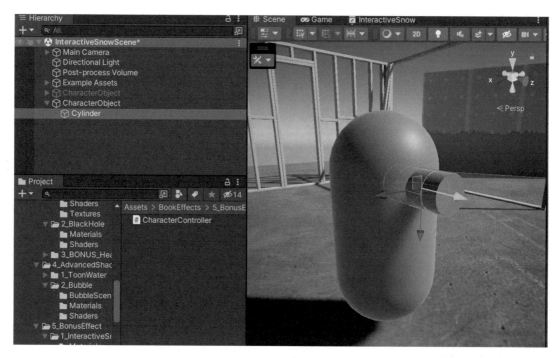

Figure 8-4. *Adding z-axis orientation indicator*

Feel free to customize your character as you want. Remember that it is the representation of the protagonist of your game.

In my case, I am using the bunny object, which is properly oriented to the *z*-axis (Figure 8-5). Remember that all the assets, including this little guy, are available in the GitHub project of this book.

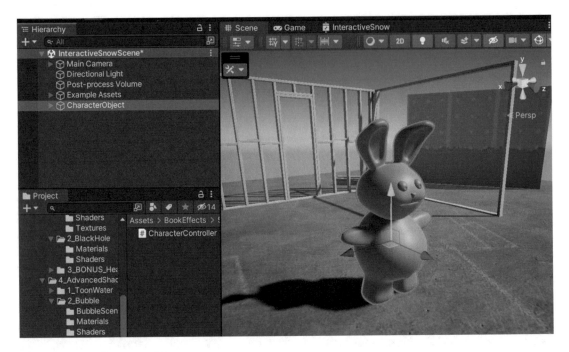

Figure 8-5. *Bunny object*

Now that we have our playground ready, we must give our character the ability to move, using the keyboard keys **W, S, or UpArrow, DownArrow** to move the character **forward** and **backward** and the **A, D, or LeftArrow, RightArrow,** to **rotate** our character around its **y-axis** so we can change its orientation.

Give Movement to the Character

To make this effect interactive, we have to be able to move the character in the scene using the keyboard. To do it, you guessed it!—we need to create a script. "But hey! This book is not about code or boring scripts." Yeah I know. This will be the first and last time we will create a script, I promise. First thing we need to do is set up our **IDE** before we can start scripting.

Set Up Your IDE

IDE stands for integrated development environment; in other words, the program that allows you to work with code and develop the features in your game—**your code editor.** There are plenty of them in the market: **Visual Code, Visual Studio, Ryder**, and more.

Each one has its pros and cons, and, of course, there is disagreement as to which one is better or worse. For this sample, I am going to use **Visual Studio Community**, since it is the one that Unity recommends to use and it's free. But if you have your preferred IDE installed and already set up, feel free to use it and jump over this step.

When we went over the Unity Editor installation in Chapter 3, there was a step in which Unity Hub asked us which extra modules we wanted to install along with the desired Unity version (Figure 8-6).

Note   Remember that to install a Unity version or add modules to a current Unity version you have already installed, open **Unity Hub** and at the left click on **Installs.** You can then install a new version, and Unity will ask you to add any modules you want; or you can click at the right-hand button with a gear icon in any of the already installed versions and select **Add Modules** to add new features to that Unity version.

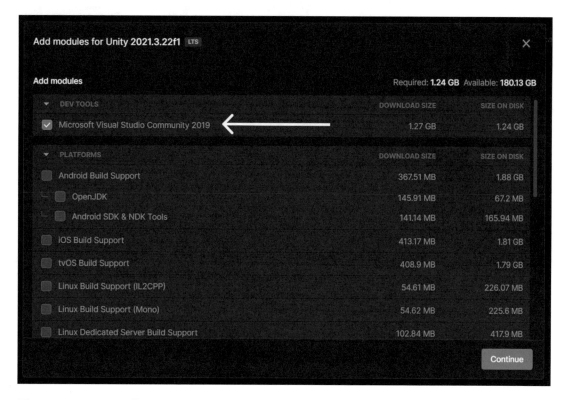

Figure 8-6. *Installing Visual Studio Community 2019*

Clicking on the Continue button at the lower-right of the screen will install or update the desired Unity version with the selected modules; in this case, installing **Visual Studio 2019**.

A Visual Studio installer will pop up asking if you want to install any extension (workload), and to select it. You must toggle the one related to Unity programming, which will enable you to use debugging and other features (Figure 8-7).

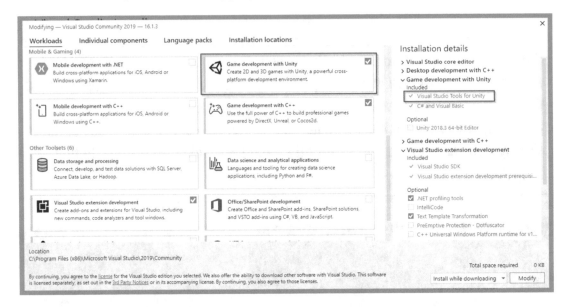

Figure 8-7. *Adding Unity extension*

Then, click on the **Modify/Install** button and wait for your computer to install everything correctly.

Now that you have your IDE installed on your computer, let's ensure that some settings are correctly set up inside your **Unity Preferences**, as follows:

- Open Unity Preferences under **Edit ➤ Preferences**, or if you are using a Mac, go to **Unity ➤ Preferences** or Cmd + ',' to open it.

- Then, click in the left tab called **External Tools**, where you can find something like what is shown in Figure 8-8.

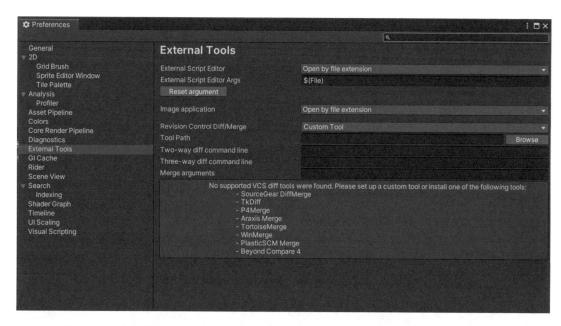

Figure 8-8. *External Tools configuration*

- Open the first dropdown setting, **External Script Editor**, and select **Visual Studio 2019** (Figure 8-9). If it doesn't appear available to select and you have followed all the preceding Visual Studio installation steps, restart Unity.

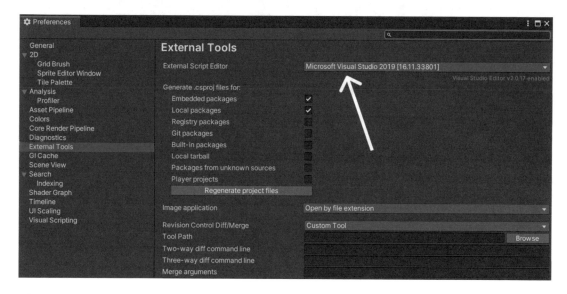

Figure 8-9. *External Tools configuration*

Now the project is ready for scripting, so we can give our character some movement.

Create a Character Movement Script

All the components attached to game objects in your hierarchy or scene (**Transform, MeshRenderer, MeshFilter, Reflection Probe, etc.**) are scripts that give a specific functionality to that game object. All of them working at the same time is what gives an object a unique behavior in your game.

In this case, we are going to create one that will provide our character object the ability to move around using the keyboard keys W, A, S, D, and directional arrows.

Right-click in any empty space inside the Project tab and select **C# Script.** A script will be generated inside the folder where the Project tab was opened, allowing you to put a name to your script. I called it **MyCharacterController** (Figure 8-10).

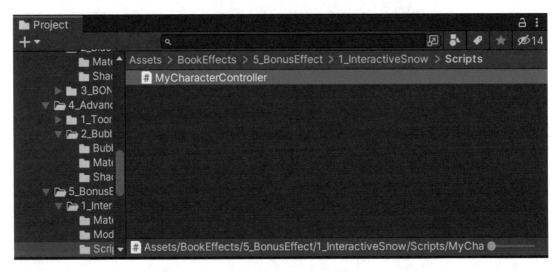

Figure 8-10. *MyCharacterController script*

If you double-click the **MyCharacterController** script, Visual Studio will open and show you the code of the script with the default **Start** and **Update** functions (Figure 8-11).

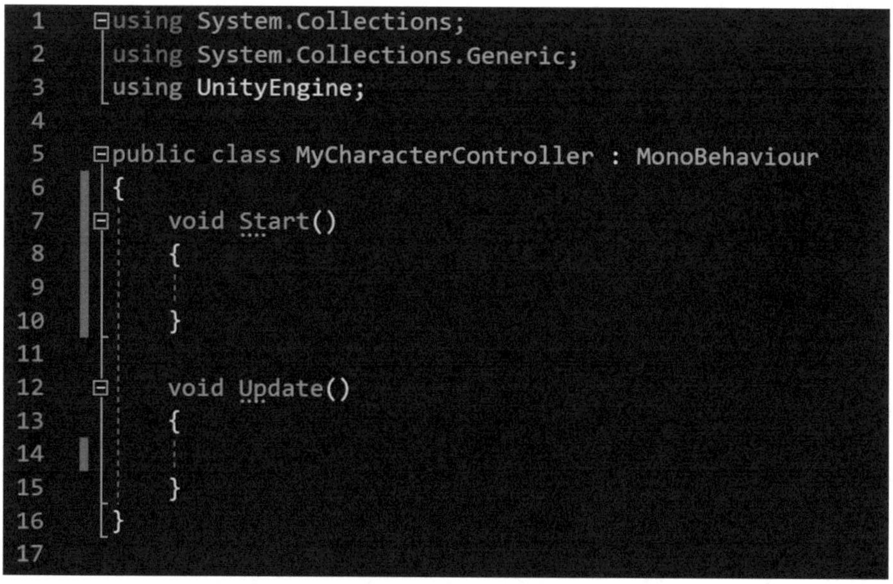

```
1    using System.Collections;
2    using System.Collections.Generic;
3    using UnityEngine;
4
5    public class MyCharacterController : MonoBehaviour
6    {
7        void Start()
8        {
9
10       }
11
12       void Update()
13       {
14
15       }
16   }
17
```

Figure 8-11. *MyCharacterController blank script*

These default functions run in certain moments during the "lifetime" of our object. Without going too much into details, the **Start** function is called once, after the game object with this script attached is instantiated into the scene. The **Update** function is called once per frame while this object exists and is enabled in the scene.

In our script, we are basically going to remove the Start method AND introduce code in the **Update** function that will be constantly reading what the player is inputting and using those inputs to change the position and rotation of the object in the scene. Replace the contents of the script file with the following code snippet:

```
using UnityEngine;

public class MyCharacterController : MonoBehaviour
{
    //The SerializeField Attribute will let you tweak
    //these variables from the Unity Editor
    [SerializeField] float speed = 5.0f;
    [SerializeField] float rotationSpeed = 300.0f;

    void Update()
    {
        // Get the horizontal and vertical axis.
```

```
// By default they are mapped to the arrow keys.
// The value is in the range -1 to 1
var translation = Input.GetAxis("Vertical") * speed * Time.
deltaTime;
var rotation = Input.GetAxis("Horizontal") * rotationSpeed *
Time.deltaTime;

// Move translation along the object's z-axis
transform.Translate(0, 0, translation);

// Rotate around our y-axis
transform.Rotate(0, rotation, 0);

// Avoid getting out of the Camera view
transform.position = new Vector3(
    Mathf.Clamp(transform.position.x, -4, 3),
    transform.position.y,
    Mathf.Clamp(transform.position.z, -9, 0.5f));
    }
}
```

All the lines have comments to describe their functionality, but let's quickly review it:

- First, as we are creating properties to set up the movement and rotation speed, we are using the SerializeField attribute to let the programmer adjust them from the editor.

- We are running the code in the **Update** function, so this whole process will be performed once per frame.

- The translation and rotation values are updated by reading the input from the keyboard, vertically and horizontally, respectively.

- The **vertical** values will be stored in the **translation** variable and the **horizontal** values will define the **rotation** of the object.

- The transform.Translate() function allows you to move an object in a specified direction by a given distance. The Vector3 represents the direction and magnitude of the movement in the local coordinate system of the object, and Time.deltaTime ensures smooth movement by scaling the distance with the frame rate.

- The `transform.Rotate()` function rotates the object by the specified Euler angles. The Euler angles represent the rotation around each coordinate axis (x, y, z) in degrees. The Vector3 we are using defines a certain rotation in the vertical axis of the object.

- Lastly, we are **clamping** the **position** of the object so it cannot go outside of the boundaries of the scene.

After modifying the script, save it using the **Ctrl+S** shortcut (**Cmd+S** in Mac) or in **File ➤ Save**. Now that the script is ready, let's attach it to the character object in the Scene view using **any** of the following alternatives:

- Drag and drop the script asset from the Project tab to the object in the hierarchy.

- Drag and drop the script asset from the Project tab to the Inspector tab while the character object is selected in the hierarchy.

- With the object selected, at the very bottom of the Inspector tab, there is a button called **AddComponent**—click it and search for **CharacterController.** Click on the found component, and it will be automatically attached to the object (Figure 8-12).

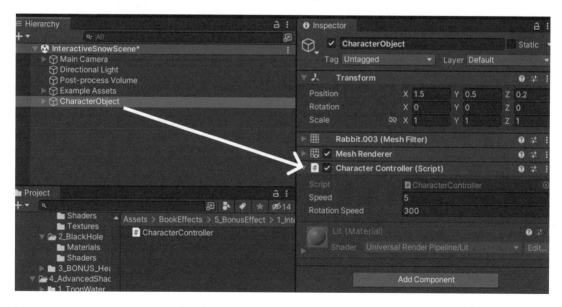

Figure 8-12. *Script attached to the game object*

As you may have noticed, the script has two variables exposed that you can change at any time. These default values worked fine for me, but you can adjust to make the object movement smooth and comfortable. They are as follows:

- **Speed = 5**: Defining how fast the object is going to move around.

- **Rotation Speed = 300**: Defining how fast it will turn around its *y*-axis.

Now, the object is ready for you, the player, to move it around the scene. Click the Play button at the top of Unity Editor and use the keyboard to move the object around! Funny, isn't it? You have just given your character life.

Now that our character is moving with the player inputs in the scene, it is time to create the plane that will be transformed into snow using our special shader.

Snow Plane 3D Object

It is really straightforward to use the already implemented plane that Unity has by default. Why are we creating a plane object?

If you take a look at the **topology**[1] of the default plane in Unity, you will see that the amount of detail is really low; there are too few vertices and polygons (Figure 8-13).

---

[1] Topology: defines the arrangement and structure of the elements of the mesh (vertices, edges, polygons)

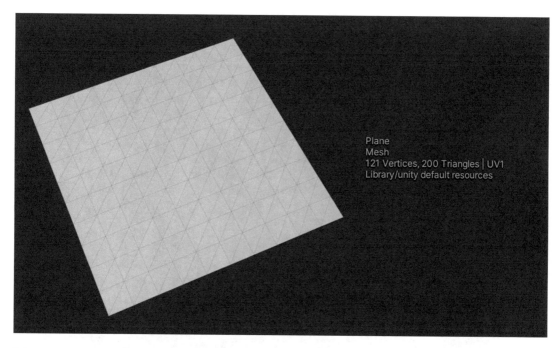

Figure 8-13. *Default Unity plane mesh*

When deforming the plane to make the shape of a snowy landscape in such a big environment, or interacting with that snow using the character, we are going to have as a result a really chunky and poor effect. I will show you a comparison of the final effect using the default plane mesh and with a more detailed topology in Figure 8-14.

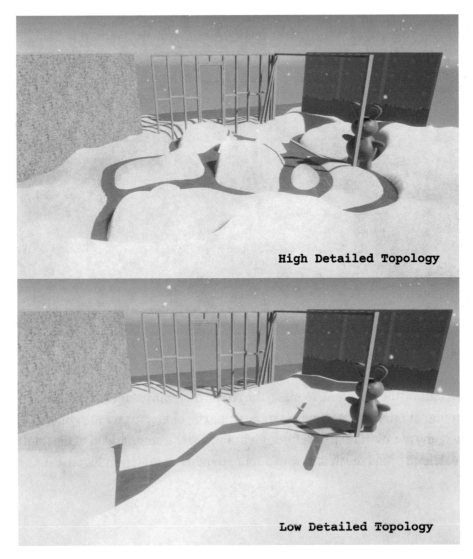

Figure 8-14. *High-detailed plane (top) and low-detailed plane (bottom)*

As you can see in the figure, the difference is substantial; therefore, we need to create a new plane mesh with a lot more vertices and polygons to work with. **Keep in mind** that using too many vertices and polygons is going to create heavy workloads for the GPU that is in charge of "painting" them. In video games, you always have to balance detail against performance.

Subdivided Plane Creation

As usual, this object is available in the GitHub project of this book by selecting **Assets** ➤ **Book Effects** ➤ **5_Bonus Effect** ➤ **1_Interactive Snow** ➤ **Models** ➤ **Subdivided Plane** for you to replicate this effect or use it in your own projects.

There are a lot of techniques available to create extra topology, like tessellation shaders, but the complexity of creating them is out of the scope of this book.

I will teach you how to create one in Blender in case you want to tweak the amount of detail of the plane.

First and foremost, download and install Blender from its home page.[2] Open it and find yourself totally overwhelmed with the huge amount of settings and options inside, even when looking at just a single cube (Figure 8-15).

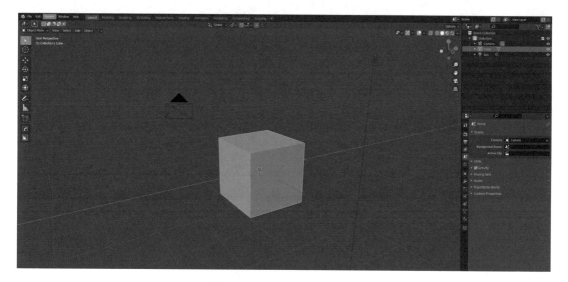

Figure 8-15. *Blender user interface*

Now, you can delete all the objects in the Collection tab at the top-right corner of the user interface by selecting them and clicking **Delete.** You should see the scene completely empty at this point.

---

[2] https://www.blender.org/

Then, we are going to create a plane object as follows:

- Using the keyboard, press **Shift + A** to open the **Add** menu in the middle of your cursor.

- Select **Mesh ➤ Plane** to create a plane object in the scene (Figure 8-16).

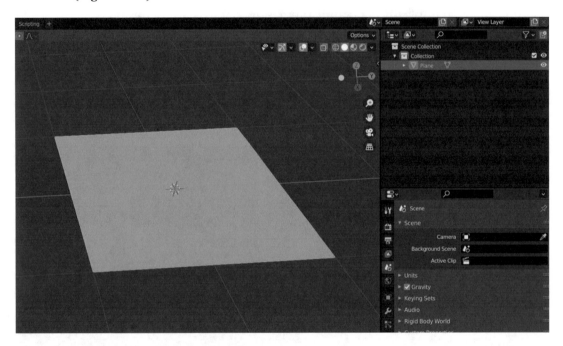

Figure 8-16. *Plane object in Blender*

You can check the topology of the objects in Blender by changing the Viewport Shading mode in the top-right corner of the Layout view to **wireframe** (Figure 8-17).

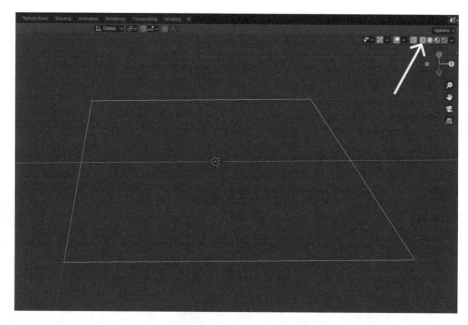

Figure 8-17. Changing to wireframe mode to see plane topology

This plane is made out of a single quad (two triangles), which is way less detailed than the default one in Unity. We need to crank the topology up by a lot. To **subdivide** the plane we are going to apply a **modifier** to our object. **Modifiers** are tools that allow us to apply certain operations to the topology of our objects. In this case, we are going to use the **Subdivision Surface Modifier**, which is going to increase the detail in our mesh exponentially. Do the following:

- With the plane object selected, open the Modifiers tab in the menu below the Collections tab. It is represented by a wrench icon (Figure 8-18).

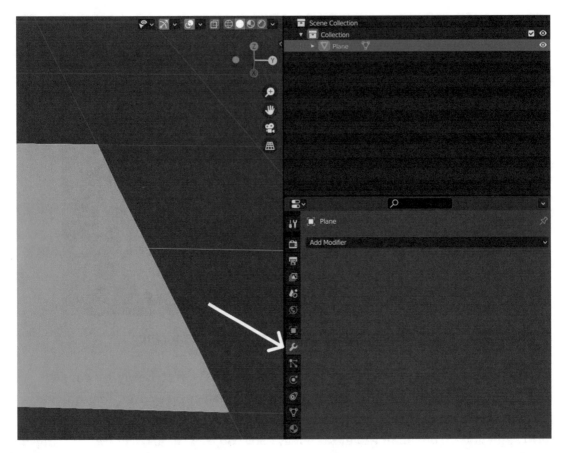

Figure 8-18. *Modifiers tab*

- Click in the **Add Modifier** dropdown to reveal a list of modifiers; select the one called **Subdivision Surface,** shown in Figure 8-19.

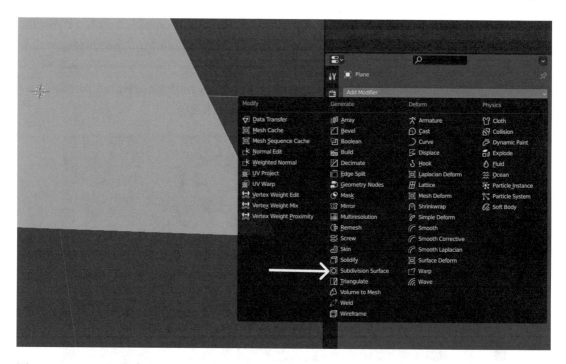

Figure 8-19. *Subdivision Surface modifier*

When this modifier is added, your plane will turn into a polygon (Figure 8-20), which is not intended, of course.

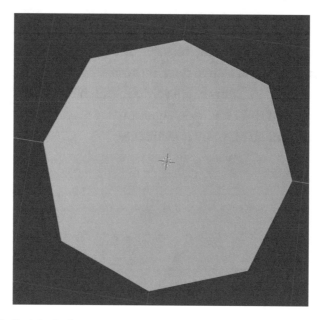

Figure 8-20. *Subdivided plane*

This is happening because the modifier is calculating the medium distance between the old vertices and generating the new vertices in that exact position. That is really useful when you want to achieve smooth and curved topology (trees, waves, cars). In our case we don't want that, so go to the Subdivision Modifiers settings at the same place where we created it and click the **Simple** button **(Figure 8-21).**

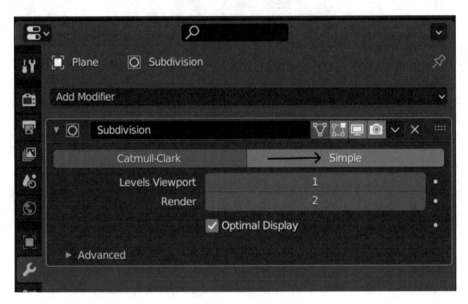

Figure 8-21. *Simple subdivision calculation*

You can also change the **Levels Viewport** to increase the level of detail of the plane's topology. I recommend you set the value of **7** (Figure 8-22), which will increase the vertices of the original mesh a great deal. Be aware that having higher levels of subdivisions results in there being more vertices, which means higher memory consumption (both system RAM and video memory for display). This can cause Blender to hang or crash if not enough memory is available.

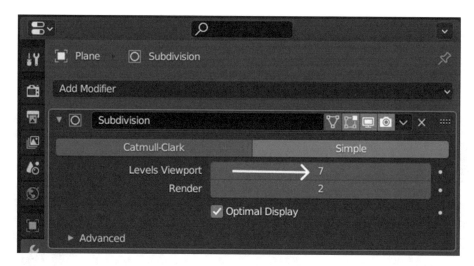

Figure 8-22. *Levels Viewport = 7*

After setting the Levels Viewport value to 7 you can apply the modifier in the top-right dropdown of the Modifier settings (Figure 8-23).

Figure 8-23. *Apply modifier*

Now, you can see in wireframe mode that the plane went from a single quad topology to hundreds of them (Figure 8-24).

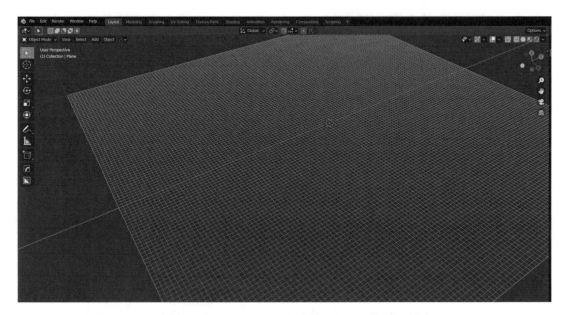

Figure 8-24. *Subdivided plane*

We are now ready to export this object as an FBX file to be used in our Unity project, as follows:

- First, make sure that the plane object is selected (with an orange outline).

- Change its name to **Subplane** by double-clicking the object in the Collection tab.

- At the top-left part of the Blender user interface select **File ➤ Export ➤ FBX(.fbx).** A pop-up window will appear for you to set the export settings (Figure 8-25).

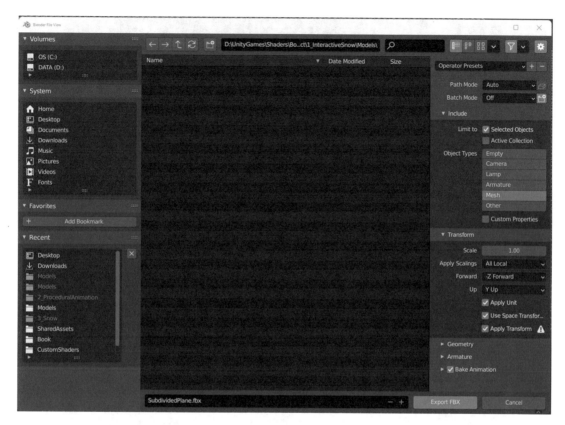

Figure 8-25. *Export FBX window*

At the top-center part of this window you can set a destination folder in which to save the FBX asset. Select anywhere inside the Assets folder of your Unity project. You can set a name for the FBX file. I called mine **SubdividedPlane.fbx**.

Now, at the right part of this window, there are several settings that we are going to tweak in order to properly save this asset to be compatible with Unity's coordinate system, as shown in Figure 8-26.

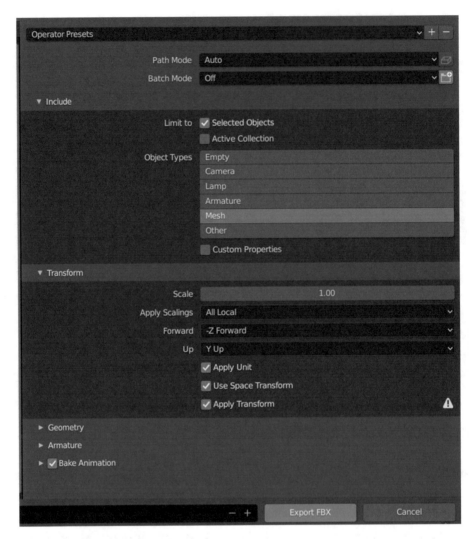

Figure 8-26. *Export FBX window*

When everything is set up the same way, click on the Export **FBX** button, and you will have the FBX ready to go in the selected folder.

If you like modeling and are interested in learning Blender, there is a Blender manual[3] for you to study as well as a lot of information and tutorials on the internet, since it is the most user-friendly CAD program.

---

[3] https://docs.blender.org/manual/en/latest/

Import the Plane to Unity

Open your Unity project and open the scene we set up in the first section of this chapter.

If the FBX file is in any other folder outside the Assets folder of your project, just drag and drop it from that folder to anywhere in the Project tab, as we did with the **Fish** and **Bench** models in Chapter 5 in the Fish Procedural Animation and Snow Effect subsections.

Then, take the FBX from the Project tab and drag and drop it inside the scene or inside the Hierarchy tab (Figure 8-27).

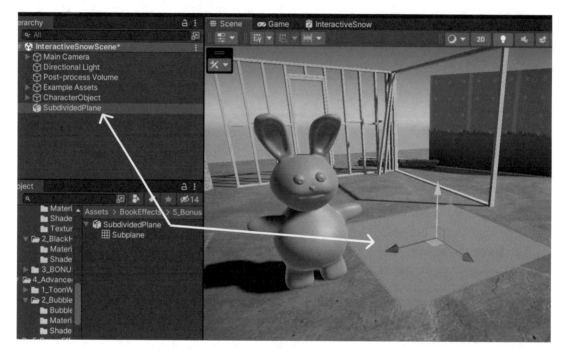

Figure 8-27. *Imported subdivided plane*

Now, change its name to **InteractiveSnow** and its **Transform** component values to the following:

- **Position**: (0, −0.01, 0)

- **Rotation** = (0, 0, 0)

- **Scale** = (6.5, 6.5, 6.5)

You will end up with the plane shown in Figure 8-28.

Figure 8-28. *Subdivided plane set up in the scene*

The **InteractiveSnow** object is now ready to be treated in order to obtain cozy and detailed snow to play with. Let's focus on what this book is all about—Shader Graph.

Note   You may have noticed that the plane is inside the floor. The shader will apply vertical deformation to create a volumetric snow, so it will be displaced on top of the floor. Using this position value allows us to create a nicer effect when the character steps on the snow.

Interactive Snow Shader Graph

Let's now create a shader graph that will display the white and cozy snow on our subdivided plane object. Start by creating the shader graph and the material.

Shader Graph Setup

Follow these steps to create a shader graph and material:

- Create a new URP lit shader graph called **InteractiveSnowShader** by right-clicking anywhere in the Project tab and selecting **Create ➤ Shader Graph ➤ URP ➤ Lit Shader Graph.**

- Right-click on the **InteractiveSnowShader** shader graph asset in the Project tab and select **Create ➤ Material** to create a material with this shader referenced.

- Finally, drag and drop the created material asset from the Project tab to the **InteractiveSnow** object in the hierarchy or scene to assign it to its mesh renderer component.

At this point, everything should look the same. It's time to modify the shader graph and create vertical displacement to the InteractiveSnow object's vertices to create a snowy appearance.

Apply Displacement Using Noise

As we did with the previous snow effect in Chapter 5, we are going to displace the vertices of the plane across their vertical axis to create a natural and cozy shape out of the plane.

To create an irregular and bumpy snow displacement in the plane, we are going to use a noise texture taken out of the **Simple Noise node** and translate its values from black to white into a displacement amount. A texture used this way is normally called a **displacement map** or **displacement texture.**

Let's start creating this setup by opening the **InteractiveSnow shader** we recently created and doing the following inside:

- Start by creating a **Simple Noise node** and reduce its **Scale(1)** default value to **50**. This will reduce the resolution of the texture, creating a subtle pattern.

- Drag out of the **Simple Noise node** and create a **Multiply node** connected to its B(1) input.

- Create a Float Input node exposed as a property called **SnowAmount** with a default value of 0.2 and connect it to the A(1) input of the Multiply node (Figure 8-29).

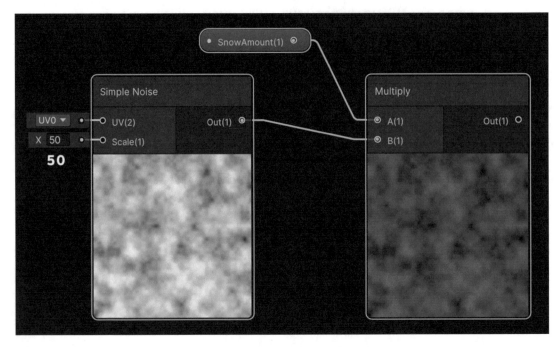

Figure 8-29. *Simple Noise node and a Multiply node to control influence*

This multiplication and property will control how much the noise texture will affect the displacement of the vertices. Using a value below 1, as we are doing, is going to reduce the influence of the texture, achieving a subtle result.

Now, as we did previously, let's store this displacement information in a Vector3, filling the coordinate we want to displace with the output of the Multiply node, as follows:

- Create a **Vector3 node** with its **input Y(1)** connected to the **Multiply node output.**

- Create a **Position node** in **object space** so we can access the original local position of the vertices of the original plane mesh.

- Then, create a new **Add node** and connect to its **inputs** the output of the **Vector3 node** and the output of the **Position node**.

- Finally, connect the **Add node output** to the **Position input** in the **Vertex block** of the master stack (Figure 8-30).

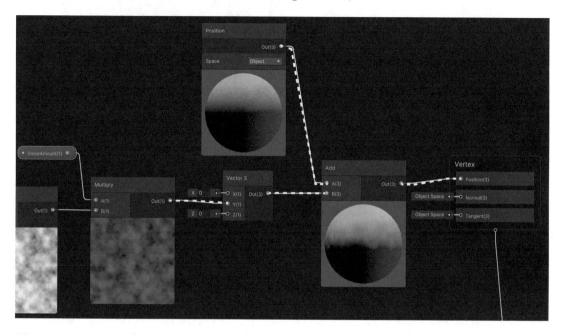

Figure 8-30. *Apply noise displacement to the vertices of the plane mesh*

If you save the asset and go back to the Scene view you will find that the InteractiveSnow object's vertices are displaced, following the noise texture pattern, by the **SnowAmount** property (Figure 8-31).

Figure 8-31. *Snow vertex displacement*

Although the snow is successfully displaced, there is an important thing missing here: the **color.** This snow is gray and lacks volume. We can tell the vertices are displaced but we barely can identify the depth of the displacement. Let's fix the Simple Noise texture, but this time add some color.

Apply Snow Color and Occlusion

Let's add some color and occlusion to the snow by using the Simple Noise node as follows:

- Create another **Simple Noise node** with the same default **Scale(1)** value of **50**.

You could use the one we already created, but that would create a connection mess in your Shader Graph; it is up to you.

- Out of the **Simple noise node** create a new **Add node** connected to its **B(1)** input.

- Set up the **A(1)** default value of the **Add node** with the value **0.3**.

We are adding positive values to the texture to lighten the darker spots of the texture a little bit, avoiding too much contrast between the darker and whiter parts of the texture.

- Finally, connect the output of this **Add node** to the **Base Color input** of the **Fragment block** (Figure 8-32).

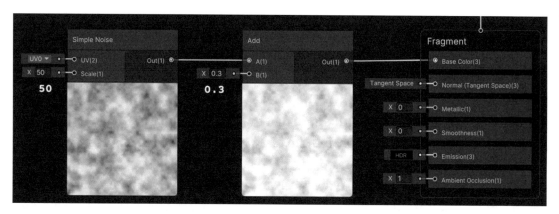

Figure 8-32. *Snow color*

After saving the asset and going back to the Scene view you will see a very nice, white, deep snow (Figure 8-33).

Figure 8-33. *Snow shader*

Very nice! We created a snow shader, but when clicking Play and moving the character around, nothing changes, and no footprints are created. In the next subsection, we are going to set up everything to let the character interact and **paint** footprints in the snow.

Interact with the Snow

First, let's define the interaction we want. The expected outcome is that the snow "stepped" on by the character should sink and disappear, as if the character is painting a path in the snow.

We can translate from this assumption that the path of the character needs to be **printed somehow**, and then that **rendered texture** must be used as an **inverted mask** to modify the displacement texture.

Imagine drawing a black line in the noise texture we are using for the vertex displacement (Figure 8-34), so those vertices will not be altered by the texture, remaining in their original position, under the floor.

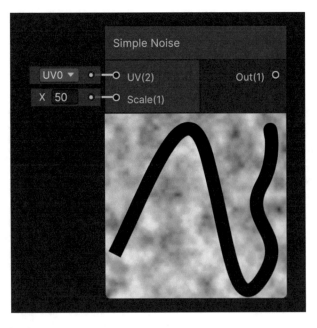

Figure 8-34. *Masked snow texture*

To achieve this real-time mask, we need to print the character path in a texture and use that texture as a mask inside our shader. But how can we print a path in real-time and translate it into a texture asset?

Using a Render Texture

In Unity, a **render texture** is a special type of asset that allows you to capture the output of a camera and use it as a texture in your game. It is commonly used for creating advanced visual effects, among other uses, like 3D UI icons. Using this technique, we can print everything that the camera is tracking into a texture and use that texture as the inverted mask we mentioned to select which vertices won't displace.

To set up a the real-time printing of a render texture we need to follow these steps:

- First, create the render texture by right-clicking anywhere in the Project tab and selecting **Create ➤ Render Texture**. (**Don't** click on the one that says **Custom Render Texture**). I called it **RT_Snow.**

- If you select the render texture asset and go to the Inspector tab you will see a bunch of settings. We are interested in changing the **size** from **256 x 256 to 512 x 512**. This way, we are increasing the **quality** of the render texture so the character path will be printed with more detail (Figure 8-35).

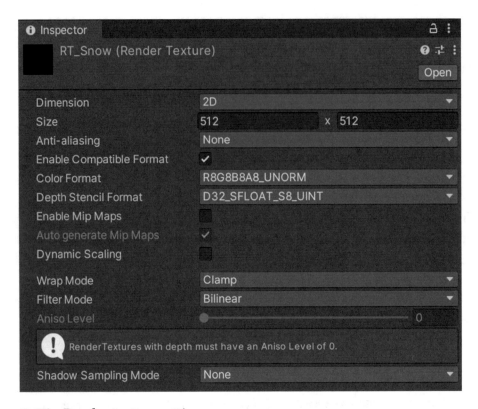

Figure 8-35. *Render texture settings*

Now is time to create **another camera**, the one that is going to record the path of the character and print it in the currently blank render texture, as follows:

- In an empty space in the Hierarchy tab, right-click and select **Camera.** I called it **RenderTextureCamera.**

Now select the camera and open the Inspector tab to make some modifications to its components:

- First, at the very bottom in the Inspector tab there is an **audio listener component**; remove it since the **main camera** already has this component.

- Now, in the camera component, there is an **Output** dropdown setting, and the first attribute asks for a render texture asset to be referenced. Drag and drop the **RT_Snow** asset to that slot (Figure 8-36).

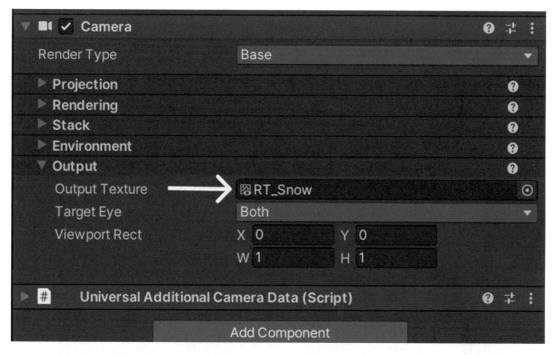

Figure 8-36. *Referencing the render texture as output texture for the camera component*

- Now, set these position and rotation values for the render texture camera:

  - **Position**: (0, 10, 0)

  - **Rotation**: (90, 180, 0)

Your render texture camera will now be facing the scene from above, perfect for recording the character movement path along the snow (Figure 8-37).

Figure 8-37. *Render texture camera recording the snow and the character from above*

Now we need to record the character path precisely without the influence of the conic perspective that the camera component has by default. To change it do the following:

- Go to the **camera component** of the render texture camera and, under the **Projection settings dropdown**, change the **Projection** value from **Perspective** to **Orthographic** (Figure 8-38).

Note   Conic perspective: Where objects that are farther away appear smaller and converge toward a vanishing point.

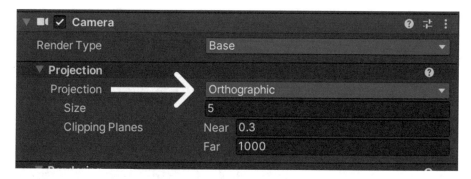

Figure 8-38. *Setting orthographic perspective*

As you can see in Figure 8-39, the camera viewport has changed to a prismatic shape that will record the character path with precision.

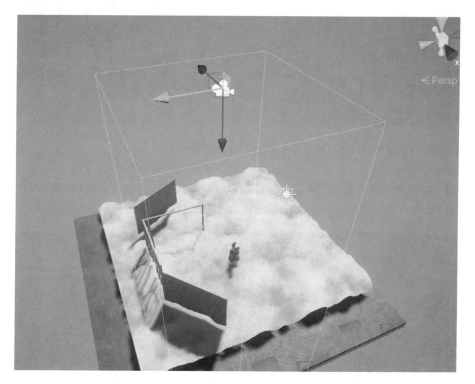

Figure 8-39. *Orthographic viewport gizmo*

Finally, if you click the *y*-axis of the coordinates gizmo at the top right part of the Scene view, you will position yourself as if watching the scene from above as the camera, but you will find that the viewport does not cover all the snow (Figure 8-40).

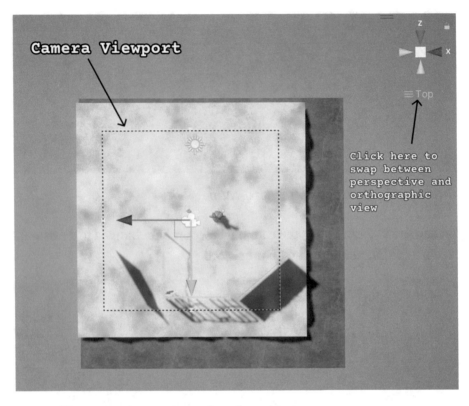

Figure 8-40. *Viewport size not covering the snow*

This is because the size of the plane is 6.5 units and the size of the viewport is 5 units. Under the Projection settings, change the **Size** setting from 5 to 6.5 (Figure 8-41).

▼ ■ ✓ Camera		❓ ⊹ ⋮
Render Type	Base	▼
▼ **Projection**		❓
Projection	Orthographic	▼
Size	6.5	
Clipping Planes	Near 0.3	
	Far 1000	

Figure 8-41. *Viewport size changed to 6.5*

The viewport is now covering the exact size of the snow plane, as in Figure 8-42.

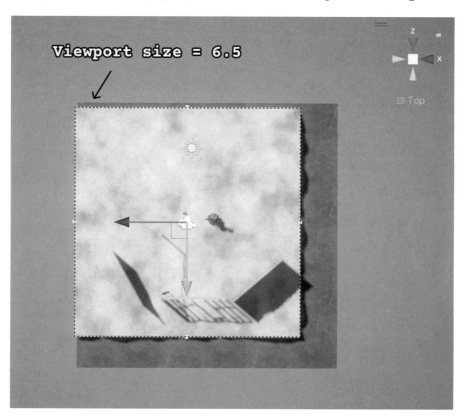

Figure 8-42. *Changed viewport size to cover the interactive snow object*

If you click Play and select the RT_Snow asset you can see in the Inspector tab that the texture is updated with the frames captured by the render texture camera (Figure 8-43).

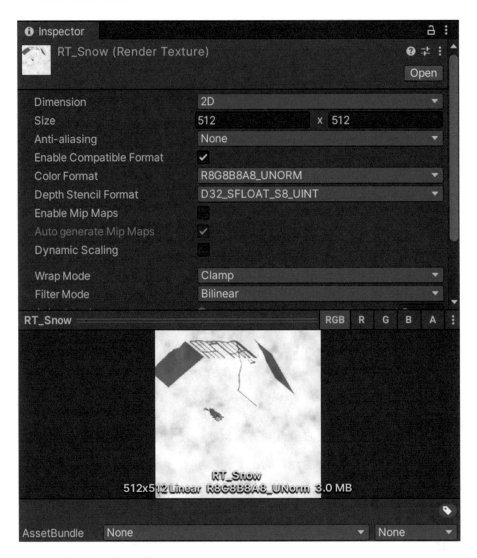

Figure 8-43. *Updated render texture*

Great! We set up the render texture to be painted with the images that the render camera is capturing. But we need to only record the path of the character and avoid the rest of the elements in the scene. How can we represent the character path in real-time visually? How can we filter the elements captured by the camera?

Painting the Character Path

In the previous section, we set up everything to record the character moving across the snow surface and printing those frames into the render texture. Now we are going to create our **brush**, a simple white blurred path that will be displayed by the character, which will be the unique element captured by the camera. Think of it as an imaginary trail that the character is leaving behind that only the camera can see.

There are a few ways of creating trails, but we are going to use the **particle system**. We can set the particle system to emit particles constantly when it is moving around. Setting this particle system as a child of the main character will allow us to create a trail whenever the main character is moving across the snow, as follows:

- Right-click in the **Character object** in the **hierarchy** and select **Effects ➤ Particle System.** A particle system object will be created as a **child** of the character controller. I called it **BrushParticles** (Figure 8-44).

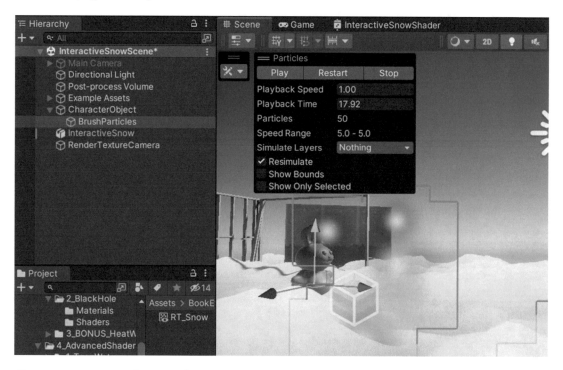

***Figure 8-44.** Brush particle system*

Now we have to change some parameters to make the particle system behave like a trail that the main character is drawing when moving around. Set these final values:

- Main module and Emission module (Figure 8-45):

  - Lifetime = 10: This will increase the lifetime so the snow sunk by the steps of the character remains for a longer time.

  - Start Speed = 0: This will ensure that the particles are still in the position of the character at that moment without moving around.

  - Start size = 2: This defines the size of the particle, which should match the size of the character.

  - Simulation Space = World: This ensures the particles stay still when appearing and avoid following the character's position.

  - Rate over time = 0: We don't want to spawn the particles if the emitter is not moving.

  - Rate over distance = 5: This spawns a ratio of 5 particles per unit of distance the character is moving.

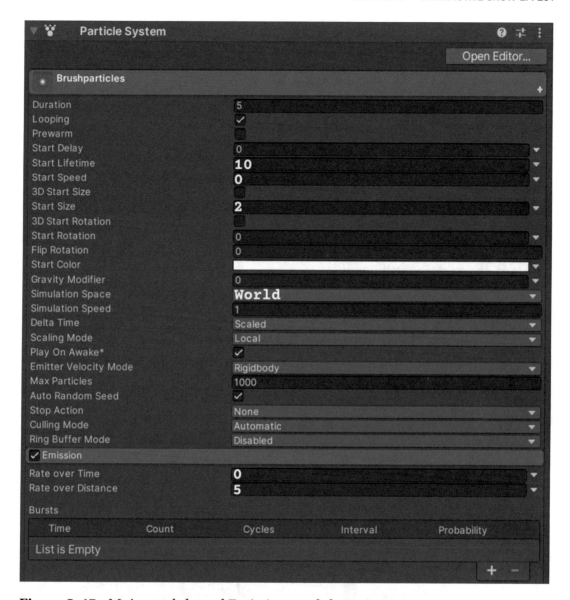

Figure 8-45. *Main module and Emission module settings*

- Shape module (Figure 8-46):

    - Shape: To edge, so we can reduce it to a single point in space.

    - Radius: Reduce it to the minimum possible so the particles spawn in the same exact point.

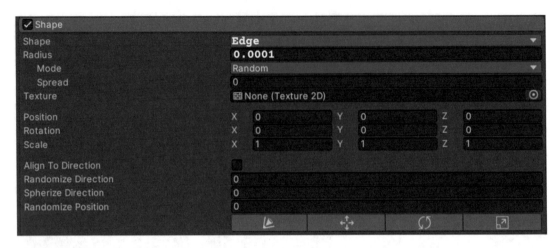

Figure 8-46. *Shape module settings*

- Renderer module settings (Figure 8-47):

    - Render Mode: Horizontal Billboard, so the particles are always looking to the top, where the render texture camera is placed.

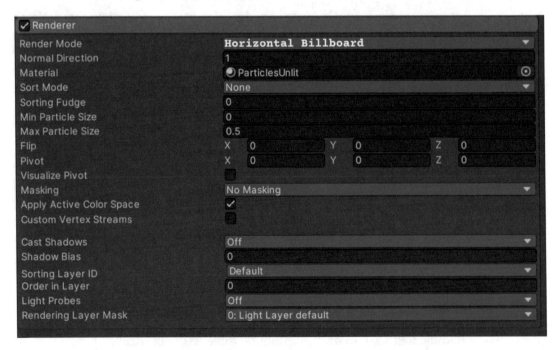

Figure 8-47. *Renderer module settings*

These settings overall will ensure that a trail of particles will be displayed according to the movement of the character and appear in the current position of the emitter. You can also change the **size** to achieve a **bigger or smaller** brush. They will also face upward always, so the render texture camera can track them perfectly. We are creating a brush to paint the path of the character.

In the Hierarchy tab, **disable the interactive snow for a moment** and click **Play** to see how the character is dropping particles as it walks across the snow, painting a path (Figure 8-48). After this experiment, **remember to enable** the snow object again.

Figure 8-48. *Path painted by the character while walking*

The path is painted correctly, but we want a totally white trail to be used as a mask in a more efficient way. We need to create another material for the particles, as follows:

- Right-click anywhere inside the Project tab and select **Create ➤ Material;** call it **RT_BrushMaterial**. This will create a default lit material, which we will change to the shader reference.

- Select the Material asset and at the top part of the Inspector tab there is a dropdown setting called **Shader.** This will change the shader loaded in this material.

- In the Shader setting dropdown select **Universal Render Pipeline / Particles / Lit.** This will assign the default lit shaders for particles inside the Unity project.

- Now, new settings will be exposed in the Inspector tab, so we are going to change the following:

  - Surface Type = Transparent

  - **Blending Mode = Additive**

- Under Surface Inputs dropdown, click on the Search button at the very left of the **Base Map** setting and search for the **Default-Particle** texture to load (Figure 8-49).

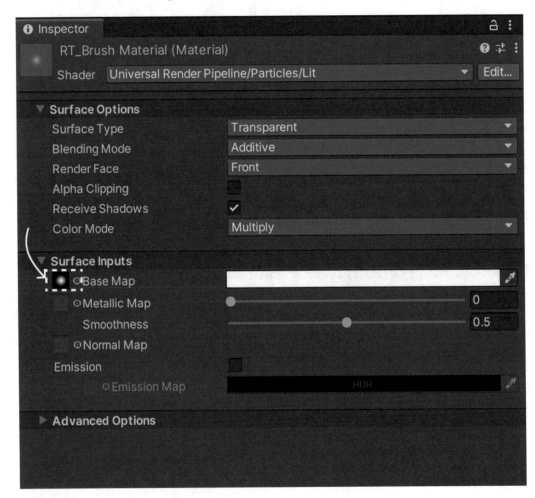

Figure 8-49. *RT_Brush material*

The BaseMap texture will define the brush intensity and shape. You can use any you want or create your own for different footprint effects.

Now, drag and drop the **RT_BrushMaterial** asset to the **BrushParticles** in the Hierarchy tab to assign this material to the **Material property** under the **Renderer module**; see it referenced in the **BrushParticles Renderer** module (Figure 8-50).

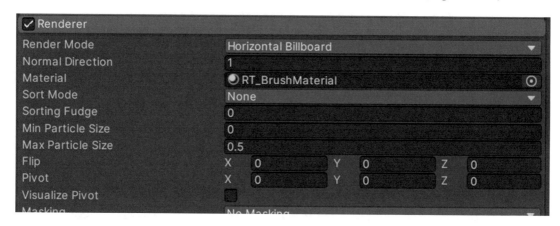

Figure 8-50. *Loaded material in BrushParticles Renderer module*

If you click Play again you can see how the particles are now more intense and whiter, without separation borders between them (Figure 8-51).

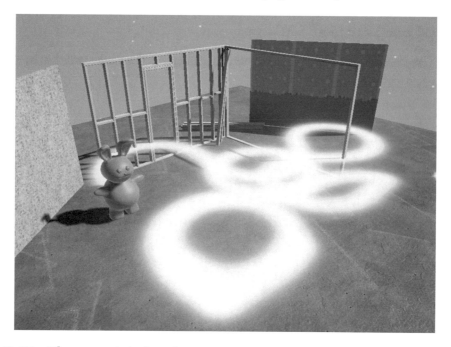

Figure 8-51. *Clearer painted path*

The trick was to set the blending mode in the RT_BrushMaterial to **additive.** This blending mode is a rendering technique that overlaps objects by adding their color values, so the particles are just adding their color information on top of each other, creating a more intense and clear path without marked borders.

Recording Only the Character Path

Now that we are painting the path of the Character using the Particle system and a custom material, we want the Render Texture camera to ignore the rest of the elements in the scene and only record this path.

Adding a New Culling Mask to the Particles

Select the BrushParticles object in the hierarchy. At the very top of the Inspector tab, there is a dropdown called Layer with the default value set up. This variable is used to assign an object a classification layer that is used by programmers to filter certain numbers of objects in different categories. Let's create a new layer so we can assign our particle system inside it to be filtered by the render texture camera, as follows:

- Open the Layer dropdown in the Inspector tab while the brush particles are selected.

- Click the last option: **Add Layer.**

- The Inspector tab will now display all the layers that are available in your project (Figure 8-52).

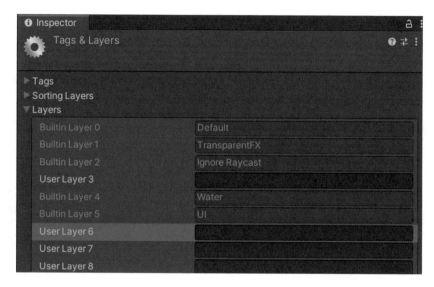

Figure 8-52. *Layers interface*

- Select an empty space that is not used yet; in my case I will use
  User Layer 6. In that empty space at the right of that layer write
  SnowPainter (Figure 8-53).

Figure 8-53. *Setting a custom layer*

Now you can select the BrushParticles object again and select the recently created
SnowPainter layer from the Layer dropdown (Figure 8-54).

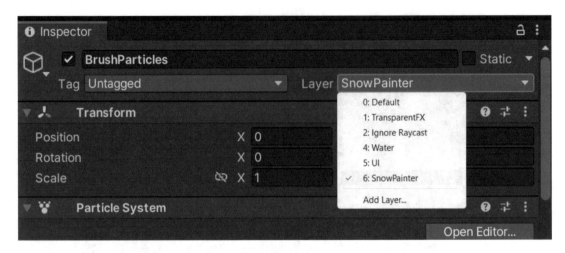

Figure 8-54. *Selecting the SnowPainter layer*

Great! We introduced our brush particles into the SnowPainter category. A category can be filtered by other classes like the **Camera component**.

Update the Render Texture Camera Culling Mask

In the **camera component** of the **render texture camera** object there is a section called **Rendering**. Inside it there is the **Culling Mask dropdown**. If you open it you will find all the available layers marked with a tick. Select only the newly created **SnowPainter**, as in Figure 8-55.

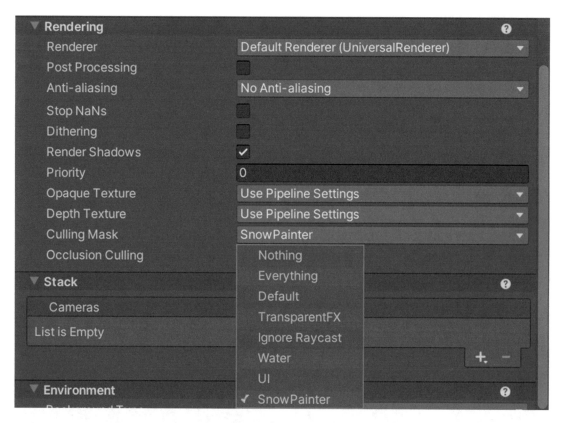

Figure 8-55. *Filtering the SnowPainter layer*

This will ensure that only the elements inside the SnowPainter layer will be captured by the render texture camera. The rest of the elements in the scene will be ignored.

Last but not least, be sure that inside the **camera component** of the **render texture camera**, under the **Environment dropdown**, the setting **Background Type** is set to **Solid Color** and **Background** is set to full black (R = 0, G = 0, B = 0, A = 0). You can see this in Figure 8-56.

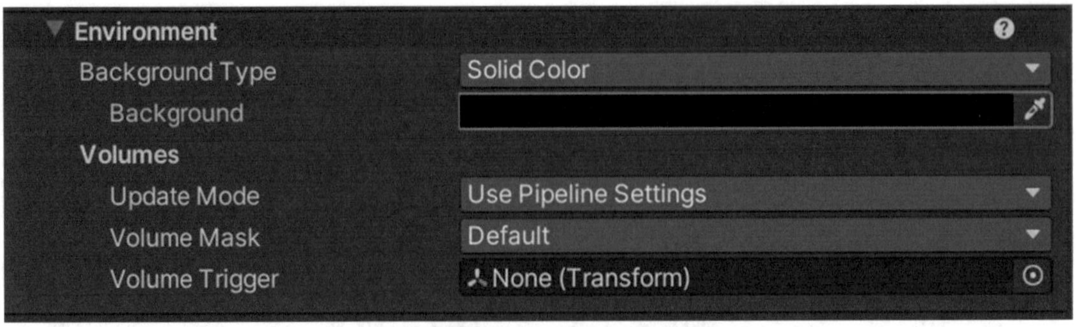

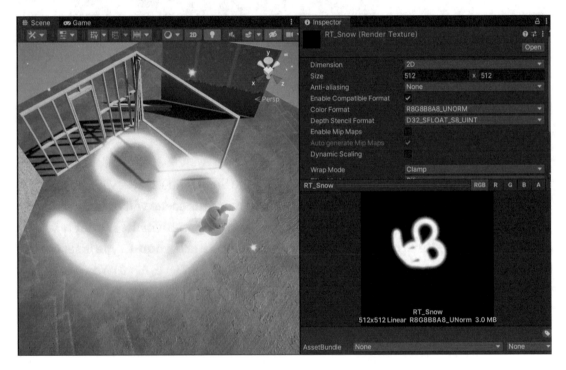

Figure 8-56. *Background type and background settings*

After all this hard work to set up, click Play again. After moving the character around, you can check that the RT_Snow texture created earlier is printing the path of the character successfully (Figure 8-57).

Figure 8-57. *Final render texture*

Note   The render texture is not updated in real-time in the preview figure shown; you may have to wait a little after moving the character to see the path painted in the render texture.

Impressive! The render texture is creating the perfect mask for our shader, is painting a texture with the path of the character, following a beautiful line and ignoring the rest of the objects.

Update the Main Camera Culling Mask

The only problem now is that we **don't want to see that trail** in the **main camera** while playing, so we will do the opposite, filtering in the **camera component** of the **main camera** object as we did in the **render texture camera,** only ignoring the objects in the **SnowPainter layer** (Figure 8-58).

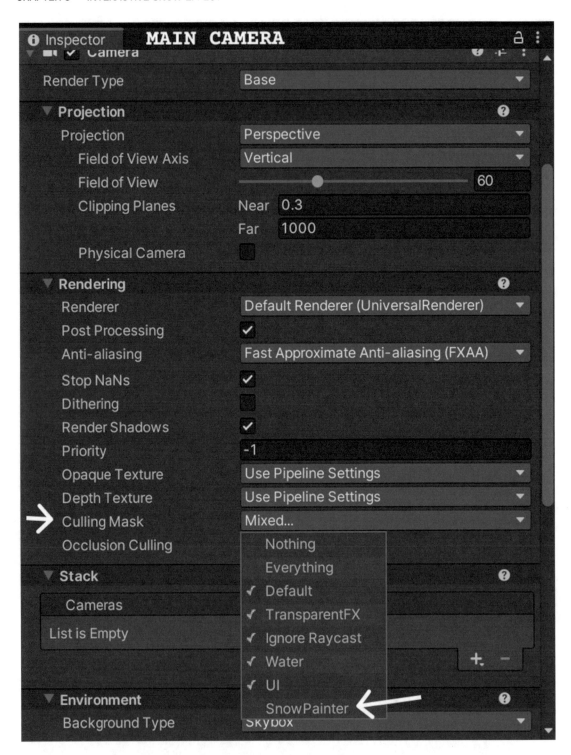

Figure 8-58. *Ignoring the SnowPainter layer in the main camera*

Finally! We have created a nice and dynamic texture that is going to be used in the next section as a mask to filter the vertices that are going to be displaced by the shader. Remember to enable the **Interactive Snow object** again.

Render Texture as a Displacement Mask

As with other textures, we can access the RT_Snow texture color information inside the shader graph. Let's add it to the **InteractiveSnowShader** graph as follows:

- Open the **InteractiveSnowShader** asset by double-clicking it.

- Now, create a **Sample Texture 2D LOD node**. This node will allow us to connect color information outputs to nodes that end in the Vertex block.

- Drag and drop the **RT_Snow texture** from the **Project tab** to the default value of the **Texture(T2)** input of the **Sample Texture 2D LOD node** (Figure 8-59).

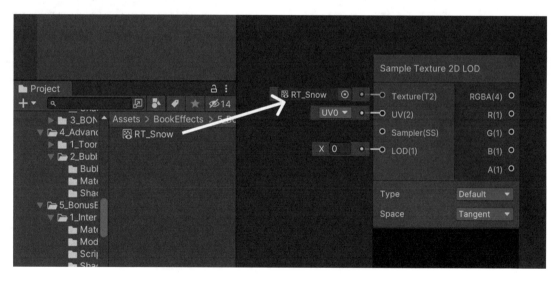

Figure 8-59. *Sample Texture 2D LOD node loaded with the RT_Snow texture*

Now, we need to invert this mask and set the character path as black and the rest of the texture as white so the displacement corresponding to those vertices is 0. Do the following:

- From the **R(1)** output of the **Sample Texture 2D LOD node**, create a **One Minus node**, which is going to invert the colors of the mask.

- Now, from the output of the **One Minus** node create a **Multiply node** connected to its B(1) input, as in Figure 8-60.

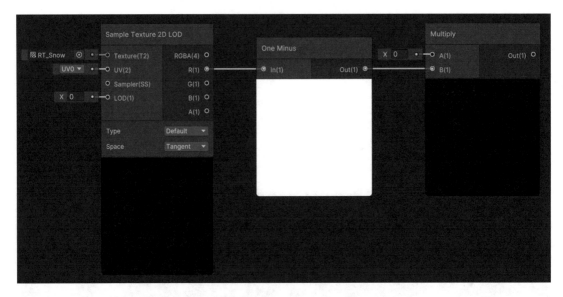

Figure 8-60. *One Minus and Multiply nodes*

The Multiply node has to apply this mask to the noise texture before it is applied to the vertex displacement calculations in the shader graph, as follows:

- Connect this new **Multiply node** between the **Vector3 node** and the **Multiply node** we created in the **previous section** of this chapter (Figure 8-61).

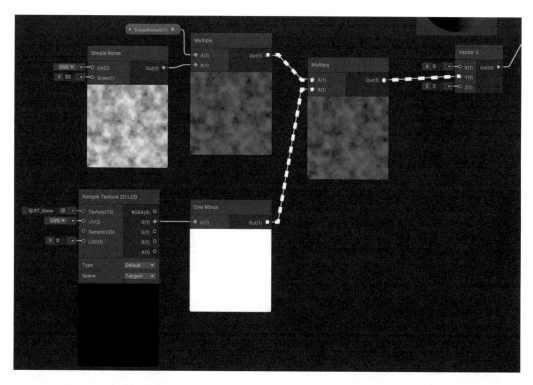

Figure 8-61. *Applying the mask to the noise texture*

We finally applied the RT_Snow texture as an inverted mask using the One Minus node. And then, we applied that inverted mask to define the path in the noise texture that is representing the snow using a Multiply node. **Save the asset** and enjoy playing with the snow (Figure 8-62).

Figure 8-62. *Snow effect*

431

If we pause the gameplay and go to the shader graph, we see how the RT_Snow is interacting in real-time with the shader, masking the noise texture (Figure 8-63).

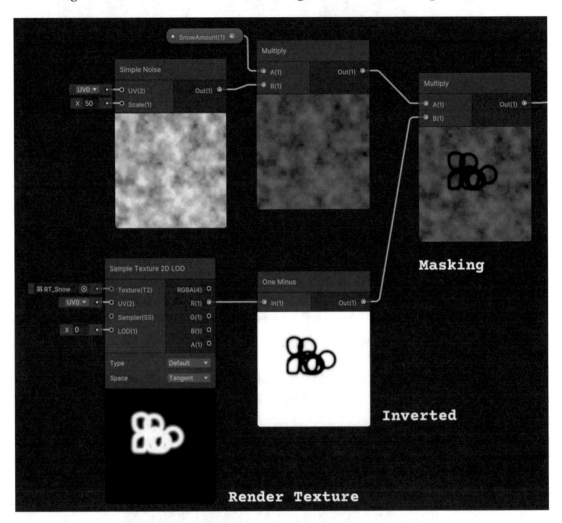

Figure 8-63. *Snow effect*

This texture is, in fact, the path of the character that can be seen from above in the Scene view (Figure 8-64).

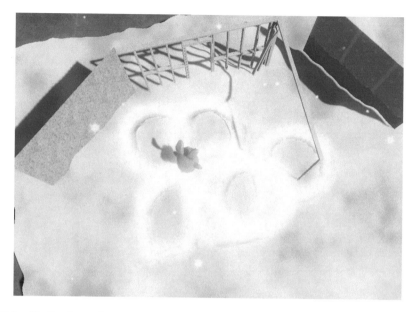

Figure 8-64. *Path drawing*

Summary

Wow! That was a really epic finale for this book. We applied tons of new techniques and Unity resources to create the most complex but fun effect of this book, in my opinion.

This effect can be used in plenty of situations; for example, when the player is walking in the water you can change the normal texture information to create waves; you can use it in a grass shader to make the character step on them, and much more.

I hope you have learned a lot from this book and that you use all the knowledge and effects you have acquired to improve the visual experience in your games, making them more appealing and fun to play. This is just the beginning of your shaders adventure. It is your time to create everything that your imagination is capable of. Good luck and have fun!

Index

© Álvaro Alda 2023
Á. Alda, *Beginner's Guide to Unity Shader Graph*, https://doi.org/10.1007/978-1-4842-9672-1

Printed in the United States
by Baker & Taylor Publisher Services